It Was Fun While It Lasted

The Douglass Eddystone and the graceful lines of the tower as viewed from the set-off.

It Was Fun While It Lasted

Lighthouse keeping in the 1950s

A.J.Lane

Whittles Publishing

Typeset by
Whittles Publishing Services

Published by
Whittles Publishing,
Roseleigh House,
Latheronwheel,
Caithness, KW5 6DW,
Scotland, UK

ISBN 1-870325-67-2

Produced by Whittles Publishing

Printed and bound in Great Britain by
4edge Ltd, Hockley. www.4edge.co.uk

Contents

1

Gas engines and violins:

the farewell to commerce

'*I* am at a loss to know', said Mr A.E. Bixby, 'what it is you mean when you say "We desperately need gas engines." I do not understand how a full-time employee of this company could have such a need, desperate or otherwise.'

If I had ever had a hope of succeeding in business, Bixby would have been my model. The spats may have been just one of those tricks of memory; but I certainly am not wrong in remembering the umbrella, the generous rotundity of a man who does not run for public transport, the silvered hair that spoke confidence and a good barber. His baby-smooth skin texture was normally a healthy pink, which could become just slightly mottled when he was provoked into firing someone for bad time-keeping; or as now when he contemplated the day's issue of the *Birmingham Post* on the desk in front of him. I saw that it was open at the correspondence page where my letter was printed. When, some fifty years later, I ask myself why I ever came to be a keeper in the lighthouse service instead of cutting an acquisitive swathe through the financial heart of London, or becoming Chief of the General Staff (both options that I had been assured had been held open to me from birth), I have to suppose there was some unfortunate mismatch between parental expectation and filial capacity. But as an explanation of the impending move from being a clerk in insurance to lighthouses it is also true that around this time several things had begun to come together, the first of them being this interview with Bixby.

The chief clerk was standing behind him and he gave me an encouraging nod. Mr Bixby, the nod told me, is an entirely reasonable man. You have nothing to fear.

'Yes, I may have over-stated it a bit,' I said. 'My feeling is we need to enlarge our holdings if we are to have more than a local success as a gas-engine museum. We've got our Pufendorf but for the moment nothing else.'

I had been working for the Alliance Assurance Company at its branch at 130 Colmore Row in Birmingham for some two years when chance made me the owner of a small gas engine. A neighbour had been going to throw it out. I had taken it in and given it a home. More, I had gone out and bought some Woolworth's gloss paints (red, green and black), done up the bits that needed doing up, polished the rest, connected the water-jacket to the kitchen tap and the inlet valve to the gas stove, and had the engine vibrating its way across the floor on an improvised plinth. Some time in the future I intended to fork out a fiver to someone to give it a glass case and a brass plate: 'Presented to the Gas Engine Club of the Alliance Assurance Company by A. J. Lane, 1952–'. I hadn't yet decided whether the space was to be filled with the year I left this world or just the year I left the Alliance.

'Puf—?' queried Bixby.

'No offence taken', I said. 'For the present I'm thinking that the gas engines we can move we will exhibit in a derelict warehouse somewhere reasonably close to the city centre. Those we can't we'll leave where they are, to be visited by appointment. I hope in due course we'll have the finances to provide a small annual remuneration to the custodians.'

With luck that would not always be necessary. Mr H.R. Blenkinsop, the Under-Sheriff of Warwickshire, was one who was unlikely to need to have his palm crossed with silver. He had been one of the earliest respondents to my press offensive. He had written:

> I see that you desperately need gas engines. I have one at the bottom of my property. Strictly speaking it is not mine, but it has been there so long that I think I could claim it as mine by adoption. I do not think any difficulty would be raised if you wished to add it to your collection. How you would do that and what you would do with it when you had got it I cannot, of course, say.

Drawn as much as anything by the careful formality of that final sentence I had been to see him and had found a grim but attractive brute weighing, I would suppose, anything up to 5 tons. Blenkinsop told me he used swing it into life every so often just for the pleasure of seeing the wheels go round.

Before I left he opened up his garage and showed me an elderly Rolls-Royce. Did I know of anyone who would be likely to want to buy it? I did not tell him that I could count on the fingers of a severely mutilated hand the number of my acquaintances who had either the money to buy or the panache to own such a machine.

My tabloid reading at the time was the *Daily Worker*, but I found myself warming to this capitalist. I had made him the first honorary member of our club.

'I think you were trying to ask me about Samuel Pufendorf,' I said to Bixby. 'He exists, though not as a gas engine. A very few people know of him as the author of *The Theory of the Imputation of Moral Actions and Its Relation to Modern Jurisprudence*, a work which it is not necessary to read to be impressed by. Nothing is known of his gas-engine expertise, but a man of exceptional brilliance in one field is often to be found expressing his talents in another. What helicopters were to da Vinci, gas engines could have been to Pufendorf.'

'It's a monumental doorstopper,' said Bixby into the telephone.

I hadn't noticed it had rung. I am notoriously inattentive when I get lost in exposition. He replaced the receiver and tapped the newspaper impatiently.

'The question is, Lane, where do we go from here?'

I liked his enthusiasm. Though I say it myself, I do tend to be pretty infectious.

'Well, there are the obvious runners: a Gas Engine Dinner, a Gas Engine Dance, a staff half-marathon, the turning points various notable…'

'I mean, are you going to put a stop to this nonsense? The company cannot have you using its address in this way.'

Perhaps I should say a word here about the job I was doing and the place I was doing it in. Insurance is a multi-faceted and immensely complex and rewarding study, rich in intellectual challenge. I was living a fantastic life. I'm surprised it didn't cause more comment than it did that I disappeared for as long as an hour at a time with a bundle of papers into the attic where the Westminster Fire files were kept. There I would go off into a brown study, devising turret clock mechanisms and interesting applications for electrode boilers. For that, and for doing some filing and pasting of endorsements into policy books on five days a week and two Saturday mornings out of three, I was given a modest but steady income.

I was working in a building that had been briefly rated one of the seven wonders of Birmingham when its expensively marbled interior had first been unveiled in the early years of the century. Later, but still in my time, the décor was to become an embarrassment when the high stools and Dickensian desks were replaced by swivelling chairs and low tubular-framed tables. Many years later a branch of the Bank of Credit & Commerce International was to die sensationally here. After that it was empty for quite a while except when they opened it up briefly to shoot the immolation scene for a television version of *Aida*.

I thought then, and still think now, it was the sort of place that very much needed a gas engine club – or even just a gas engine – to lighten the mood. I suppose it was when Bixby made it plain he wasn't with me that my heart went out of insurance. I wound the enterprise down and turned to the violin.

It wasn't easy. Start up a gas engine, or a gas engine club, and it develops a momentum that is hard to arrest. I had written the letter to all four of Birmingham's papers. Three printed it. The fourth wanted to send a reporter and a photographer. When I had to tell them not to come, plans were already well advanced for a member of the typing pool to pose lubriciously beside the Pufendorf in something like a bikini, sultry-mouthed, one hand caressing the water-jacket. I had found my model, no great shakes but the best the pool could offer, and had nothing more to do but persuade her to the seriousness of mind necessary to bring her fame as 'Miss Alliance Gas Engine Club of 1952'. I doubt whether such an opportunity ever came her way again.

In the meantime my correspondence was bringing to the front desk of the Alliance people who were more interesting in my view than premium payers and claimants: old gas-engine men from way back turned up in their overalls, wanting to join. It was pathetic.

I found the violin a great comfort.

The Pufendorf was no more popular at home than it had been at the Alliance. It now had its plinth and its glass case and a brass plate. These set it off but increased its living space. I wrote off to Birmingham Science Museum in a state of controlled excitement (' ...Its provenance is uncertain, but at least one authority believes it may be an early Pufendorf...') offering it on indefinite loan. They accepted it, sight unseen, and presently something the size of a Pickfords van, with an electric tailgate, drew up outside the house. Four men came to the door with an hydraulic trolley. 'We've come for the' – the foreman consulted his paperwork – 'engine'. One of them carried it out under his arm while the other three got out their manicure sets.

I had come to the violin by accident. My brother had downsized the score for a local church group production of something like Wagner's *Ring*, matching it to the three fiddles and a xylophone of the amateur backing group. We went to the first performance and I was much struck by the noise that is made by three violinists whose intonation is not secure. It was strikingly unpleasant.

I lost no time in having cards printed, 'The Zeeman String Ensemble', bought one old violin, found another, and was in business. I knew about music, so learning to play the device was not a problem. Jones, a colleague at the Alliance, was less fortunate. It did not matter that he was tone-deaf, indeed that helped to preserve him from harm, but he had somehow to be taken beyond the simple concept that the up-notes were at the top of the stave and the down-notes at the bottom. It was for him that I devised the Lane Method of Violin Tutelage that has been the salvation of the amateur practitioner ever since. Simplicity is its essence. The strings are numbered from the left, 1, 2, 3, 4, the fingers similarly, and a figure in brackets after a string number indicates which of the fingers should be pressed on that string. The bow is then shoved to and fro. A baboon could do it. To provide against the possibility, admittedly remote, of a baboon and myself coming recognisably together at any instant I took the precaution of tuning the second fiddle half a semitone flat on each string. *Viola!*

So far as the hardware was concerned we were ready for the off. There was then the matter of the software, the music. Not, obviously, anything with too high a striking rate of notes per minute. It wouldn't do for the pianist and me to have to keep on marking time waiting for Jones to catch up. I found a *Praeludium and Allegro after the style of Pugnani* by Kreisler that seemed to fit the bill. The Allegro had to go of course; our combo tempo was strictly largo; but the Praeludium was tailor-made, jumping nicely around in a way that would demonstrate our qualities. We were quite certain to be all over the place. Then would come a switch to the grand tune, the Intermezzo from *Cavalleria Rusticana*. That was enough for the programme.

All we needed now was a straight man on the piano to accompany the two straight performers on the violins. I found him at the Birmingham School of Music and hired him for five shillings. He was a student but we billed him as Gerald Moore, the celebrated accompanist. He slipped into the role like a dream and I was particularly impressed by the way he shot his cuffs before rolling up his sleeves. The public of course gave no sign of knowing any different: for them a pianist was a piano-player.

We gave two performances before being run out of town, one at the Alliance annual dinner with Jones; and the other at the Beehive, a large department store where my sister worked and where she took over second fiddle from Jones because anyone could.

The Alliance gig, in front of an audience that included representatives from Head Office, was the warm-up. It went very well. While the pianist murmured his way decorously through the introduction to the *Intermezzo*, Jones and I plucked softly at our strings, checking the tuning and making sure it was off. We hit the first note of the big tune on the beat, and notably apart. Other notes followed at intervals. The audience made no sound with the exception of one uncouth titter, quickly rebuked. We finished, and they applauded with that special hysteria always induced in British audiences by a thoroughly bad experience. We bowed as do performers who are being offered no more than their due. We nodded to each other and to the pianist and went on to hit them with the Kreisler. Afterwards we resumed our seats, discussing with professional gravity whether at some point Jones might have played a 3(2) instead of a 2(3). The Head Office representatives applauded with the rest and leaned towards Bixby, their expressions earnestly enquiring. For us, any doubts we had had about our success were removed. We were obviously quite awful.

The second venue was a more lavish affair. The Beehive had hired a professional compère. We were to provide the culture spot between a comedian and a juggling act. The compère asked for a few particulars which he jotted down on a card. He announced our pianist as Gerald Moore who unfortunately had to dash off after our performance for a concert at the Wigmore Hall so – 'a big hand ladies and gentlemen for the Zeeman String On Somble…Thank you', who were going to play something from *Cavalry Rustic Anna*.

After it was over he took me by the lapels in an anteroom in what I believe was technically an assault. He obviously thought I had done it on purpose, a charge to which I would have pleaded guilty but insane. I felt it had gone quite splendidly.

The Alliance (assets £283 million) did not long survive the scandal of the Gas Engine Club and the Zeeman String Ensemble. Presently it was obliged to merge with the Sun (assets £450 million) to become the Sun-Alliance, and then to vacate the premises at 130 Colmore Row in order to escape the attention of elderly gas-engine men who came to the counter with offers of help. I believe the Birmingham branch of Sun-Alliance is now holed up elsewhere in the city, probably ex-Directory.

By then, anyway, it and I had gone our separate ways, ending a relationship that had never been comfortable. My period of probation had been extended, probably uniquely, from one year to two, and I was then asked to provide two references. I thought this was a bit off. Who did they suppose they were dealing with, some kind of eccentric? As to the references, I found myself in a difficulty. I couldn't think who to ask. I didn't seem to know anybody and anybody who thought they knew me was unlikely to want to write me a reference. At that time I was hiring a room up the street for ten shillings a week from a Mrs Croydon. I used to go there in the evenings to write a picaresque novel about the fortunes of a family of East End knackers and glue-boilers over three reigns. Mrs Croydon was doubtful but only because she had never done anything of the kind before.

'I'll tell you what', she said, 'You write the reference and I'll sign it.'

As I recall it was quite a good one. The other was provided by Blenkinsop on the basis of our half-hour acquaintance. Somehow I was in, but not for long.

Other things were beginning to come together. Captain Carlsen of the *Flying Enterprise*, with the help of mate Dancy of the tug *Turmoil*, had brought his crippled Liberty freighter to within sight of Falmouth before going down off the Lizard. It was very exciting and radio programmes were interrupted with up-dates. There was obviously another world out there beyond the Alliance. And a fellow clerk was retiring after about eighty-five years' service. I had a look at his presentation watch and didn't think much of the movement. It didn't seem worth waiting for. Also I was rejected by Anne Phillips, who operated the switchboard and to whom I had never spoken before I proposed to her. Broken-hearted, I handed in my notice.

I was uncertain what I was going to do in the long term. The French Foreign Legion was a possibility. P.C. Wren had written enthusiastically about it. First, though, I must write a novel because every young man must write a novel. My knackers and glue-boilers had been mere muscle-flexing. It was time I got down to the real thing.

I did a word count and found that the average novel was 75,000 words long. At the rate of 2,000 words a day I would finish it in 37½ days. I set off. Some days I was a few words short, some days I banked a few, but I finished on schedule. People make a lot of fuss about novel writing. There's nothing to it really. I typed it out and sent it off to a publisher. For a long time I heard nothing but then discovered it had gone to Hollywood, where it was revamped in an American setting by Margaret Mitchell to re-emerge as *Gone With The Wind*. I never made a penny out of it.

I'm not bitter. These things happen.

With that out of the way I went up to Scotland and, of course, to John O' Groats. Nearby is Duncansby Head and the lighthouse, open to visitors. The keeper showed me round and I asked him what he had to do. 'Nothing', he said morosely. I had already taken in the cold, impersonal magnificence of the sea, the vastness of the sky, the absence of people, the drama of the coastline, the landscapes discouraging to vendors of household comprehensive insurance, and the remoteness from Birmingham. Probably it was at that moment that I decided 'This is for me.'

I returned the 450 miles from Drumnadrochit to Birmingham in one ride of 24 hours on my underpowered motorcycle, falling asleep in the saddle towards the end and waking up in unexpected parts of the road. You could do that sort of thing in those days and get away with it. Then I wrote off to Trinity House, London, offering my services as a lighthouse keeper.

2

New employment and the first posting: Dungeness

I have not been entirely truthful in my description of the events that led up to my switch of employers from the Alliance to Trinity House. To give my first chapter what we novelists call a satisfactory structure I skipped a spell in the Forestry Commission. It was obvious some sort of intermission was necessary. If 'Trinity' (as I was to find the Corporation of Trinity House was always referred to in the Service) was to require references, I was not going to be able to count on a glowing testimonial from Bixby; and I felt I had tried Blenkinsop's patience to its generous limits.

I needed a new previous employer, someone who could offer something short-term and closer to home than the Sahara, yet withal carrying a suggestion of open spaces. The Forestry Commission seemed to offer possibilities. I sent away for the brochures. They had several forests on offer. I had a look at the map and chose one at Bala as seeming as far removed from civilisation as was possible without leaving mainland Britain.

I had chosen well. Everyone in Bala was satisfactorily poor and depressed. This suited me. Disillusioned with my two-year foray into commerce I was ready to embrace gloom, though I wouldn't mind if the women chuckled a bit. The town was unrelievedly bleak and drab. I have been back since and find it now bears the unmistakeable scars of affluence. On Sundays in the 'fifties its thin reserve of vitality was expended in the chapels. On that day the newspapers arrived from Corwen in a closed van with outriders and were sold surreptitiously from a tin shack at the end of town, the vendors receiving a routine summons and fine for this breach of the Sabbath, very likely from magistrates who had themselves been among the customers.

On the other six days the town was hardly more lively. Dostoievsky would have been happy there – well, perhaps not happy, but at home. I latched on to the association and began an epic in his style.

I shared rooms with three or four other forestry workers at the house of a Mrs Foley in Tegid Street. Her husband had been killed in a quarry rock-fall and she made ends meet by taking in lodgers. Her daughter was on the stage in London, a career choice of considerable daring, it seemed to me, for a daughter of Bala. She returned home once while I was there, probably smuggling herself in and out in the newspaper van, and made an impression both exotic and voluptuous. She sat at the piano and sang us songs from the shows, inviting us to join in, but quietly.

It was late winter and the days were still short. The routine was that we rose at six, had breakfast, and waited in the main street opposite the town clock for the lorry to pick us up at 6.45 and take us the twenty-minute drive south into the hills towards Vyrnwy. There we planted trees on 30° slopes. If we planted 600 in a day we went on to bonus rates. It was not a figure I ever reached. We returned at 4.30 when dusk fell.

I had not done anything of the kind before and found it physically quite hard. Sharing my room was a youth called Trevor who also seemed to find it tiring. One evening, when he had taken to his bed early, I let him sleep for half an hour, then dressed myself in my working rags and boots and shook him awake – not without difficulty for he had just enjoyed an exceptionally short night. I urged haste, then went down and alerted the others. Thus we were all ready to accompany him as he stumbled downstairs, unwashed, late and breakfastless, and out into the street on which a cold, bitter drizzle was falling. Bala at nine o'clock on a winter's evening was hardly more vibrant than at a quarter to seven in the morning. We took up our position to wait for the lorry. The rain fell steadily. A single doomed native passed us eating chips *au naturelle*. The whiff of vinegar and warmed potato must have hit Trevor like breakfast. Under the brim of his dripping hat he raised his eyes to squint at the illuminated town clock. It showed a minute to nine. I saw he was trying to order his thoughts.

'Stopped', I said in explanation. 'Pigeons, probably.'

At that instant it struck the hour and we all returned to widow Foley's, exchanging amusing anecdotes as we went.

I ceased to be a forestry worker after only a few months, though it seemed longer. But it had provided me with the previous employer that I needed. At four o'clock on the day I planted my last tree the local weather showed what it could do in the way of the spectacular. In forty-five minutes bridges were washed away and roads, or rather the one road between Bala and Lake Vyrnwy, destroyed. On one particular quarter-mile downhill stretch two parallel chasms were carved to a depth of 5 feet. This I proved by later jumping in; only my head showed above the tarmac. The following day I looked in the national press for any mention of this impressive natural event. There was nothing. It had happened in Wales.

That evening I returned home. I had already applied to Trinity House, London, and had been for an interview and medical examination at Holyhead Depot. The doctor established that I had two each of arms and legs, could walk and talk, and had enough teeth in my head to masticate my food properly. He advised me against becoming a lighthouse keeper. On Monday 13 July 1953 I caught the 10 am train to London, paying for the ticket with the last of my savings.

London meant the Trinity House depot at Blackwall. I had not previously lived in 'the Smoke' and like any provincial I found the prospect exciting. The year 1953 saw one of nature's better attempts at a summer and Blackwall was hot and malodorous.

Ready to embrace new experiences I was prepared to overlook the general awfulness of the pub in which I stayed. It had been 'recommended', I forget now by whom, which I suppose means there must have been places that were even worse. The flies seemed to enjoy the food and for the most part I left it to them. The shared bedroom faced south and was an oven night and day. It could have been designed to weed out the faint-hearted. It weeded out my colleague, who on the second night returned drunk. I woke in the small hours to hear him urinating on the floor between our beds, behaviour for which my exquisite rearing by nuns had not prepared me. He left next day at the request of the management.

My new employer had given me a booklet prepared by whatever was the equivalent of the DHSS in those days, and I spent my generous leisure moments in consideration of an interesting hypothetical case set out in its pages. It had to do with pension rights. 'If you had retired because of ill-health on the day you died…' was the proposition, and there followed a statement of the consequences that could follow this odd combination of events. I suppose the booklet exists on file somewhere. It deserves a reprint. I would like to be reminded of the advice it must have gone on to give about the funeral arrangements you should make when you found yourself dead. Over forty years have now passed. The wording has stayed with me verbatim and I still have not made sense of it. At the time it reduced me to recurrent fits of laughter in which there may have been an hysterical component.

The main work at Blackwall, as was the case with the other Trinity depots round the coast, was the maintenance and reconditioning of buoys. The workshops were lit with the fitful flashes of welding arcs. The training hut was an afterthought. There were perhaps half a dozen of us there at any one time, a floating population that changed with the arrival of some and the departure of others to play their role in relieving various lighthouses. In this phase we were Supernumerary Assistant Keepers (SAKs) and for a year or so we would move around the coasts of England and Wales (Scotland was administered by the separate Northern Lighthouse Board) filling in as required to replace keepers who came ashore on leave from 'rock' stations. In due course we would ourselves be appointed to a particular station as an Assistant Keeper (AK) and, if we stayed the course, thirty years later would receive our final elevation to Principal Keeper (PK).

Who were 'we'? In the full employment of the 1950s there was no need for anyone to be a lightkeeper if he did not want to be. 'Better' jobs, in terms of pay and conditions, could always be found outside, whatever the level of qualifications. My midnight slasher had left claiming he was homesick. Others may have been there because they were sick of home. Still others are likely to have been on the run from wives, their own or other men's, from debts, or from the more personal ills that bedevil the human condition. None of these would stay long. They were unquiet souls who left when they found lightkeeping did not provide the remedy they had hoped for.

Then who did stay? That is harder to answer. If the others were misfits and casualties, these were perhaps natural nonconformists. I don't know whether Ken Skinner stayed – I never heard of him again after Blackwall – but he was the type who might have done. He showed me photos taken in his days with the Railway Company of the Royal Engineers in the Middle East. It was the sort of experience that could have unsettled him for a routine job outside the army. And much later there was Genghis, who had fought a sort of war in Palestine and who certainly did stay. These men were of the type for whom the Corporation of Trinity House provided an occupation different from the eight to five, home-and-family and annual two weeks at Clacton that might be the only alternative.

Blackwall as a training establishment could not be taken seriously. We had an instructor called Cooper but he had other jobs to which he frequently disappeared. He was a quiet, pleasant man whose reserve did not desert him even when he had to don his regimentals in a hurry and found some hooligan had stapled his braces together throughout their length. We spent much of our time in the depot's curious stump of a tower. It overlooked the river and was equipped with the various sizes of Hood burner, on which we practised 'lighting-up' and 'putting-out'. The burners were set on pedestals on which we developed that other traditional skill of the lighthouse keeper, brass polishing. The brasswork, I recall, tarnished within hours in the foul local atmosphere. Other than this we learned how to tie a bowline and were shown an oven in the depot kitchen. I don't remember that we actually did anything practical on our visit to the kitchen, which was intended to prepare us for our future role as part-time cooks.

We visited the Trinity House tailor to be measured for our uniforms. The query in gentlemen's outfitters: 'On which side do you dress, sir?' was here replaced with 'Are you right or left-handed?'. This meant nothing to me at the time. I came to see the point of it only after I was settled on a tower rock, where the opportunity for exercise is either round the setoff at its base (if it has one) or round the gallery outside the lantern. Right-handed keepers tend to walk anticlockwise, viewed from above, and left-handed keepers clockwise. The resultant extra muscular development of the 'outside' leg in each case is allowed for by the Trinity tailor in a slightly more generous cut of the cloth in the appropriate leg of the trousers, which is also given a half inch extra in its length. It might be thought that this would give a lop-sided effect when viewed from a distance, and so it does, but only in SAKs. Surprisingly soon after his appointment to a lighthouse and a few exercise sequences the keeper fills out to match the uniform, and the asymmetry disappears. Thirty-six years after leaving the service my left leg still looks withered when both legs are viewed together and if blindfolded and given no guidance I will walk in tight leftward circles.

This imaginative tailoring provision was the initiative of a Captain Harcourt, a nineteenth-century Elder Brother. So far as I know it is unique to Trinity House. In correspondence with a Mr Akiyoshi Arai of the Japanese lighthouse service I once asked if anything similar existed there, but I do not now recall his answer.

Towards the end of my time at Blackwall I had the opportunity of going to the

Chapman light. It was, I was told, a rather rickety timber structure in the Thames Estuary. I decided it did not sound very interesting, but I was wrong. Presently it began to lean in a very interesting way indeed. Then the men were taken off and it was abandoned. Soon after that it ceased to exist. It was a useful lesson. Never judge a lighthouse by appearances; you can never know when it's going to turn up trumps.

My first two Friday wages had been of £4 each. (Had this, I had to ask myself, been a wise career move? As a forestry worker my weekly wage had been £5.10s.) I put none of the money aside. I visited the Science Museum twice and did the round of the art galleries (out of which I got nothing: a blind spot). I queued for the first night of the Proms and got on to the floor for two shillings and sixpence. I went again and heard Campoli 'who looks like a plumber' but who I suppose played rather more deftly. Overall my first month had not been a month to be regretted. And by a miracle I had not been laid low by dysentery.

On 11 August, still in civvies, able to tie a bowline, self-taught in Morse and semaphore and capable of identifying an oven, I was posted to Dungeness. I wasn't at Dungeness because I was needed; it was just somewhere to send me for the time being. It was an odd place and an odd station. Uniquely, so far as I know, it had a complement of four keepers, made necessary by the quarter-mile separation of the main tower and a subsidiary light and fog signal.

It was more usual for shore establishments to have a complement of three keepers with married quarters provided on site. Sometimes there would be additional accommodation provided for keepers from 'rock' stations (the PK at the Eddystone, for example, had married quarters at the Lizard lighthouse) but this was not general. Holiday entitlement in the 1950s was two weeks, pretty much the average for employees in most occupations at that time.

'Rock' stations also had a complement of three keepers, but an appointed staff of four. (The designation 'rock' could be applied to an isolated tower, an inhabited island, or even, rarely, a lighthouse on the mainland. The qualifying factor was whether a station had accommodation for keepers' families.) The rotation sequence of the normal 'rock' station was necessarily rather complicated. A turn of duty for an individual keeper consisted of two months, followed by one month ashore free of duty. Two of the keepers, usually the PK and the junior AK, would come and go together in what was known as the 'double turn', and their two months would overlap with that of the third man. While this double turn was on leave it would be replaced by the fourth, appointed, AK and an SAK. That AK would of course stay for two months, but the SAK would need to stay for only the one, having then fulfilled the role of 'filler-in' for which he existed.

I found Dungeness to be 'a shanty-town defecated on to miles of shingle', its air of dereliction emphasised by an abandoned Southern Railways branch line from Lydd. Forty years later, as with Bala, I was to find it scarred by money, but less disagreeably so. In the 1950s it seemed to perform the function of outstation for the Research and Development department at Trinity House. Two weeks before I arrived a radio beacon had been installed which, by triangulation with beacons elsewhere, provided a navigational aid to shipping. It was a promise, or threat, of what was to come in the lighthouse service.

In too many ways I found Dungeness to be a hive of activity. It was a 'visitor station' and visitors are notoriously dirty. Typically they use the brass hand-rails to save themselves from falling as they climb the stairs to the lantern, which is something no keeper would ever think of doing. In consequence the middle watch from midnight to 4 am was spent polishing, sweeping the tower top to bottom and repairing the day's depredations generally. The compensation was in the takings at the door as the visitors left, in which SAKs did not share.

There was also the distraction of the three-hourly telephone call from the Meteorological Office, for Dungeness was a reporting station. For this it was necessary to visit the thermometers in the Stevenson Screen, to make an estimate of wind strength, wind direction, cloud height and type, and note barometric reading and tendency, dew point, precipitation if any, and visibility. Reference was then made to tables and the whole lot encoded into figured groups which were read over the telephone when the call came. It was a service for which the keepers were paid.

Bird watchers were also liable to visit whenever the weather became 'thick', particularly in the migratory season when the birds lost their star map and swarmed round the lantern. We would telephone to say there was traffic and the birdmen would come with their clip-boards and make a note of breed and number. It occurred to me that perhaps the birds were drawing their own conclusion that *Homo duffelcotis* also navigated by the stars because it was so often to be found on lighthouse galleries in fog.

Altogether there was too much going on at Dungeness. This was not what I had joined for. Surely Trinity House had its equivalent of Arabia's Empty Quarter. Well no, never quite that, and not yet anyway. On 24 August I boarded the boat train from Waterloo to Southampton, bound for Alderney.

3
Hornsbys and birds:
Alderney and Casquets

The *Isle of Sark* pulled away from the quay at a quarter to midnight. I had seriously considered running away to sea as an alternative to the French Foreign Legion and I was now to discover how lucky it was that my visit to Duncansby Head had pointed me in a slightly different direction. I had been looking forward to this night crossing to the Channel Isles, my first deep-water venture since I had sailed to New York in 1945 to learn how to bomb Tokyo. (I wasn't needed.)

If that had been a fun-trip it was probably because the boat then was a sister ship of the *Titanic* and perhaps I was a bit luckier with the weather. Now I was to discover a most disastrous lack of sea-legs. I survived for long enough to identify the Needles, then abandoned myself to a depression as deep as the one that had cancelled the previous night's sailing. Shakespeare had pitched on 'lawyers in the vacation' as an example of those for whom time 'stands still withal'. I decided that either the man was set on knocking lawyers, or he had never made the crossing to the Channel Isles in a heavy swell. The seven hours' run to St Peter Port amounted to a near-death experience which left me quite ready to embrace the real thing. I stepped ashore with aching ribs and 'a mouth that felt as though it had been rinsed with caustic soda'.

Yet no experience is more transitory than sea-sickness. If you haven't actually died overnight then dawn is the best of pick-me-ups. A wish to go on living returned on the brief twenty-minute flight in the BEA Rapide to Alderney.

I was still in civvies (the cap and jacket had come through but we had been told of a bottleneck in asymmetric trousers) and on the plane I was aware that I was being eyed by someone wearing the whole outfit. This was John Jarvis, Assistant Keeper at the island's lighthouse, returning from a month's leave. We dropped in at the store for provisions. The airfield on Alderney is at one end of the island, Quesnard lighthouse at the other, and Braye, the only village, in the centre. The store proprietor was an ex-Trinity man from one of the depot ships, with a remarkably scarred face. The story was that he had been serving on one of the district tenders engaged in hoisting a buoy for maintenance when a leak of acetylene gas caught fire and he had been trapped inside the cage superstructure. He had a dog with an infallible nose for keepers, identifying them by the paraffin on their trousers. I forget now whether he exercised this skill by biting them, or by sparing them and biting the general public instead.

The lighthouse was the usual neat, walled structure with a kitchen and three bedrooms. On the other side of the tower from the living quarters was the engine-room with two large horizontal Hornsbys for driving the fog signal. The Hornsbys dated from 1908. Trinity House's machinery was always of the best, it was well maintained, and it tended to last for ever. The downside to this was that equipment doing the same job tended to vary from lighthouse to lighthouse. Alderney had Hornsbys; Casquets, nearby, had Blackstones, perhaps for no better reason than that they were the 'in' engines of their time, just as Hornsbys had been of theirs. One had to learn 'on the job' what it took to get the best out of a particular type of engine, which was why our 'training' at Blackwall had had to be so limited.

It followed that a piecemeal rotation of lighthouse staff between stations was necessary to ensure continuity of experience, each newly appointed keeper being taught what he had to do to keep things working. Later I was to experience at first hand at the Longships what could happen when this continuity was lost. A better example might be provided by the Wolf Rock, though I write of this from hearsay. Not only had the lens at the Wolf Rock been shot up in the war so that (quite visibly from Longships when I was there) it suffered periods when it displayed an erratic light, but the fog signal was a reed driven by some small notoriously 'difficult' engine. When the engine refused to run, there was a sort of stand-by 'bicycle' pump (as it was described to me) which the keepers had to take turns to ride, twenty minutes on and forty minutes off. In periods of prolonged fog, life must have been difficult. Most of the time, of course, the engine could be persuaded to run. Within a short period, all four keepers (three plus the man ashore) were transferred, continuity of experience was lost, and the new crew knew none of the tricks needed to keep a rickety station in being. There was then no alternative but to bring forward the major refurbishment that had been delayed by the war.

The lighthouse at Alderney had survived German occupation virtually untouched. It was said that the only damage the station sustained was inflicted by a relieving British tommy who broke open the never-used main door when he found it locked.

I thought every aspect of the Hornsbys very impressive: their 4-foot flywheels, their 8-foot length (memory may exaggerate), the flailing con-rods, the eccentrics, the governor. Their breathing capacity was such that, when they were running, the twin swing doors to the engine-room were in constant matching motion. Despite their size they were surprisingly quiet in operation, in contrast to the roar of the blowlamps which pre-heated the bulbs which provided the hot-spot ignition for the paraffin vapour. The pre-heating process took about fifteen minutes during which the flywheel was turned to just after TDC (top dead centre) for the first stroke, the toggles were lifted on the oil drip-feed bowls and we oiled around generally. Once the engine got going it oiled both itself and the engine-room and cleaning up afterwards was less fun. The signal used large volumes of air at relatively low pressure, built up between blasts in large tanks. A run finished with a filling of the tanks to about 125 lb ready for the next start.

John Jarvis was a congenial companion. It was my first encounter with that oddity, the secret conductor. Like a field-marshal he carried a baton in his knapsack, and when the other two of us were out of the way he would move the chairs back to stand in the middle of the kitchen, find something suitable on the domestic radio, and conduct orchestral works *molto appassionato*. After a while he left to join the Probation service. I do not doubt he is still alive. Conductors tend to live to a great age.

My own eccentricity, at least as I practised it, was cooking, and it carried greater risks. I recorded in my diary:

> Picked some blackberries and made a blackberry pie. The pastry was excellent and I am now feeling a little unwell.

Presently I was moving into areas uncharted by Mrs Beeton. It was late summer and blackberries were plentiful. The next day:

> Prepared a rice pudding with blackberries and an egg added – not unpalatable.

Perhaps not, but I have never tried it since.

The routine of lighthouse work pursued its invariable course.

> Up and on duty 0400–0800, the first morning watch I have done. It entailed stopping the lens and putting out the light at 0622, cleaning the vapouriser, dusting the lantern chamber and watch room and wiping the slate floors, putting up the curtains, dusting the stairs, sweeping the kitchen and living-room and taking the others tea at 0900.

The rest of the morning might be considered recreation.

> After breakfast by bicycle into town to buy a few things. A beautiful day. Back and down to the beach for a swim, the first for some years, in the clear water.

This gives the flavour of an exceptionally pleasant posting, but a lot of people had found the island less agreeable. Alderney had been evacuated at the beginning of the war and its residents replaced by an army of labourers who included Russian prisoners. As Russia, for reasons of politics, had never acknowledged the Red Cross, their countrymen received no protection and suffered appallingly. As ancillaries of the Todt organisation they created, at the cost of probably some hundreds of lives in Alderney alone, a third set of fortifications to add to those of the Napoleonic and First World wars. It was part of the *Festung Europa* so derided by Rommel when Hitler sent him on a tour of inspection. And indeed it was all for nothing.

> Saw the crude cemetery of fifty or more DPs [displaced persons, the term current then]... Only five are named.

There was another large mound which was presumably a communal grave. I was told Russian representatives had recently paid a visit to the island, and some time later a memorial was erected at the site.

Alderney was a rock station in hardly more than name. The daily plane, though it was the only regular means of communication in winter, brought mail and news-papers, including an at first inexplicable letter from a Mr Purser requesting the pleasure of building an aeroplane with me. What madness was this? He attached a cutting from the *Birmingham Mail* containing some embarrassing nonsense obviously cooked up by a cub reporter with a few column inches to fill. This so unsettled me I threw down my latest tart (by now, probably, a rice pudding baked in pastry with blackberries and chopped bacon) and dashed off a vituperative letter to the editor.

I gave the matter of press irresponsibility some thought. It seemed a pity the custom of horsewhipping errant editors had fallen into disrepute. Perhaps it could be revived. I composed a letter to the Superintendent at East Cowes asking whether the Corporation would be likely to object if I horsewhipped the editor of the *Birmingham Mail*, provided any period of imprisonment arising from the assault was confined within my period of shore leave. Captain Williams replied a few days later declining to give such an assurance and counselling moderation.

I looked forward to being placed beyond the reach of such irritations. Perhaps my next posting, to the nearby island of Casquets, would oblige.

The arrival of my relief ended my month at Alderney but a gale meant that I had the luxury of hotel accommodation at the *Rose and Crown* for one night while the weather moderated. It was the following day that I boarded the fishing vessel *Burhou* to go out to the Casquets.

Up to now the matter of provisioning had presented no problems. Both Dungeness and Alderney had had shops within easy reach. Casquets was a different matter. Faced for the first time with the need to provide for myself for a month I made the usual mistake of greatly over-estimating how much I would be likely to eat. A paper calculation suggested a figure based on three meals per day, twenty-one per week, eighty-four per month; say half a ton of assorted produce. The reality was different. There was only one daily meal, supplemented by top-ups. Even then you would over-order if you based your calculations on what an active man would eat ashore. Food, after all, is only fuel. Except briefly when the supply boat called there was very little demanding physical activity on a lighthouse. For exercise, on a tower rock, you could walk on the gallery round the lantern or on the set-off at its base – *if* the tower was one that had a set-off (the walk-way round the base of the tower) and *if* it was not being swept by seas. Otherwise you moved up and down stairs between rooms.

Casquets, in the demands it made for food as fuel, lay somewhere between the extremes of an island like Alderney, and a tower. It was a pile of rock of some 200 metres diameter, the centre of which had been flattened to provide a surfaced court-yard which acted as the drinking water catchment area. At one end was the tower, at the other the Blackstone fog signal engines and diaphones. The radio beacon room and the accommodation took up the other two sides. The surrounding rocks were accessible but inhospitable. The tide differential in the Channel Isles is very great and I think at Casquets it could be of the order of 32 feet. The entire aspect of the periphery of the island could change in the course of a few hours. The courtyard was therefore the practical limit for exercise.

If you add to inexperience the normal human anxiety at the idea of running short of food, it isn't surprising that a first-time keeper tended to grossly over-provision himself.

The East Cowes depot tender, the Trinity House Vessel (THV) *Beacon,* chose the month I was there to stock Casquets up for the winter. A catalogue of the hiccups in the procedure gives an idea of the general difficulties involved. She made her first call on a Monday in the late afternoon and landed stores for three hours. The following afternoon she called again, but the sea had freshened and after hanging about for some time she went off back to Guernsey. Two days later she called at 0500 by radio for a report on how things were. At that hour of a bleak November morning hardly anything looks good. In pitch dark we went down to the landing to assess the situation by torchlight and reported unfavourably.

> At mid-day conditions were better and they arrived at about 1500 and from then until well after dark (when by searchlight) they unloaded coal and oil.

Bear in mind that Casquets was only one of several stations needing this sort of attention, in an area that included a length of England's south coast.

Such provisioning was one function of a THV; the other was the relieving of lighthouses and lightships. Some reliefs were 'local' and did not demand their attention. At Casquets, for example, the relief was carried out under contract by a local boatman, and so were those of the Longships, the Eddystone and the Bishop Rock. But most were not. The reliefs of the Smalls, South Bishop, Skerries, Bardsey and the Wolf, as well as the reliefs of all light vessels, were done by depot tenders. And when they weren't busy with that, they were maintaining and positioning buoys and marking wrecks. Trinity House vessels were not often to be seen in port.

Socially I had arrived at Casquets under a cloud of my own making. I found very few lighthouse colleagues boring, but Walter, the Keeper-in-Charge that month (the PK was on leave), was one of the exceptions. We had had a couple of casual encounters on Alderney in circumstances I now forget. It was after the second that I had had to note that he was 'a crashing bore', and in the belief that bores often bore themselves I decided I would make his life more interesting by hinting that I had a spectacular past. This, I let slip, included a conviction for 'uttering a gas engine with intent to deceive'. Walter, intrigued, wanted to know more, but I made it plain it was not a matter I wished to discuss. John Jarvis stirred the pot with the story of a trip I had made to Marseilles to audition for the post of second violin with the French Foreign Legion symphony orchestra. Unfortunately all this backfired when we got to Casquets. Walter declared grandly that so long as I showed a steady light my past would be no concern of his, and for the rest of the month he adopted an irritatingly paternal approach. This did not, unfortunately, make him any less boring. It is true, I might have got more out of his company if he had not been toothless. He claimed his dentures had been lost or, somewhat improbably, 'stolen' on the boat, but when I found we had shared the same crossing from Southampton I decided he was, like me, simply a bad sailor and that he had parted with his teeth overboard. He showed me the operation of the radio-telephone, bellowing 'I've lorse me teef' to anyone who might have been listening.

Walter's conversation, so far as it could be understood, tended to what I came to recognise as the Heroic Confrontational, the opposing parties usually being a keeper and the District Superintendent. The standard pattern was a conversation in which the Superintendent cowered in his chair while an aggrieved keeper carried on at him about something or other. The formula was so unchanging I gave it the acronym ISIS – 'I Said to the Superintendent I Said'. Some years were to pass before I was to meet its finest exponent at Portland Breakwater lighthouse.

Our table-talk could be amusing, but it could also be repetitive. I had noticed, pasted to the ceiling in the kitchen, the word BALLS, apparently made up from news-paper headlines. It had clearly been there for some time. I was told it commemorated a brief victory over a Principal Keeper who had over-taxed the patience of his two colleagues with the length and unlikelihood of his anecdotes. It was the man's habit to make his points by stabbing the meal-table with his forefinger whilst glancing up-ward over his glasses, a trick that gave rise to the belief that his mother, while carrying him, had been frightened by a balloon. I suspect any check in the narrative flow brought about by the reproach would have been temporary. Walter's own flow was as unstoppable as it was incomprehensible.

At Dungeness there had been occasional migratory birds congregating at the tower. At Casquets they now arrived in their thousands. At midnight on 15 October 1953 I went out to stand in the yard, alerted by birds flying up and down the lighted corridor within the dwelling. It was an extraordinary sight. Around the lantern countless birds wheeled like driven snow, many hitting the radio beacon masts and aerial and drop-ping into the yard, dead or injured. The station cat sat in the middle of the carnage, doing nothing, just looking. In the morning I picked up and threw into the sea 220 corpses. One carried a tag marked 'N. Museum, Praha – Csr K133254'. When, many years later, I found out that the reporting station for such finds was the British Mu-seum, I learned that the bird was a song-thrush that had been ringed as a nestling on 12 May that year on the southern outskirts of Prague. Forty more birds, alive but crippled, were trapped behind the stone balustrade of the gallery and had to be cleared. Besides those I threw into the sea there were probably twice as many hop-ping among the outlying rocks, broken-winged or otherwise injured. They would feed as best they could over the ensuing days, then die.

The Royal Society for the Protection of Birds (RSPB) provided two palliatives. One involved the erecting of perches around the lantern as extensions of the gallery rails. This failed because it provided for hundreds when provision was needed for thousands. Every inch of alighting space would be occupied by birds, and then birds would perch on birds. The other method was paraffin floodlights set up to illuminate the tower itself, which I met later on the Skerries. This helped by providing an object to which the birds could relate, as against the point-source of the navigation light above. Numbers remained the problem: most of the birds still went on wheeling in the rays and continued to stun themselves against the lantern or hit other obstructions. These were, as I say, palliatives; perhaps there could be no complete answer.

During the war Casquets had been raided by our side. That probably explained the small arms cartridge cases that were to be found lying around, though the German garrison must have banged away often enough themselves out of boredom. It was said that the commandos had arrived to find everyone in bed, which seems to show excellent judgement on the part of the garrison commander. If you post sentries they raise the alarm and people get needlessly shot. There was a reminder of the occupation in a compass rose painted on the yard with an O (*Osten*) for East.

I left Casquets on 20 October. I think Walter was disappointed that I had not produced any fireworks. He wasn't to know how close I had come. If I had held myself back during his seamless and incomprehensible monologues it was because I could not have borne his chiding 'Tut, tut' and paternal pat on the head.

I have a memory of the *Burhou* momentarily stopping dead as she came out of the slack water in the lee of Casquets, caught by one of those vicious tidal races so characteristic of the Channel Islands. The following day I flew painlessly north from Alderney to Southampton in a BEA Rapide, threading through fair-weather cumulus to a let-down through stratus at Southampton. I had been told that after Casquets I would probably be transferred to Penzance District 'to be nearer my home', a somewhat doubtful premise since my home was in Birmingham and just about equidistant from everywhere; but I associated Cornwall with hard rocks and bad weather and that was what I wanted. When I wrote to Penzance to ask for instructions their reply told me to get myself vaccinated – for the third time in four months! I had been vaccinated at Blackwall and again at Dungeness. But experience was to show how right they had been. Not once during my six and a half years in the Service did I have a single day off work with smallpox.

On 9 November 1953 I caught the train for Penzance *en route* to Pendeen.

4

Krishnamurti and the Hood burner: Pendeen and Bishop Rock

*P*endeen came into the category 'standard shore with modifications'. In its basic form such a lighthouse would have a paraffin-fuelled Hood burner for the main light, a diaphone fog signal powered by paraffin-vapour reciprocating engines (as at Alderney), and a resident staff of three keepers with accommodation on site for their families. The variation here was that the light was electric and was supplied from the mains, with an on-site generator as standby. As at Dungeness the accommodation for an SAK was entirely separate from the married quarters of the appointed keepers. Pendeen, though, was much quieter than Dungeness. It had its quota of visitors, but situated as it was at the extreme south-western tip of England, they appeared in relatively small numbers. It was November, too, and holiday-makers had long since gone home.

There was no social visiting between an SAK and his married colleagues, so the SAK saw them at the change of watches and hardly at all otherwise. It was a solitary existence, agreeable or not according to temperament.

The PK was 'Policeman' Davies. I never discovered whether he had once been a policeman or whether it was a nickname earned by his stolidity, which was both physical and temperamental. He had the enviable knack of never needing to be called for watch; at five minutes to midnight or 4 am he would simply appear as though he had never been to bed.

On a half-day I hitched to Land's End and visited an acquaintance I had met before joining the Service. Hedda Carington lived in Sennen Cove in an adapted store-house filled with books, weaving machinery, spinning and potters' wheels and painting materials. It was difficult to get into and would have been impossible to get out of in the event that it caught fire, which in the light of her improvised cooking arrangements, a single primus set on the floor amidst all this clutter, seemed likely to happen at any time. Her husband, Whateley Carington, had written a book on telepathy which I had found sensible on a topic that interested me. He had fallen ill and died in Sennen and Hedda had had a set-to with the undertaker. The man had wanted to charge her £12 for his services, which would have included the usual trappings. She wanted a plain box and a hole in the ground; and she beat him down to £3.10s.

It was in accord with her view of things, which had been shaped by the teachings of the tennis-playing mystic Krishnamurti. German and Jewish, she got out of Germany in the nick of time on the excuse of attending one of Krishnamurti's seminars at Ommen in Holland. There she met Whateley. She was a rather unusual woman. On my way back that night I called in at Sennen churchyard at the top of the steep hill from the cove. Following her general directions I looked for evidence of Whateley Carington, who had written that sensible book on telepathy. Was he under this unmarked mound or that? (I had always resented the carelessness of the gravedigger who alone saw Mozart's body to its grave, then afterwards was unable to remember where he put it.) I left the churchyard pulled by Hedda's logic in one direction, by sentiment in the other.

The following day I was told I would be going on a temporary posting to the Bishop Rock.

The *Scillonian* was designed exclusively for the service between Penzance and the Isles of Scilly, some 25 miles south-west of Land's End, which meant she had a shallow draught to allow her to get into St Mary's, the islands' port. She didn't have the stabilisers of a later replacement and she rolled and pitched with every punch the swell threw at her. As we came abeam the Wolf Rock lighthouse, never one of my stations and perhaps the most difficult of all the English and Welsh lights to relieve, I noted wanly that it looked an interesting situation. Hedda had lent me some slim red volumes of Krishnamurti's talks and I had dipped into them. 'Acceptance' of whatever might befall seemed to be the key to inner contentment. I tried it on my nausea without obvious effect.

It was 14 November and I was providing relief for a keeper with toothache. The understanding was that as soon as the tooth had been attended to he would return to the Bishop and I would return to Pendeen. And that, surprisingly, was exactly what happened. At that time of year it was much more likely to have been otherwise, and probably the keeper I was relieving hoped it would be. If things had gone his way he might have found himself spending Christmas at home. In common with every other tower rock before the coming of helicopter reliefs the Bishop's relief was vulnerable to bad weather. In 1946 Edward Ward of the BBC had been trapped there for a month after arriving to make a Christmas Day broadcast.

At St Mary's I had had my lost breakfast obligingly replaced by lunch prepared by the wife of the Bishop's Principal Keeper, and now I lost that too over the side of the launch just five minutes before we arrived at the tower. The Bishop is much bigger than was originally intended, because it was re-cased in the mid-1850s after doubts had arisen about the stability of the original structure. This enlargement gave it its chief feature, an unusually high set-off. The method of landing-on was one that had been proven over generations. The launch moved in, dropping an anchor and then paying out a stern-rope until it was some 20 feet from the set-off. A keeper would throw a heaving line to which would be secured ropes attached to eyebolts either side of the tower. These were hauled in and were secured to the bow of the boat, which was now effectively held in place by a triangulation of ropes; one from the stern and two from the bow. This limited movement to a rise and fall on the swell at a safe distance from the breaking water around the base of the tower. The unloading of men and materials could then start.

At this point arrangements varied slightly between towers. At the Bishop a two-handled winch, normally stowed in the entrance room, was bolted to the set-off. A rope from the winch passed over a pulley on the lantern gallery and then down again to the boat, its free end having been attached, like the bow ropes, to the heaving line. Men were moved before stores, and it was always men on before men off: for better an overmanned than an undermanned lighthouse if for any reason the boat had to

Although taken at the Eddystone, this usefully illustrates the relief whaler tethered, with a line paid out to a stern anchor and two bow ropes secured to eyebolts either side of the tower. The oars are stowed, there is at least one keeper on board, and a full stores box is on its way up or an empty one down. The vantage point is the winchroom doorway.

cut and run. The transfer from the boat upwards and over the often boiling froth of broken water to the set-off looked hazardous but required no judgement, just simple faith. One foot was placed in the loop at the end of the winch-line, the other leg crossed over it, and the rope grasped firmly with the hands. With that stage completed, stores boxes would be lashed on and hauled in in similar fashion; then, in reverse order, the empty boxes. Finally the man or men to be relieved would be taken off, followed by the empty food boxes and their personal baggage.

After forty-three years I do not remember much of my experience on the Bishop, which lasted only two days. I was given the caution that the spiral stairway on the Bishop rose to the left instead of the more usual right (if I had formed the wrong habit elsewhere I might have pitched myself downstairs in the dark) and my diary records that the 'effective' rooms, in order of ascent, were kitchen, bedroom, office (!), and service room. I noted that the PK, Charlie Cherrett,

> ...just remarried, seems to be particularly missing his wife. He was trying to spy her through the telescope in the afternoon.

I would have thought him an optimist if he had not so obviously been a pessimist. At that distance I was unable even to identify St Mary's, let alone his house, and certainly not the lady who had so kindly given me lunch. Cherrett was an anxious man and his anxieties provided me with an uncomfortable experience when he called me for watch at four o'clock the next morning. The wind had freshened slightly during the night and he was worried that the ropes might chafe; they had been left in place in the expectation of the early return of the relief launch. Within a minute or so of being woken he had me on the gallery in very little clothing, heaving away with pounding heart at a dead weight of rope while he lashed the slack to the gallery rail. In an otherwise sedentary life one had occasionally to rise to such demands, though rarely so abruptly.

We then went down to the kitchen and I became acquainted with the watch-changing routine which varied so little between stations. Nominally watches changed at midnight and at 0400 and this was what the monthly Journal, with its three-hourly entries for outside and inside temperature, wind direction and speed, and visibility, supported by the keeper's signature, showed. In practice it could vary. The calling procedure, however, did not. The keeper to be relieved would prepare a pot of tea, climb to the bedroom, shake his relief awake, and carry on up to the lantern where he would enter the lens from below and, as it rotated around him, 'prick out'.

The standard illuminant in the 1950s was the Hood burner, which had been introduced some thirty years before. It was itself an adaptation of an older principle. A jet of vapourised paraffin emerged from a nipple and entered a burner head where it was mixed with air. Part of the gas then burned round a self-forming collodion mantle to provide the light, the rest being deflected downwards into a retort to play two banks of flame on to the tube in which the paraffin was vapourised. It was not economical in terms of light output against fuel used (though much better in that respect than the Argand wick lamps it replaced) but it *was* robust and reliable. Lighting-up from cold involved pre-heating the retort from a pan of methylated spirits. At the last gasp of the spirits a micrometer valve would be opened and a taper used to ignite the gas above the mantle and in the retort. (It was said that the Germans, meeting Hood burners on the Channel Island lights, made the mistake of igniting the gas where it issued from the nipple of the vapouriser. The result was a loud roaring noise and a rapidly melted burner head.) Two vapouriser tubes were used in rotation, the morning watchman drying out the discarded tube on the Cornish range before drilling out the accumulated carbon and replacing the nipple. The orifice in the nipple was quite small, of the order of half a millimetre or so (it varied according to whether the mantle was of 35, 50, 75 or 100 mm diameter) and pricking out at the end of a four-hour watch consisted of inserting a wire to clear it of any carbon that might have accumulated.

The relief keeper, dragging himself from sleep, would note this pause in activity, then the clicking of the back-stop ratchet as the weight of the lens clock was wound up to the bell. This was the signal for him to stir. Only one activity remained. Footsteps descended to the Service Room where, in the light diffusing down from the lantern, shelves of spare parts showed behind the doors of glass-fronted cupboards. Here were also the 'IOBs', an abbreviation that I always believed stood for Incandescent Oil Burners, though as such it was something of a misnomer. They were duplicated tanks of paraffin, each with a larger tank of compressed air below. The burner itself, either single or tandem, was inside the lens in the lantern. Two gauges were provided: a glass contents gauge for the paraffin; and a Bourdon pressure gauge for the air, a typical operating pressure being 70 lb per square inch. The function of the compressed air was to force the paraffin up to the lens and into the burner. As the paraffin level fell in the course of four hours so would the air pressure, which was brought back up at the end of a watch by a hand-pump.

The relieving watchman would by now be relieving himself, walking to the landing window (perhaps three paces: all horizontal distances in tower lighthouses are very short), opening it, and bringing in the discarded fruit-tin from its place between the inner window and outer storm shutters. (If the wind was contrary he might go down the spiral stairs to the next landing and another window, from which the contents, when he threw them out into 'the big locker', would be less likely to return.) By now he would be listening to the clatter of the pump as the man upstairs restored the lost air pressure in the tank. Finally, as he dressed, the Service Room door would open and close with the special quietness of the night-time keeper, and his colleague would pass silently down to the kitchen to pour the tea.

The theory was that lantern watch was kept. In practice it was not, either at shore stations or on rocks. It might have been necessary to keep lantern watch when the light was provided by Argand concentric wick lamps, which could 'run away', but the Hood burner was of a different order of reliability. Lanterns are rarely very cold because of the moderating influence of the sea (I can recall only two freak occasions on the Eddystone when the temperature fell to anywhere near freezing) but they are cold enough. The kitchen, by contrast, especially when the door was sealed with strips of old blanket, was agreeably warm with the heat from the Cornish range. The keeper on watch would sit in a particular chair facing a window in which a mirror was canted at an angle of 45°. Perhaps the fog signal jib outside the lantern had been wound partly out and from where he was sitting he could watch the successive rotating beams as they progressed along the jib. That is where and how he would spend the next four hours, going up to the lantern once an hour to wind the lens clock.

For the first hour or so he had the company of the keeper he had just relieved. They would talk, two men in a society of three. What about? Anything and everything: personal histories, anecdotes, colleagues – and the colleague on leave particularly. They would both have been on other stations with other keepers; they would have lived other lives, both inside and outside the Service. Sometimes the conversation would catch fire; sometimes it would be halting. Sex did not figure very much. Insofar as it was touched on it would usually be fact devoid of salaciousness. I recall a colleague telling of a visit to a Paris brothel with his father. I decided the story was too improbable to be untrue.

Either in the ordinary course of administration, or from wisdom acquired through experience, or because of the development of a 'situation', the Corporation rotated the complement of rock stations on a fairly regular basis. The maximum length of stay for a man at any one station was three years and this seemed about right. It would be noticeable that towards the end of such a period of co-habitation by any two men the change-of-watch conversations would have become shorter and the silences longer. It must be remembered that the environment was not stimulating. There was no television (then), no newspapers, nobody visited – if bad weather intervened no outside face might be seen over a period as long as six weeks. There was the radio, but that meant the regulars (the Goon Show was in its heyday) because there were no printed programmes to consult. The open radio-telephone supplied some discreet Service gossip of a quickly exhausted kind. The Seafarers' Society provided a box of library books which was exchanged at the relief, but not everyone read, and if I recall a conversation about some short stories it is probably because it was the only one. The analogy with marriage, particularly a long-term marriage, provides a useful illustration of the differences: there, although the partners may long since have exhausted each other as objects of surprise and delight, the cycle of mutual interests continues by way of children, their illnesses, their education, their marriages and divorces, grandchildren and, perhaps, great-grandchildren. On a lighthouse, what a man had to offer was what was in his head and it was a miracle if two men could still have something interesting to say to each other at the change of watch after a much shorter period than three years.

I don't believe there is a parallel anywhere to the tower rock lighthouse society of the 1950s. Even in a three-man prison cell the door is unlocked from time to time to allow association with other prisoners. To be confined in a lighthouse was not to be confined in a cell, true; but in the level of its social insularity I cannot think of a rival.

The weather held and the launch came out in the middle of the second afternoon to end my brief and only acquaintance with the Bishop. The transfer was made without difficulty but 'I thought it more pleasant going up backwards than going down forwards'. To my astonishment I kept my lunch down on the return trip to St Anne's; but we were going east and moving with the swell which is always less demanding. Two days later – the *Scillonian* did not sail every day in winter – I was back on the mainland.

Pendeen had its compensations. I got out and about a good deal, typically walking to St Ives and St Erth and then catching a bus to Penzance to have tea at Tonkins. I was enjoying Cornwall before it ruined itself in a rapacious pursuit of the tourist, after which it would never be the same again.

Presently I received news of the where and when of my next posting. It was to the Longships and I would probably be going there on 9 December.

On the 8th I left Pendeen for Penzance, paid a brief visit to the THV *Satellite* to get my radio-telephone certificate (probably a Board of Trade requirement; I have no memory of the instruction; it cannot have been much) and went on to Sennen where I was to lodge for the night with a Mrs Tregean. I had time to call on Hedda Carington. The visit was brief. She was entertaining fellow-artists. The air was electric with creativity and I left them throwing pots.

5

Christmas on a tower rock:
the Longships and the Eddystone

As my experience of the Longships lasted only a month over forty years ago my memories of it are sketchy and I have to rely mainly on my diary for what follows. It was a posting that began what was to be a curious run of seven successive Christmas Days spent on rock lighthouses of one kind or another. I didn't seek this, nor was it imposed on me; it was purely how the 'turns' came out.

The relief was one of the 'local' ones and it was done from Sennen Cove by a Sennen boatman. The morning was unseasonably quiet. I settled with Mrs Tregarn; she asked, diffidently, eight and sixpence for bed and breakfast; I gave her ten shillings (50p). Down at the slip we loaded the stores and, with two crewmen, another keeper and a passenger, we rounded the headland and Longships came into view. There was a moderate swell and I describe the landing as 'sticky'. As I recall, we each chose our moment and jumped ashore on to an extensive landing area.

Because it had the relative protection of a substantial reef the tower's entrance was set at its base on the landward side, not, as was more usual, several feet up and to be reached only by gun-metal dog-steps. Except that it lacked the Bishop Rock's 'sitting-room', the internal dimensions did not seem much different – until I retired to my bunk. I am a moderate six foot; the bed seemed to be six inches shorter. This may be a minor inconvenience for a night. Over a month I found it irritating.

It could be overcome to some extent by sleeping corner to corner. This may seem an odd solution but it has to be remembered that the bedroom of a tower lighthouse, like every other room, is circular. On one axis it is some ten or twelve feet in diameter, wall to wall, but considerably less in the other direction because of the space taken up by the spiral staircase, which winds upwards from below to a landing outside the door and then continues on up to the next level. The need to make the best use of limited space produces a furniture-maker's challenge: everywhere the fittings match the curvature of the walls. The three bunks, set end to end behind curtains to provide some privacy, are curved. Above, reached by a ladder, are two more bunks for visiting mechanics. You can cut a mattress to a curve, but nothing of the kind can be done to sheets and blankets, so there are minor problems in bedmaking. Below the bunks are curved cupboard doors opening to reveal curved drawers.

After a month of Procrustean discomfort I decided that if I was to be appointed to a tower rock it should not, if possible, be the Longships.

The light was occulting, which means that the period of eclipse was greater than the interval of light. The lens did not rotate. Instead the light was displayed throughout the 360° and was given its characteristic by a cap which periodically descended to cover the mantle.

I have mentioned the problems that arose when there was a wholesale change of staff at the Wolf. We may now have had an experience of that kind. The keeper with whom I went out was newly appointed. Whether that was also true of PK Roberts I do not know The indications are that it was, for the occulting light proved a minor nightmare to all three of us throughout the month. The Hood burner here was fitted with the largest size of mantle, 100 mm. The problem we experienced was that as the occulting cap came down over the hot gases the burner might take it into its head to howl in protest. This it would do without warning after behaving perfectly for an hour or two, lulling us into a false sense of security. At the first howl the watchman would have to rush up to the lantern from wherever he was, for at the second or third descent of the cap the fragile mantle invariably shattered and it would be necessary to fit another. Consumption of mantles was prodigious: we had them lined up on the burner platform on spare carriers. These episodes got on my nerves so badly that, when I got home on leave, for the first day or two I behaved like a Pavlovian dog. A locomotive whistle was enough to set my heart racing for the dash to the lantern. I suppose the problem was caused by a resonance setting up in the gas flow. What we never found was the solution, which I learned a long time later. Because of the volume of gas being passed in this large burner, the nipple had three orifices instead of one. The trick was to leave the cleaning wire in one of them. It is probably the only thing we didn't try.

At Blackwall we had spent some time learning semaphore. I was now to see it used here – but never thereafter. Trinity Cottages at Land's End were situated on the headland in sight of the tower and provided one element in a complex chain of communications:

> Wrote a message home which in the evening P. sent by radio to his wife at the cottages which Mrs R. acknowledged by Aldis lamp.

The procedure therefore was that I wrote the message, P. read it over the radio, and his wife took it down and acknowledged it phrase by phrase – and this was before the involvement of the ordinary processes of the Post Office. Land's End Radio discouraged such use of the working frequency and from time to time would cut in to tell us to get off the air. It was after one of these blitzes that the PK went down on to the landing and reverted to semaphore which his wife read through binoculars. Evidence of this activity can be seen to this day from Land's End in the outlining in white of the lighthouse entrance door against which the semaphoring took place.

THV *Satellite* was meanwhile pursuing its labours of Sisyphus in what presently became the usual difficult December weather. We must have been lucky with our relief day for I note that the boat paid six visits in the course of the month and succeeded in landing stores only twice. Typically:

> Sunday. A day spoiled by an abortive visit from the *Satellite*. Awoken at 0800 when she arrived. We fixed up the tackle on the landing but after dithering for some time she decided against it and left, whereupon we dismantled the gear, cursing.

The *Satellite's* crew had even greater cause to curse. I have said that Trinity vessels spent little enough time in port and now it was a Sunday too. Apart from the need to get jobs done their captains may have been subject to more subtle pressures. THV skippers were the depot Superintendents of tomorrow. Meantime the Superintendents of today tended to frown with disapproval when they looked out of their office window and saw the depot vessel tied up at the quay.

I have mentioned food. As important was the matter of water.

18 December: Had a stand-up bath.

The only sink in the tower was in the kitchen and it had two taps. One delivered rainwater from storage tanks underneath the lantern. The catchment area there was no more than the diameter of the lantern gallery. Rain that fell on the lantern roof dissolved first the seagull droppings, then the salt-rime, then the chemical film deposited by the fog-signal charges, before passing this interesting solution down the astragals to flow across the pitch-covered gallery to the outside gutter cut into the topmost course of the granite, and thence into the storage tank. It rains no more often at sea than on land and the demands of a population of three barely matched supply. In a good summer the tank would certainly run dry. At the best of times the supply needed to be husbanded. When you had the luxury of a sit-down bath it was because the tanks were full.

The other tap supplied drinking water from a small header tank in the kitchen which was topped up by hand-pump from cisterns set into the granite base of the tower. Care was even more necessary here. I seem to remember a figure of 70 gallons a week as being needed simply for cooking and tea-making for three men, and such supplies did not come easily. Barrels had to be off-loaded from ship to launch and then pumped up via a hose, usually in difficult conditions. It was sensible to assume there would be at most one delivery in the winter months.

The very effective hot water supply, of what water there was, was simplicity itself. A large copper tank stood on the hot-plate of the Cornish range. You lifted the lid, poured the chemical mix in at the top and drew it out hot as required by way of a tap at the bottom.

Duties rotated on a three-day cycle and I was to find myself cook on Christmas Day, which meant attempting something a little different:

> Had Mock Turtle soup and Christmas pudding for extras. Afterwards we listened to the round-the-world hook-up and the Queen's speech. For tea I opened a tin of red plums. From 1030 each station – Bishop Rock, Round

> Island, the Wolf, with Seven Stones light vessel as MC, contributed a carol.
> And in the evening, at the request of those ashore in Trinity Cottage we
> repeated ours, 'Silent Night', finishing with a bucolic rendering of 'Nellie
> Dean'.

Was this the year that the Irish lighthouse, Tuskar Rock, went quite berserk, carrying on for hour after hour with uniquely Celtic abandon? On reflection, no, it wasn't this year, it was every year.

Looking back on those Christmasses I reflect that it is not only the world of manned lighthouses that has passed. Radio then meant BBC radio, with Radio Luxembourg providing the solitary commercial exception. The round-the-world hook-up might already have declined from one that linked an Empire to one that linked the Commonwealth, but we all took the Queen's speech with some degree of seriousness; and no doubt at the end of the day the BBC congratulated itself that most of its laboriously constructed landline connections had worked. Now there are no such miracles. Communication is instant and effortless and (as was claimed one year to the irritation of some who thought it meant something else) Christmas now 'means ITV'.

Memory of that Longship Christmas supplies one particular image. It was a beautiful day but with a heavy sea coming in from the south-west. In mid-morning I watched from the gallery as a collier come round us, rolling heavily as she turned broadside to the swell and headed north for Bristol or Cardiff or Liverpool. In the wheelhouse doorway a heavily built man stood and gazed impassively at us. I suppose he must have been up to a mile away, but I saw him so I suppose he saw me. Neither of us waved. For him, too, it was business as usual.

We were as lucky in going ashore as we had been in our arrival. Relief was delayed by only a day, which could be described as fortunate for January.

> We [PK Roberts and self] embarked at about 1300 and perhaps thirty minutes
> later stepped ashore in Sennen Cove.

I was given about £30 pay at the depot in Penzance and seven days' leave. My first month on a tower rock had been much as I expected. It had not been a disappointment; it had not been boring; the hours had never dragged as they had often in the insurance office and sometimes in the Welsh hills. When I had noted 'No relief because of rough sea' I had been able to add: 'But beautiful weather and it was hardly a penance to stay aboard'. It was a sentiment I was sometimes able to echo on occasions of more prolonged overdue in the future.

In due course I was to be appointed an AK at the Eddystone, but my first visit there was as an SAK. I was lucky in getting sixteen days' leave before leaving for Plymouth on the 0230 train from Birmingham. The relief was not due until the following day but I needed to arrive in time to order my stores.

Messrs Blights was that necessary institution that is to be found in all ports, the ship chandler. They had been provisioning Eddystone keepers for years. They knew the routine and no one would have thought of going anywhere else. They made up the boxes of food, non-perishables first, adding the perishables only after the call had come through from Rame Head Coastguards, who would pass on the Eddystone's radio message that conditions were favourable. And they provided the van that took the keepers and the roped-up boxes into the docks to where the tug waited at the quay in Millbay. On this occasion it was to be an unexpectedly long wait.

The relief was due Wednesday 27 January. It took place ten days later on Saturday 6 February. Plymouth at this time of year was not welcoming to a stranded lightkeeper. Having been thoroughly bombed it had been redeveloped as a megalopolis in the conventional post-war style: clean, cold, windswept and inhospitable. I spent one night at a bed and breakfast – 'fifteen shillings and not worth ten' – the rest at the Seamen's hostel – 'four shillings a night', breakfast extra. The one fixed point in each day was the visit to Blights at nine in the morning to get the Eddystone's radio report; the rest of the time was my own. I visited the parts of Plymouth that were still worth visiting. I took a bus inland, then walked five miles to Princetown:

> ...a fine day but very cold and with a keen wind. Had lunch at a pub in the town then walked to Buckfastleigh, about fifteen miles across Dartmoor.

All quite enjoyable, but the eventual promise of a 'good landing' was welcome when it came.

In comparison with the launch and fishing boat that had taken me out to the Bishop and the Longships the harbour tug seemed elephantine. We smoked our way past Drake's Island into the Sound and with tatty regality gave a blast on our whistle as we came abreast the Breakwater. A tea-towel fluttered from one of the windows of the tower in response. I don't record that I lost my breakfast; perhaps it was now too habitual to be worth mentioning.

The story of the four Eddystone lighthouses – Winstanley's, Rudyerd's, Smeaton's and Douglass's – has been told elsewhere. On 12 June 1957 I took a photograph of the stump of Smeaton's tower to mark the bicentenary of the laying of its first stone, an anniversary that almost certainly went completely unremarked in Plymouth. How different from the level of the town's interest in 'their' lighthouse in 1882, when enough money had been raised by public subscription to have the upper part of Smeaton's tower taken down and re-erected on the Hoe.

A word might be said here about the tugs that carried out the relief. There were three, and I believe it was the owner's boast that one of them had been built this century. They were certainly very old and it was my feeling that, like the elderly dowagers they were, they ought not to have been let out on the open sea unaccompanied. I can remember on a murky day being out of sight of land and the Eddystone, leaning back against a lifebelt and feeling it crack in half behind me. The on-board boat which we might have used had the tug's bottom fallen out was filled with the bric-à-brac of ages and it is doubtful if room could have been made in it for us within the span of time allowed by any ordinary emergency. I suppose there must have been a radio, for how could a tug communicate otherwise, even in those days, but I have no

It Was Fun While It Lasted

Smeaton's Eddystone, the stump, illustrating the shelving in the reef to which the tower had to be accommodated. Five partial courses preceded the first complete one.

recollection of seeing one. Emergency flares? I saw none. An engineer/stoker, one of the three or at most four crew, once invited me below to listen to the piston 'toppling'. He explained that this happened when a piston was so worn in its cylinder that it flopped from one side to the other between up-stroke and down-stroke. I wondered where Lloyds or any regulatory body having to do with safety came into any of this. It was little consolation to know that a coroner would have been critical on several counts.

The relief procedure at the Eddystone was much as it had been at the Bishop. The tug hove to a quarter-mile to the north while the boat we had towed behind us was drawn up alongside and the stores, two keepers and two of the tug's crew embarked. The major difference was that the winching here was done not from the set-off but from the winchroom a third of the way up the tower, operated on the instructions of the third man in the doorway. Men, as before, were landed on the set-off, but the boxes were hauled straight up to the winchroom.

The Bishop was slightly taller, as was the Skerryvore (which was burned out the following year in a chimney fire) but on the approach the Eddystone looked impressive enough. If the tide was low the concrete coffer dam would be exposed, and rising from it the cylindrical base of the tower, both of them encrusted with sea-growth. If the tide was high the dam would be covered, but in either case breaking seas would be coming round the tower to froth under the boat. Recessed into the base below the set-off were 'dog-steps', gun-metal rungs set into the granite. These were continued on the wall of the tower itself, suitably spaced to provide foot- and hand-holds to gain the entrance door some 15 feet above the set-off and beyond reach of any possible assault by the sea. On perhaps two reliefs out of eleven in the course of the year it was possible for the boat to tie up to the steps so that there would be a 'step-aboard' relief; but this required the coincidence of a high tide, a prolonged spell of quiet weather beforehand, and the balmiest of days. More usually it was a stand-off relief, a hauling out of the boat, a glance back at the tower, a cry of 'Lower away', the set-off beneath the feet, contact, an instant of insecurity in the act of disengaging from the rope, then up the dog-steps to the entrance and thence up the stairs to the winchroom to take the place of a colleague who, dressed, unusually, in white shirt, tie and Trinity uniform, would help to bring the boxes over the sill before going down to leave from the set-off. Empty boxes from the previous relief were sent down at speed, the winch-

The Douglass Eddystone. The base of the tower and the SE reef. High water, depending on how high it is, will come up to somewhere short of the top of the cylindrical set-off. Low water here has exposed the concrete coffer dam within which the laying of the lowest courses of granite took place in 1880.

handles flailing, the winch being slowed on the hand-brake. More carefully, the weight of the man was lifted from the set-off and the winch drum unwound on the handles as he was drawn out towards the boat, until a slackening of tension told that he was on his back on the heaped life-jackets in the bow. The ropes were cast off, the boat rowed back to the tug, and with a blast on her whistle she would be off back to Plymouth. The new month, the first of two, had begun.

On the boat out I had been surprised when the third hand, Dee, with whom I was going aboard, confided that if the Principal Keeper 'gave trouble' – he didn't say of what kind – we should stick together. PK Matey Rictus, I was to understand, had a reputation as a holy terror. The Service, then, had its equivalent of the RSM. This would be interesting.

I have suggested that lighthouse society was unique. The interdependence of three men had the effect of discouraging extremes of behaviour. When clashes occurred they tended to be across the generations, where there could be a forty-year age gap between a Principal Keeper and a young Assistant. However, there were more favourable factors working for harmony than outsiders might think. Even on a tower rock, keepers were not always in each other's company. Rather the reverse. Over the twelve hours between 2100 and 0900 the next morning only one man at a time would be up and about; between lunch and tea only two men and, of those, one might be fishing from the set-off, or by kite from the gallery, the other baking or engaged in some other domestic chore. And though society was static for a minimum of a month at a time, it would then change. Every month one (or two) men would go on leave and one (or two) return. Every three years at most there would be a more radical refreshment as someone was moved on and a replacement appointed. It was a self-sustaining society with curiously effective checks and balances.

Within these limits, though, it has to be said that getting along with Principal Keeper Rictus was not always easy. There was, I sensed, a predisposition to bleakness in his temperament. In a man who must have been close to retirement age, his features had the strained lines of someone whose pattern of introspection is not naturally joyous. His eyes were normally cold but could glitter with a spurious warmth when he told jokes; and his jokes generally managed to include an account of someone's unnatural death. He was a fierce defender of the Service as it had been, yet equally fiercely anti-Trinity. He claimed – I have no way of knowing with what justice – that he had often been treated disgracefully.

On the credit side he undoubtedly had the indefinable quality of command, allied to a disconcerting knack of catching one in the wrong. Like Glendower, but with more certitude, he could probably have summoned agues from the vasty deep. He could certainly summon fog. I recall a beautifully sunny lunchtime, with visibility extending several miles in every direction. He had been amusing us with a story, probably involving a child's death in a combine harvester, when he interrupted his anecdote to stroll to the window. 'Thick as a bag', he remarked conversationally. And so it was. It was probably my watch and I would have stumbled up the stairs, cursing, to start sounding. I don't think I was alone in crediting him with occult powers.

After those ten days of waiting in Plymouth the weather had opened just that one-day window for us. Of the following day, a Sunday, I recorded:

> Up 0400. A wild night with high seas: blowing a full gale...Cook. Did cabbage, baked and boiled potatoes, rice pudding.

A day or two later I was glad to note:

> The standard of cooking is decidedly lower here. The PK's lunch today was very unambitious.

It was a welcome decline insofar as every lunch on the Longships had had to conclude with a steamed suet pudding; the PK had cooked one for us, so we, his two colleagues, had had to cook one for him. For the significance of this as a hazard to health I refer you back to the comments on food as fuel in the chapter on Casquets.

Lighthouse watches were four hours on, eight hours off, throughout the twenty-four hours, with the exception of the one from 0400 to noon which was of eight hours. This produced a progressive rotation of the watches and the three-day cycle of duties. Going off watch at midnight was one's 'all night in', 0000–0400 was the 'middle watch', and 0400–1200 the 'morning watch'. The morning watchman was cook. Each man took his own food aboard but the cook of the day prepared the meal for all three using his own fresh vegetables – for as long as they lasted.

It was understood that up to lunchtime the kitchen belonged to the morning watchman. Meantime his colleagues would be filling up the IOBs with paraffin, or liming the set-off, or pumping up water, or sweeping down the stairs, or constructing such one-offs as a wind-break for fog-charge loading. All this was pretty standard as between stations.

I was soon to learn the background to Dee's comment on the tug. He and Matey had been with each other before and had already learned to dislike each other. This produced early skirmishes. And because no one can be an outsider in a society of three, I became involved in such exchanges as might occur. Part of the problem was that Dee didn't belong at the Eddystone; he was here for this month only. Perhaps for that reason he seemed to have no occupation. He didn't read, and he had no hobbies. This is always bad. Matey, too, had no distractions that I can recall. He either brooded or he talked. I preferred the brooding. In conversation I found it best to restrict myself to a 'Yes' or a 'No' or a 'Really?' – uttered with careful lack of irony. If I did rashly query something that seemed unlikely the temperature rapidly rose.

> I thought of Thurber's maid, the one who went berserk while doing the dishes [we were washing up at the time] and withdrew to preserve the crockery. Tempests within, high winds without.

Two days later:

> Before and during a breakfast a splendid brouhaha. I refused to comply with

> Matey's absurd demand for my services as a witness [to whatever was taking
> place between himself and Dee]. Presently there were reconciliations though
> Dee declares his unwillingness to stay in the event of a recurrence.

This was an interesting rhetorical flourish; it was not the time of year for swimming the fourteen miles into Plymouth.

If I report these difficulties it is because they were of a kind that could happen, and that the public expects to be a commonplace of lighthouse life. Really they were quite exceptional. I was to spend prolonged periods in the future in the 'double turn' with PK Rictus and, though he was never easy company, things were never quite as lively again. (I make this comment, but it should be remembered that he might similarly have complained that *I* was not 'easy company'.) He and Dee simply did not like each other and were refighting old battles.

Three weeks into the first month we acquired a visitor when the Stuart Turner charging engine ground to a halt with ominous suddenness and could not be revived. This produced the happy result that instead of listening in on the radio-telephone every two hours in case *Satellite* called (calls which rarely came) we listened once a day only to Rame Head Coastguard station to conserve batteries. We were sent a mechanic.

> Up at 0820 as *Satellite*'s smoke could be seen on the horizon. We put the
> ropes down and waited on the set-off in the warm sunshine until conditions
> improved and the boat came in.

The mechanic was our first visitor in 3½ weeks and as such was welcome: the three-handed games could become four-handed. At this distance I cannot say for sure how this affected the gameplay. I would guess that Matey became temporarily less saturnine and embarked on a re-run of his anecdotes. Relief for him was nominally only three days away. He had already had ten days' overdue, at the end of his first month, and must have been looking forward to getting ashore. Perhaps that cheered him up. Then, too, Bill Spicer was a real outsider, a Stuart Turner man, not a Trinity mechanic – who would also have been to some extent an outsider in the sense of not being a keeper. (Tony Parker, in his book *Lighthouse*, brings out these distinctions.) This would have encouraged a certain reserve while at the same time topics would have broadened. In the case of a long-stay privileged visitor (fortunately they were discouraged by Trinity House and I had experience of only one) there would have been an undercurrent of disfavour. Visitors disrupted the pattern of things; they had to be cooked for; they did not sit comfortably at a table for three; they tended, however amiable, to be around at times when one would normally have wished to be on one's own.

Within a day of his arrival Spicer had the engine going. He had been surprised to learn that we had been running it on a 60/40 mixture of diesel and an upper cylinder lubricant that was at that time popular on the forecourts of garages. Matey showed him the memorandum from Trinity House. It made no sense to Spicer. In his view a diesel engine was designed to run on diesel fuel and nothing else. The curious insistence that we should use large quantities of this expensive additive in our machinery caused much speculation in the Service at the time.

There was an embargo, later relaxed, on a relief being attempted on the first Sunday after it was due. Fortunately it had not lost us an opportunity on this occasion because at midnight on Saturday a gale was blowing. At 0830 on Monday Dee gave Rame Head a favourable report

> ...but we were to be disappointed. The swell increased and though we put the ropes down and the tug hung about for a couple of hours till about 1330 the swell made it too risky and she made off back to Plymouth with our mail, our food and our relief. In the evening the sea became calmer and a landing would have been feasible.

Two days later the light stopped. There is a story (quite possibly told by Matey: it has his mordant stamp) of an old retired keeper recovering from an operation in hospital who is visited by a younger ex-colleague. 'Your light's stopped, Principal Keeper', the visitor cries cheerily as he enters the ward, whereupon the old man starts up in bed with a terrible cry, his eyes glaze, and he falls back dead. The trouble with a stopped light is that it is so *very* conspicuous. The term is a misnomer of course; the illumination continues but the lens has stopped rotating. Like the others I made a practice of stopping the lens when sounding in thick fog, and even then I found the still rigidity of the beams unnatural and unnerving. In clear weather one sensed that every ship within seventeen miles would be noting in its log 'Eddystone light erratic'; though there probably wasn't a ship within seventeen miles, and as for everyone ashore they were sensibly tucked up in bed and not interested anyway. None of this mattered in the sheer horror of the moment. The light stopped at a little after 0400 just after I had handed over to Dee. He leaned forward in disbelief, peering at the mirror, then flew up the four flights of stairs and gave the lens a push. It started, and never stopped again. At breakfast Matey's joyless features were even more sombre than usual as he muttered about a 'Three Page report'. This sounded impressive but proved a little disappointing, the second and third pages of the three being carbon copies of the first. The third was retained; the first two went to the District Superintendent.

Reports marked the occurrence of Extraordinary Happenings – though what constituted extraordinary was a matter of individual judgement. One Keeper-in-Charge thought the loss of a broom handle from the inventory was not something that could be overlooked: 'Dear Sir', he wrote to the Superintendent, 'I regret to have to tell you that one handle, broom, cannot be found and must be considered lost...' However, he also believed that an entry in the Three Page report book, like a page in a policeman's notebook, once written, must not be discarded. On the relief with the first report went a second, which was a correction of the first: 'Dear Sir, With reference to my report herewith concerning the loss of a handle, broom, I am now able to tell you that the handle, broom, has been found and is no longer lost.' Of the two originals and two copies that went to the depot Superintendent, one of each would have been forwarded to Trinity House at Tower Hill. No doubt there was a notice board there on which they pinned that sort of thing.

The Superintendent, Penzance, was now to enjoy a three-page report from PK Rictus, accompanied by a plea in mitigation from SAK Lane. Why bother, it may be asked? Well, it was possible the lens had been stopped for as much as five minutes which was difficult to explain in terms of the fiction that we kept lantern watch.

'How about a duster falling into the lens clock', I proposed; 'It would have taken five minutes to disentangle it from the cogs.'

Matey objected that they would want to see the duster.

'Then let us pass a duster through the clock.'

It was verging on farce. I don't know what Bill Spicer thought of it all. He probably wished he was at home. Finally I sank my teeth with some enjoyment into a bit of technical writing. We had been sounding for fog from 1410 the previous day until 0220 and perhaps the oil on the lens carriage had formed an emulsion with the moisture, etc. etc. I may have been right, though it scarcely mattered. Like the First World War our nonsense wasn't sensible, or of the least importance to anyone ouside our own small world, but it supplied the need of the time.

Meanwhile one day of adverse weather succeeded another and we sent a message via Rame Head requesting permission to broach reserve provisions. This gave Matey the opportunity to tell us how, as an AK at the Longships, he had experienced a spell of prolonged overdue during which they had virtually run out of food. The epic had attracted the attention of the media, which in those pre-television days meant newspapers and radio, and a small contingent of reporters had descended on Land's End. What incensed Matey then was to hear over the radio the Corporation's assurances that the keepers were well provided for when, in fact, the larder was bare of food. It was understood that we provisioned ourselves in the expectation of four weeks' normal duty plus a few days' possible overdue. Thereafter, in earlier days, there would have been nothing.

I cannot vouch for the truth of Matey's story – he was a bitter man – though it seemed circumstantially persuasive. Certainly at some point the Corporation made it its business to provide every rock station with a store of reserve provisions kept under lock and key in a cupboard. At the Eddystone we had 200 tins of corned beef (this is the figure I remember, though it seems excessive), tins of butter, tinned flour, and even some tobacco. There was a price list and we bought individually as required. It was stodgy stuff but it was food. After ten days' overdue I noted:

> The stomach is far from happy at the present absence of vegetables. At the
> moment the staple diet is potatoes, corned beef, bread and Bovril.

At one time stomach trouble had been a common complaint in keepers as a result, it was said, of their tendency to do fry-ups, quite likely in fat that was added to but never renewed. Education took care of that and by my time things had improved in this as in other respects. There were three refrigerators on the Eddystone (of the absorption type, paraffin powered), one for each man, and this greatly eased the storage of such perishables as butter and bacon. It would also have made possible the use throughout the month of live yeast for breadmaking, but coincidentally dried yeast had just come on the market to provide an alternative. The practice previously had been to use live yeast for as long as it lasted and thereafter to make soda-bread.

Storage of meat had also been difficult. There still existed at the Eddystone one or two oak buckets in which meat had been kept in brine, but it was hit and miss in its effectiveness and had been superseded in my time by the jam jar as a means of preservation. Here the meat was cooked immediately after the relief, cut up, packed tightly into jam jars and then covered with hot fat which cooled to make an effective seal. When this method was used the meat seemed to keep indefinitely.

I had myself come round to a more fundamental solution to the diet problem after studying the Ministry of Food's *Manual of Nutrition* (HMSO 1953, Two Shillings Net. A splendid work. I still have it). I had noted with misgiving that on the two days out of three that the preparation of my lunch had been given over to my colleagues, their treatment of it seemed designed to reduce its value as food as near as possible to nil. The technique was to boil vigorously whatever it was for an hour or so before decanting it at one o'clock with a cry of 'Grub up'. This did not seem to be a prescription for long-term inner contentment. However, it was a ticklish area. Complaining would not have been wise and would probably have been unproductive; and I couldn't really reproach them with not having studied Dr Magnus Pyke's *Manual* which was too thorough to be easy reading. My provisions list for my second month, sent over the radio via Rame Head, therefore represented a radical departure and set the pattern for my following six years. For breakfast I would have a fried egg and a rasher of bacon; for lunch, invariably, a tin of vegetable soup; and for the evening an orange – plus, of course, bread, jam and so forth. A small bar of chocolate eaten on each Wednesday and Saturday would mark the passage of the weeks. My reasoning with regard to the soup was that the contents had probably been cooked and sealed in the tin within a day or so of coming in from the fields in the raw state and that, however vigorously my colleagues chose to heat the tin in water (suspended on a string in the hot water tank), no deterioration could take place until the instant the contents were decanted into a bowl. It was then up to me to get outside the stuff as quickly as possible before Vitamins A, B, C, D, E and K could escape into the Atlantic. I say 'the stuff'. Over the next six years I must have eaten some hundreds of tins of vegetable soup. It kept me well. I have never willingly eaten it since. At the time monotony seemed a small price to pay for freedom from a ravaged digestive system.

(I do not think the Longships, when I was there, can have yet received their refrigerators. There we had kept our bacon between the inner and outer windows of the kitchen where it grew in maturity as it diminished in quantity in the course of the month, a string barrier providing a defence against a particular seagull which had learned that we kept it there. This did not discourage the bird, which was distinguished by a round hole in one of its webbed feet, from flying in through the opposite window and landing on the table in what I can only describe as a querelous mood. Seen at close quarters in the confines of a lighthouse kitchen a seagull is enormous. As it seemed likely to register its protest in a way peculiarly open to it we quickly persuaded it to leave.)

After ten days of overdue we missed a chance. It was difficult to make a risky call when the tug had already had one abortive call-out. This was never discussed, but I am sure it was in the mind of all of us that Trinity would not be pleased to have to pay the contractors three times for one relief. In fairness it must be said that we never received a reproach on this score. Thus:

> On 0400–1200. There being a great improvement in the conditions I called out the PK at 0907. He dismissed the possibility of a landing out of hand but later seemed to come round to the opinion that perhaps my optimism had been justified, for in fact the improvement continues.

But the following day:

> Yesterday's promise disappeared overnight. At 0730 a wind came up and with it fog.

Eddystone relief day. The Douglass tower with the stump of Smeaton's. The normal complement of the relief boat, a Plymouth harbour tug, would be three or four. The extra heads are those of visitors who have come along for the 14-mile ride on what seems to be a fine summer's day.

It had now been six weeks since I arrived on board and my second month had yet to begin.

On 21 March, at last, the relief.

> On 0400–1200. I was doubtful what prospects to report to Rame Head and might have said No, but fortunately Dee happened to get up and staked his ten years' experience on a Yes. So I gave Rame Head that at 0830.

As I have indicated, making a decision was an anxious business. It was best done from the set-off, watching a succession of seas break round the tower and deciding whether, not now but in three hours' time, the occasional large one was likely to fill a boat sitting fifteen or twenty feet off. After ten or fifteen minutes' observation you might decide to give the go-ahead, and then even as you turned to climb the dog-steps back into the tower, something awful would come crashing through the Gut to revive your doubts and the assessment would begin anew. You knew that objective judgement was being corrupted by the wish to get the thing done, but you never knew by how much, or how far you were over-compensating.

There must have been an irregularity in the relief pattern for the choleric Dee, who would normally have stayed for a second month with me, in fact went ashore with the acerbic Matey and the mechanic, to be replaced by Fred Moffatt and Frank Roach. At once the atmosphere lightened. They were men of exceptionally placid temperament and I record no discordancy in the month that followed, which was spent scrubbing the interior granite from top to bottom. Whose idea this was I do not know; we never, in my subsequent years on the tower, did it again. I confess I suspect the malign instruction of PK Rictus, for it was a disagreeable job which left the granite looking exactly as it had before, like granite. Three days later:

> Satellite called at 1530 with a request for the weather entries from the Journal for the 11th, the night the lens stopped. The message requested I be informed that weather particulars should always be included in such reports. From which I tentatively assume that my account of the disaster has been accepted.

We heard no more of the matter.

> 12 April: Made an attempt to get to the Stump.

There was no particular difficulty in swimming across in calm conditions, though care was necessary. It was important that the tide should not be running faster than one could swim. My first attempt was baulked by the weight of line I attached to the life-jacket but two days later, dispensing with the line, I was successful – only to discover, to my annoyance, that the top of the conductor, on which I had planned to invert a plum-tin in celebration, was beyond reach. Later, with developing confidence, the life-jacket was discarded also. It was a peculiar experience to look across at Douglass's tower after having been confined for so long in and on it.

Relief day approached. A few days before:

> Rame Head came on at 2215 with the message that the relief, due the 20th,

Assistant Keeper Ken Monk gives scale to the tower. The SE reef is ompletely covered and the quiet sea shows no movement that would betray the existence of the hazard below the surface.

Tuesday, and not the Monday as we had expected, would bring a Supernumerary to replace me, and not the Old Man. Conjecture as to what has become of the old b.

I have already commented on the practice of not attempting a relief on the Sunday until we were into overdue. Now we had a postponement, because of the Bank Holiday, of a relief already so much delayed, which could lead to further delay if it was an opportunity missed. If relief arrangements did not reflect a better sense of priorities the fault may not have rested entirely with the Corporation. There was little push for improved conditions. Nominally keepers were members of the Transport and General Workers Union (TGWU); in practice their dispersal and consequent difficulty of communication meant they were poorly organised. And there was opposition to change from within the ranks. The 'old soldiers', as represented by Matey and other long-service career keepers, certainly took the attitude that what had been good enough for them in the past was good enough for the present generation. For them 'improvement' was synonymous with 'softness'.

I found the lack of recognition of the extra time spent on overdue particularly irritating. It could have been so easily remedied. I was to step ashore in Plymouth twelve weeks to the day since I had arrived for a nominal eight weeks' duty – and I would still get only four weeks' leave as an AK, perhaps only two as an SAK. It would have been administratively simple to have kept a record of a man's cumulative overdue and, when occasion offered, to have given him an extra month's leave. Again, not everyone felt like this. Tony Parker instances a keeper who regarded his tower more as 'home' than his home ashore, and who could not wait to get back to it. Some of those who served on the Wolf, from which they seemed to emerge so rarely, must surely have been in that category; but I suspect they were in a minority. Leave was necessary. 'Month on month off' later became the rule (though not for any reasons of health). I felt a quite perceptible mental 'dulling' towards the end of two months' confinement; it was simply too long.

It was odd to be on the pavements of Plymouth and to walk on the level and in a straight line, and to be surrounded by so much activity and noise. Keepers celebrated their release in various ways. One would go on an immediate binge and stagger on to his train home with a label attached to his lapel asking that he be put off at his destination. Our wages, though boosted by rock allowance, were probably no more than was appropriate to a semi-skilled labourer at the time, but having spent nothing except on food for two months we came ashore to what seemed a small fortune.

I took train likewise, but without binge or label, saying goodbye to a Cambridge geologist with whom I had chatted about the £3,000 instrument he had taken the opportunity of setting up briefly on the set-off to discover the density of the rocks beneath the tower. I had been introduced to the Eddystone. I was not to know it had been the least agreeable of the fourteen turns I would spend there.

6

Halcyon Devon days:
St Anthony in Roseland

A pre-war commercial picture postcard of St Anthony in Roseland lighthouse shows the usual neat building on the waterline at the end of a promontory, and behind and above it a thickly wooded slope. But war and the destructive hand of the military had overtaken the scene. The timber had been felled to leave nothing but an exposed path down to the lighthouse from some unused or under-used barracks at the top.

Apart from this loss the setting was superb. Up the river Fal was St Mawes and Howard Spring country, across the estuary, Falmouth and du Maurier. It was spring and the tourists were beginning to arrive. My father had turned up to see me off from New Street station. I noticed he was limping. I half-wondered if it was the bit of shrapnel from the Smyrna explosion, a memento of an episode in the First World War when he had played a prominent part in the blowing up of the Ottoman Bank. It was an episode of which he himself never spoke, for the good reason that at some early age I had invented it. Now only some small part of my mind still believed it was true. Therefore it wasn't shrapnel. Instead it was the cancer that was presently to kill him. He had turned up to tell me of a job with, presently, a four-figure salary. He was still thinking in terms of the diplomatic service and worldly success. I regretted that I could not take advantage of it at present. He limped away. I play the scene in my mind and wish it could have gone another way. So much ventured; so much irretrievably lost.

The route from Bristol was an evocation of the West Country: a change at Truro, then to Falmouth where I walked through the early morning streets to the Prince of Wales pier to catch the ferry across the river to St Anthony, and finally a taxi.

St Anthony was an oddity. There was permanent accommodation for the Principal Keeper but not for the two assistants. So it was administratively a shore/rock station mix, with the AKs enjoying the usual two months on, one off, without the disadvantage of overdue. It was fully electrified from the mains with an occulting light and an electric foghorn. The watch sequence was uniquely odd. Having done the 2000 to midnight turn the keeper on duty went to bed for four hours and then was up again from 0400 to 0800 when, inevitably, he turned in again for more sleep. It had the compensation of leaving one free for 24 hours until 0800 the next day. For once 'all night in' meant just that.

The PK was a sleepy, taciturn man who stayed for the regulation tea-drinking hour after calling me for watch. Later he was to have an eye knocked out in an accident with a flailing winch-handle. As he invariably sat with one leg tucked under him on the chair he would thereafter have given the impression of a man with one leg who also had only one eye, suggesting to an impressionable SAK a riskier job than he thought he had signed up for. I do not recall that he ever said anything memorable.

The third man, Genghis, I was later to be with on the Eddystone. He had gone for the option of becoming a 'Bevin boy' in the mines as the alternative to doing military national service. Later he had been in the Palestine police at the time of the 'troubles'. One of the high points of his life seems to have been to rumble through a village in an armoured car, pointing his machine gun this way and that. He had little regard for those he referred to as the 'A-rabs' and was scornful of their habit of hiding their rifles in sand, then getting them out and, of course, 'blowing their own —ing heads off'. I was never able to decide why he was in the lighthouse service. I felt he was waiting for another war, which was never to arrive, at least in the time we were together.

Meantime he diverted himself by laying women whenever opportunity offered. He had been on Skokholm Island when one of the visiting bird-watchers invited him to share a hide. He accepted the offer at face value and for some time they observed kittywakes and great black-backs. Presently his companion remarked sourly: 'You're a bit slow, aren't you?' 'I wasn't after that', he said with satisfaction.

On one occasion our conversation turned to religion, a subject on which he had strong views. His opinions went some way beyond scepticism. 'The Pope wants his arse kicking' is a remark the memory of which I treasure for its breathtaking simplicity and directness. There was a particular woman he wanted to marry, and couldn't, because Catholicism came into it somewhere on the other side and divorce was not possible.

His current woman at St Anthony was living in a caravan somewhere nearby. Her husband was away at sea, she was missing him, and Genghis was obliging by filling the gap. There was a period when he would call me for watch at midnight, roar off on his fifth-hand motorcycle, and return at 0400 to take over again. It seemed a remarkable exhibition of stamina. Apart from the practical difficulties, or perhaps because of them, the relationship was marked by storms. I suspect it was the usual problem: he just wanted a good screw while she presently wanted something more. On one occasion he had to cope with hysterics and returned the worse for wear, categorising the lady crossly as a 'dizzy cow'.

I sense that I am describing an England that is lost. It was high summer, and 'glorious Devon', and on those free days I walked for miles through places with names like Philleigh and Percuil and Trewithian and Treluggan. Sixteen miles was not exceptional. Sometimes I walked to St Mawes by road and returned on the ferry: 'Caught a boat full of artists to Place …' It was artist country. Typically:

On 0400–0800 then to bed till 1030. A strenuous day ensued. Left 1115.

45

> To Gerrans then Cockins, then on to King Harry Ferry where paused for 30
> minutes. Beautiful weather and the country the other side of the river is good
> to the eye. Through Feock to Restronguet Point where I ferried across, then to
> Penryn and so into Falmouth at 1810. Caught the 1900 ferry to St Mawes,
> then walked back thence via Percuil Ferry, calling at Ward's café for strawber-
> ries and cream'.

I was, do not forget, being *paid* for living this life.

There was a regular flow of visitors except for a brief interval when the military closed the fortifications at the top of the path. We protested and the siege was lifted, which was fortunate for our income. Visitors gave tips which individually might not amount to much but which cumulatively were a useful addition to our wages. My outgoings were modest. I had no obligations and the pay seemed quite adequate. Perhaps it had not always been so. Pig-pens were a feature of many shore stations, I was told, because they had helped keepers to supplement a subsistence income. I do not know whether this was true: certainly I saw none used as such in my time. It seems at least as likely that they reflected an age of self-sufficiency that has now disappeared.

At certain plum visitor stations the takings from tips were considerable. I was later with a PK whose son was a doctor and I believe a main part of the expense of his six years' medical training was met by contributions from the public while his father was an AK at the Lizard. This may seem surprising but it is quite possibly true.

I had seen the technique in action at Dungeness The keeper would precede his conducted party down the tower and stand by the table as they left, his features composed in an expression that could vary between expectation, dark disapproval, and then condescending gratitude as at a reward well earned when they coughed up. Already on the table would be enough silver to encourage a sense of obligation to contribute, but not so much as to suggest that the keepers were already on to a good enough thing. The takings were usually split three ways.

The money, though, was worked for. During the night the day's depredations had to be made good. Keepers are clean from self-interest, for what they undo they have to do. The public have no such scruples. Notoriously, they handle brasswork, which is something no keeper ever does if he can avoid it.

I did not welcome visitors, other than for the contributions which helped to pay for my lunches at Pickles' in Falmouth. The people who visited were on holiday, and often bored, and therefore boring. Or they were disturbing:

> Took a Birmingham party up: father, mother and two daughters, one of whom
> was so enchantingly beautiful I at once lost my heart to her.

Or riotous:

> Helped the PK cope with about 100 girls from St Trinian's, Truro.

Off-station there were other encounters. With Miss Pryce of the Typewriting

Agency: 'For some reason she wants me to meet clergymen'. (Why?) With a girl who 'stopped me last Friday to ask what service I belonged to'. Believing that in minor matters it is more important to be interesting than strictly truthful I told her I was on secondment from the Special Boat Patrol of the Peruvian Navy. To an elderly lady on North Road station, Plymouth, I said nothing at all when she peremptorily instructed me to convey her luggage to the opposite platform. I accepted her tip and touched my forelock with a 'Ma'am' as to the manner born. I had not been wearing my Trinity hat and she had mistaken me for a porter.

After eight halcyon weeks I went home and the following day did forty minutes' aerobatics in a Tiger Moth at Elmdon. I was air-sick shortly before landing. It was the end of a flirtation with Club flying that had begun during my previous leave. I decided that what had been enjoyable when the Royal Air Force was paying for it was now merely expensive. The club's Chief Flying Instructor had a large pencil drawing of himself in a pilot's leather helmet pinned up in his office, a relic, I suspected, of more glorious days. When I saw him again some months later in the centre of Birmingham he was in chauffeur's uniform and avoided my eye as readily as I avoided his. *Sic transit gloria...*

I rode back to St Anthony on the same underpowered motorcycle on which I had once returned from Scotland, covering 270 miles in fifteen hours, with only one hour off the road, and arrived just five minutes before I was to go on watch at midnight. The lighthouse was still under martial law but the prohibition did not discourage one visitor to whom I confided that he would be doing us a great favour if he took away, purely as a souvenir of his visit of course, the board on the gate at the top, forbidding entry. This he obligingly did.

I had returned to a new colleague, an agreeable fellow with an extraordinary gabbling style of speech which verged on incoherence. When he seemed to say he had found a dead swan floating in the sea I thought I had misunderstood, but it was true. We improvised a stretcher, recovered the corpse, and in the gathering dusk carried it up from the beach, a curious cortège had there been anyone to see us. Swans are surprisingly heavy – or at least this one was. The body was fresh and we could only suppose it had for some reason flown into the cliff. The following day we buried it in the garden by the old paraffin store, its head pointing inland to where it ought to have known it belonged. Its immolation was symbolic of mine so far as my time as an SAK at St Anthony was concerned. Within a day or so I heard from Penzance that I had been appointed AK at the Eddystone with effect from the 14th. of August 1954.

7

Spectacular seas:
the Eddystone, winter 1954–5

*U*ntil I came to read my diaries I had always wondered why the winter of 1953, so vividly remembered by most, was a blank to me. The answer was that it had been spent as an SAK on the Eddystone, where all it had meant to us was the series of gales that had produced so much overdue. Now it was high summer. Instead of lighting-up in the late afternoon and putting out at eight the following morning we exhibited for a mere seven hours – I noted a 'false dawn' as early as 0230. There were days of flat calm, and warm evenings spent on the base of the tower with a gently undulating

The Smeaton taken from the Douglass Eddystone, with Principal Keeper A.J. Freathy fishing. This illustrates the reef at its most treacherous, with an oily sea, a spring high tide giving almost total coverage, and no broken water to provide warning.

spring tide lipping the set-off, the only sound the slow thrash of the screw of some distant vessel passing in ballast unseen in the haze. Memory is usually generous; but what seem magic days in retrospect were probably pretty good at the time.

Yet it was still the English Channel and the English climate as we were reminded in a 'turn' that, nevertheless, was one of only two not marred by overdue.

> **9 September: Down to the set-off to admire truly romping seas going by like a mill-race – the result of a wild night.**

It may seem surprising that in such conditions one could be on the set-off at all, but on the lee side it was possible to be there in all but the worst weather and be wetted only by spray. On the seaward side the advancing march of the grey swells was sinister and I gave them only a sideways glance round the corner – unlike a colleague who horrified me with an episode of behaviour which belied his surname of Prudence. We were standing in the lee in rather doubtful conditions with seas repeatedly sweeping half the set-off when he suddenly took off at speed, defying not only the sea but also centrifugal force and the slight outward slope of the set-off. We had no rope rigged and if a sea had come at him he could only have hoped to grab one of the eyebolts set into the wall of the tower. He got away with it but I don't remember him doing it a second time. The following day:

> The gale continues; the best I've yet experienced. After lunch stood watching it attacking the Stump and regretting that I hadn't a cine-camera.

This illustrates the effect of a moderate sea on Smeaton's stump. The stump was complete in the 1950s. Reports in the 1990s are that it has begun to lose some of the granite blocks of its upper courses.

In such conditions the Stump would be completely obscured. Smeaton's daughter made a drawing of her father's tower being swept by seas. It has been criticised as being too fanciful but I don't find it much exaggerated. Unless the glazing of the lantern was perfect it must have been a very damp tower to live in. Smeaton's inclined base encouraged the dissipation of the sea's energy upwards and a lucky shot of the Wolf, taken from a Coastal Command Shackleton and showing it two-thirds obscured by spray from a breaking heavy ground swell, is an excellent illustration of the effect on a similar tower. Even with Douglass's cylindrical base it was still sometimes necessary to close the kitchen shutters, two-thirds of the way up.

Wave-strikes in a storm produced a marked tremor in the tower and were accompanied by the characteristic upward fling of the sea, but only at a certain state of the tide; and this was true irrespective of the violence of the storm. This oddity is easily explained. As with a heavy sea on a beach, it was the rising level of the seabed towards the reef that caused a swell to topple and break. At low tide it would break early and dissipate its energy before reaching the tower. At high water it flowed round and broke beyond it. Only at half tide did the break occur just sufficiently short so that a falling weight of many tons of water would impact the base to rise vertically and throw spray to a height of sixty or seventy feet. This was sometimes accompa-

Smeaton's stump taken from Douglass's Eddystone. Getting this photograph was a matter of sitting on top of the lens and waiting, not for very long, for a gale-driven sea to completely obscure the stump. It must be taken on trust that the stump is in fact centred in the middle astragal.

nied by a curious metallic clang which I tend to explain in terms of the compression and release of air trapped against the tower by a falling sea; but this is guesswork.

The effect as viewed from outside was probably more impressive than anything we experienced within, which amounted to no more than a generalised hullaballoo. The impression on us as residents was that we were inhabiting a very substantial structure. The keepers on the Bishop Rock are said to have retreated to one of the lower rooms in a major storm, but this story almost certainly refers to an occasion before it was cased in the 1850s. We were never in the least alarmed; though that is not to say we were not impressed. Storms, when they occurred between reliefs, were interesting and welcomed as a spectacle.

> 25 August: Baked on middle watch. The weather included a brisk breeze which did not prevent the *Patricia* from arriving at about 1615 and her launch tying up to the set-off while Captains Galpin and Chaplin came aboard. Their tour lasted about twenty minutes. They found the station 'well kept and clean' and had the fog gun fired. They asked us individually if we were happy. We made the expected noises.

The *Patricia* was the Corporation's flagship. She was based at Blackwall and for most of the year carried out some of the usual functions of a depot tender; but each summer she conducted a tour of the English and Welsh off-shore stations. The inspecting Elder Brethren (EBs) were not always able to land; certainly they gave the Eddystone a miss one year. On this occasion they had asked us to detonate a fog signal. They might have asked us to start the lens and then timed it. This they would do by placing a coin on the lens carriage and consulting a watch while it made its three-minute rotation. It was said that on one occasion a half-sovereign had returned as a florin, a keeper on the other side of the lens having made the switch. If true I would have expected the EB to have rewarded the opportunism with silence. They seemed agreeable enough men.

I was now more self-sufficient than I had been on my first visit. I had bought a small paraffin lamp at Blights so that I could read in my bunk, and had put together a one-valve radio which drove a pair of earphones. From a recumbent position in my bunk, and from a height of some hundred feet, I enjoyed a unique view. With my head on the pillow I could see the winking of the Breakwater light, and beyond, the street lights of Plymouth and an arc of perhaps fifteen miles of coastline to the west. As at St Anthony, although it was a more restricted life, it sometimes seemed a little indecent to be paid for enjoying such an agreeable situation.

There were, though, distractions. The Eddystone in summer was really quite a lively place. We even had an irregular mail service, provided by Pearn's motor boats from Looe. During the tourist season he came out on most fine days. Fine simply meant a calm sea, not necessarily the absence of a swell, and often our first indication of the approach of the boats through the telescope would be from the white water at the bows as they bounced from crest to crest. On those occasions a proportion of passengers must have lost all interest in lighthouses within fifteen minutes of leaving

Pearn, from Looe, juggling the throttle as he eases in to exchange mail with Assistant Keeper Ken Monk. The vantage point here is the entrance door.

harbour. On such days we ourselves would be surrounded by white water and he would simply circle us while those capable of movement waved wanly, we waved back, and then he would return to Looe. When conditions were better he could nose into the set-off and one of us would hang out from the dog-steps so that mail and newpapers could be exchanged. On 20 August conditions were so good that 'a half-dozen of the male passengers came aboard'. I have no idea whether there was any formal prohibition but I think it unlikely that visitors could be officially approved of. Even though those were less litigious days, had a visitor chosen to fall off the dog-steps at any point between the set-off and the entrance door fifteen feet above, the impact would have been considerable, and not just for the visitor. On these occasions, which were rare simply because the conditions that made them possible were, an AK was usually in charge. I think PKs preferred not to take the risk.

When Pearn was able to come into the reefs but not up to the set-off, passing mail proved more of a gamble.

> I prepared the Ovaltine tin. We had some difficulty getting the tin to the boat by throwing it with a line attached, so at the fourth attempt we let it drift out. A clerical gentleman nearly threw himself overboard in an attempt to retrieve it.

Variants were tried. I swam out with a line to the north-east reef where there was an eye-bolt set in the rock. The other end we took to a window half-way up the tower. Theory suggested we should be able to run our tin down the line to dangle more or less at a height convenient for Pearn to retrieve it. The problem here was that Pearn, as a one-man crew, had to do everything himself: cut the throttle and catch the swinging tin as it passed somewhere nearby, the wire meanwhile tending to snag on the short mast above his wheelhouse, and the passengers falling over each other in an excess of helpfulness.

We considered the howitzer approach, using a Tonite fog charge as a propellant inserted into a substantial steel pipe. This would have thrown our correspondence well clear of the reefs in some style and would have provided a spectacle for the passengers, but I couldn't see how the sort of containers available to us would not have been destroyed by a full 4-ounce charge. We thought of cutting a charge up with a knife. Tonite was a docile enough explosive in ordinary use but we decided we would like to have the manufacturer's assurances in writing before proceeding further in that direction. We were a long way from hospital – or the mortuary.

There were other entertainments. Occasionally a large pleasure-steamer, the *John Hawkins*, came out from Plymouth. 'She gave us a blast, we fired a detonator and ran up a pair of trousers on the flag-mast.' More transient visitors were Vampire aircraft based at Exeter. These approached low from Plymouth, came past the tower at gallery height, turned, climbed to 3,000 feet or so and returned to some point over Dartmoor before repeating the run. We were being used as a reference point for whatever it was they were up to – possibly providing a practice target for radar operators.

The relief was done to time. I had gone aboard with two Johns: one a fellow AK, John Prudence, the other John Broseley, a Trinity mechanic who did some maintenance work or other and left on the *Satellite* half-way through the month. Already aboard had been Genghis, who now went ashore to be replaced by PK Rictus of whom my memories were not over-warm. I thought enviously of Jesse James 'who never yet met a man he didn't like' and wondered how he managed it. But perhaps Matey had decided that, after all, we had to survive each other in what might be a lengthy association. And I for my part tried to practise moderation. It was difficult to keep quiet when he disclosed a conviction that the pile at an atomic power station fed molecular activity directly into the electricity grid, but 'The month has been socially very quiet and rather than prejudice the peace I sacrificed the vanity of better information to silence.'

Eddystone relief day. The working rope is being paid out from the boat, which has been rowed in and is now secured to the tower by two bow ropes, one of which can be seen running to the right. It is obviously an exceptionally low tide. Assistant Keeper Prudence is looking behind him at the set-off on to which he will be lowered when he has been hauled up sufficiently by his colleagues in the winchroom – who he hopes at this moment are also his friends. The man in the foreground seems to be praying. Perhaps he has noticed that Prudence's foot, which should be lodged firmly in the loop of the bowline, is nowhere near it. The entrance door is off the top of the picture.

My interest in cookery seems to have flagged. 'Prepared a steamed pudding for tea. It was a distinct improvement on the cast-iron lemon curd tart the excellent John served up for lunch' is the only culinary reference After seven and a half weeks 'John gave my hair a trim – the first since I came off.' Bread-baking was do-it-yourself but haircutting had to be mutual. The entry for 9 October describes a typical day:

> On 0000–0400. John stayed for a while [after calling me] reading a western which evidently impressed him. He quoted a situation where the hero asks for a lemon squash and carries the day against the barman who at the point of a gun tries to insist that it shall be a whisky. John, I noticed, had just made himself an orange drink, clearly identifying with the hero. In the morning scrubbed the lower floors: almost the last act of the relief clean-up. Somehow felt like it. Another fine day. I write this up to date in the kitchen in the afternoon. Matey is in bed, John on the gallery in the sunshine. A heavy, noisy swell is rolling in from somewhere. I am boiling my shirt for Tuesday (mentally putting a query after the day) and hoping my bread will rise above the circumstance of too hot a mixture. (It didn't.) In the evening read Arnold Bennett's *Journal* in the lantern, for the latter part of the time while sounding for fog.

This suggests contentment, yet there were evidently anxieties. I twice mention anxiety dreams:

> As before towards the end of my time aboard, my sleep at night is disturbed by a sudden starting up in my bunk to look at the rays moving across the sky and wondering why I am not up, whether I have fallen asleep on watch, and so on. Very annoying.

And there was another:

> Dreamed of M. Had a peculiar impression of the divinity of her body. Rather poignant in its effect.

The relief was done to time and there is an indication of wage levels in the mention of cashing money orders of £35 for August, £40 for September. The amount for August was less because it would have included rock and victualling allowances (of the order of three shillings a day each) for only half that month.

Also awaiting me was a letter from the BBC at Bristol. This was the latest in an exchange that had been going on since I had sent them a draft talk on lighthouse cookery from St Anthony. They had wanted to do an interview. I declined with a shudder: it was to be a talk or nothing. An interview ought to be given by someone whose long service had earned it: Matey, for example, could certainly have given them something to think about.

Returning to Plymouth after my leave I found that the Seamen's hostel had been refurbished. Instead of innumerable rather grubby cubicles there were now five well-fitted rooms. Bed and breakfast was six and sixpence. It was as well for 'The weather dealt a fearful blow in the night, winding up to half a gale', with the inevitable consequence. I went on tour again, to Looe; and on another day 'took the 1030 bus to Dousland and walked from thence to Princetown' where I looked round the church built by French prisoners in the Napoleonic wars – surely the grimmest of all churches and the grimmest of all churchyards.

> Ate a half-pound of chocolate biscuits and had a pint of cider. Then at about 1400 started to walk back along the winding railway track. Climbed King's Tor and eventually mounted the one-coach train at Ingra Tor and so back to Plymouth.

Three days later:

> A satisfactory weather report at 0830, and an eventful trip out to the Eddystone ensued. The water in the harbour was flat calm but as we passed beyond the breakwater the wind began to freshen and it was blowing about a 5 and raising whitecaps. About half way out the boat we were towing suddenly filled – or rather, suddenly went under to the gunwales, having been progressively filled by spray. The next twenty minutes were spent pumping her out and another fifteen searching for the oars which had drifted away. Meanwhile no doubt Genghis and company on the tower were keeping up an interesting commentary on our progress. Having left the quay at 1030 John and I stepped aboard at 1330, both of us having parted with our breakfast.

> Genghis seemed pleased to see us, having had what was for him a rather odd month with mania of Matey and the incoherence of Albert [the SAK with whom I had buried the swan at St Anthony]. Had a feeling of genuine pleasure at being back, and not merely because 'back' was firm ground.

> November 14: Lunch was a protracted meal, made so by Genghis's dissertation on the Union, and how little it stands for. [Some time earlier I had noted posting five shillings to Jack Beale at Pendeen in union dues; so it did exist.] Two new chairs having come aboard for the kitchen, the idea of sawing a hole in the seat of one of the heavy oak ones thereby made redundant and lowering it over the lightning conductor on the Stump, had immediate appeal and it was resolved to put the business in hand at the first opportunity. Lighting-up is now at about 1630 and putting out about 0730.

> November 15: Up 0400. A fine morning and therefore drilled out the centre of the chair. The sea was not as calm as we would have liked. Failed in a first attempt to go across with a heavy line so returned and took the cod-line as I did on the first occasion. Even then only just made it. Hauled across a thicker line, then the chair, which I found I could not quite get over the top of the conductor. John therefore swam across so that I could stand on his back. Then I found I hadn't made a big enough hole so had to haul hammer and chisel across. After half an hour we left the chair wedged on the pole with its legs two or three feet from the stump and we returned with a sense of something idiotic well done.

Smeaton's chair installed — the view from the entrance door.

On 19 November we were on the air:

> Laid for tea and afterwards sat in the kitchen waiting, whether we cared to acknowledge it or not, for 1945 and the programme on the Eddystone, *The Infamous Rocks*. As it progressed Genghis grew red and restless but at about 2025, at the end of the programme, on went the whine of our transmitter and he spoke his piece without a hitch. We were all three of us relieved and pleased. The programme was much better than it might have been.

That comment may seem uncharitable but the media's capacity for whipping things up into a froth of nonsense was unlimited then as now.

We had installed Smeaton's chair just in time.

> 22 November: Up 0930 to a fine gale and after breakfast I set the chair on the table in the lantern to admire it. The hullaballoo at times was daunting. After lunch, the weather clearing somewhat, I took photographs of seas, some of which were real rompers.

> 26 November: Writing this in the lantern at 1641 while looking down on the angriest sea yet. It isn't merely the occasional swell that rockets over the Stump: most of them do. And I am beginning to wonder whether I was rash

> this morning in negotiating a bet with Genghis that Smeaton's Chair will still
> be there on June 1st.
>
> After lunch spent most of the afternoon admiring the seas going over the
> Stump and up us. The tower, as I continue this in the lantern at 1856, is
> flexing continuously at a low frequency. The gale has freshened still further
> and the roar is reminiscent of a large blast furnace. Apparently the flooding
> ashore is very serious. Without doubt a memorable year for weather.
>
> *27 November*: Up 0400 after a rather poor night. Wind and sea had moder-
> ated by dawn and the tower was shaking less. At 0930 *Satellite* called round
> the group to ask for reports of any storm damage. The South Goodwin light
> vessel was stranded on the Goodwins, the crew trapped inside Not freed by
> this evening. A coaster apparently lost off the Lizard, a tanker broken in half in
> the Irish Sea etc.

The report on the South Goodwin was optimistic. The crew were, in fact, lost, the only survivor being an ornithologist who was seen waving from what was left of the wheelhouse at first light and who was rescued by helicopter. This month provided the only occasions on which I saw the spray thrown up from Douglass's tower illuminated by the beams of the light at 140 feet – though by then carried several hundred feet downwind. It was impressive, too, to look down from the Service Room window directly below the lantern and see the stern lights of some afflicted ship repeatedly extinguished as she laboured for Plymouth and safety, pooped by the following seas. By a not very remarkable coincidence this particular gale occurred on the anniversary of the Great Storm of 1703 that destroyed Winstanley's Eddystone lighthouse, taking its builder with it.

I thought it fortunate that the crews of lighthouses and lightships were not interchangeable. I certainly would not have had the stomach for the other branch. Indeed, a lightship crewman was supposed to have served two years as an able seaman before being accepted, though I believe this was not always strictly observed. Their turns, too, were different, being one month on, two weeks off. The loss of the South Goodwin was an exceptional event in exceptional circumstances. Lightships depended entirely on their moorings for position-keeping and safety and here the moorings had parted – even though the mooring chains were more substantial than those specified by Lloyds for vessels of similar tonnage, and were normally replaced every three years.

The weather was not finished with us.

> *30 November*: Up 0400. The sea was giving us a better battering by far than
> we received in the celebrated gale on Friday night. There was a much more
> metallic quality in the occasional clang. From time to time the spray came high
> enough to be illuminated by the beams before I put out and was often up past
> the kitchen and Low Light room windows.

The relief tug.

*The whaler rejoining the tug
with the relief completed.*

> *8 December*: A gale is increasing in strength and there are, and have been all
> day, recurrent thunderstorms. Amazing weather! Only an idiot would be
> optimistic about the relief being done to time on Monday. Both Bishop Rock
> and the Wolf are a week overdue.

Our only visitors in these conditions were aircraft.

> A Shackleton came past at lantern height and I had just time to collect my
> camera and get back on to the gallery for her second run in.

And there was the occasional diversion:

> In the afternoon HMS *Devonshire* left Plymouth under tow for breaking up.
> Deeply moved I sent an Aldis signal to the master of the tug: 'God rest your
> plates, noble Devonshire', and noted in the monthly Journal that I had done so.

As expected, relief day came and went unobserved, but two days later

> I gave the OK to Rame at 0830 in the belief that in the otherwise favourable
> conditions the swell would disappear with the falling tide. The tug arrived at
> about 1215, her boat rowed in and had already dropped her stern anchor
> when three spectacular seas came round the tower and discouraged her. She
> stood off for a while, then returned to the tug and the tug to Plymouth. The
> spirits prove astonishing resilient to this sort of body-blow, though a sense of
> mental dis-ease, inseparable from any relief, is accentuated.

It was a disappointment that conditioned attitudes the following day, when

> Most of the day there was an excellent landing, but as it was a little doubtful
> at 0830, and there had been yesterday's debâcle, Genghis said no. One of
> those things.

Due on the Monday, spoiled on Wednesday, the relief was finally done on the
Saturday, 18 December. 'Genghis ashore and the old man aboard, as much the Corporation's victim as ever'. For an hour that evening he brought me up to date on his
angsts. Unfortunately, 'with his preoccupations with bad turns done to him he has
done one to us by failing to bring aboard any newspapers or even a *Radio Times*'. The
latter, for us, did not cease to be useful after the week of publication. More welcome
was the Christmas mail, which included the usual parcel from the boys' school in
Dumfriesshire. We were not alone in being adopted by a school: most of the well-
known towers had such affiliates, either groups or individuals, and the school sent a
parcel for each of my three Christmasses at the Eddystone. Nor was it only the school.
The following day:

> We unpacked the large Christmas box from the ladies of Redhill, feeling, as
> John remarked, that we didn't merit it any more than the next man. An
> individual parcel, each with sweets, cigarettes, razor blades, a scarf, etc.; and
> a great deal of tinned food which we shared out. The hardest task ahead of us
> this month will be eating our way through it all.

Early in the month I had had my 29th birthday. The Court Circular records:

> The day was spent quietly. No cards by necessity. Celebrations began with the putting out of the light at approximately 0800, continued with the cooking of the mid-day meal, and were resumed after lunch with retirement to bed for the afternoon...

Christmas Day also passed quietly, lacking even the modest zip of the previous year's on Longships:

> Awoke at 0920 and from then until 1200 read back numbers of the Sunday papers. Matey cook. Tinned chicken, which to me tasted excellent. [The chicken would have been in one of the parcels.] Afterwards, as yesterday, a cigar and also a sip of John's wine, more horrible to the taste than the most beneficial medicine. Spent the afternoon listening to the wireless and reading magazines. Likewise in the evening. To bed at 2100.

I expect Matey told us jokes about important people he had known who had met violent deaths on Christmas Day but I was too dispirited to record them. John's wine was a brave effort in difficult circumstances. He kept the bottles under his bunk in the bedroom where they popped their corks from time to time in mild explosions.

At this point I abandoned Letts' diaries with their informative asides like 'Pheasant Shooting opens' and 'Mohammedan Era 1374 begins' in favour of the more open format of a plain notebook, so that hereafter my entries become more expansive. Half-way through 1955, too, becoming dissatisfied with my fist, I switched dramatically to italic script.

> *New Year's Day*: Worth recording is a recent *mot* of Matey's. Speaking of someone or other he said: 'He had personality. He could get on with anyone. I knew him very well'.

If we thought we saw a contradiction here we kept it to ourselves. Later:

> At 0930 Matey heard from Wolf that PK F. of St Anthony had an eye knocked out by the crane handle a few days ago. Initially we all felt very sorry about it but Matey presently brightened at the thought that now he might get St Anthony as was at one time intended'. [Later he did.]

> *3 January*: Winter is decidedly on us. The tower gets colder and colder as the present easterly gale continues. The day finished with sleet showers. ... A thoroughly dirty day and evening; miserable weather. ... In bed in the afternoon slept little because of cold feet'.

These conditions had their usual social concomitants.

> *4 January*: Matey went into a paddy about various things that John and I are alleged not to have done – wiping the rollers [of the lens], washing the lantern floor, etc.'

Beyond the weather it was usually worth looking for another explanation of a sudden change of mood. I recalled that the previous day John had blossomed into a sudden affability. I worked at this and decided, probably correctly, that my fears had been realised: word of the miserable Christmas Eve talk had filtered through from the western rocks. John might be amused; Matey would certainly not be. Hence the paddy. Worse, it had temporarily unbalanced our relationships, leaving Matey on the outside, so that the diatribe was directed at both of us. In case all this seems over-subtle, I have to insist that it is not. Like the weather, we experienced the varieties of personal interactions in a peculiarly pure form on lighthouses. Fortunately the pull towards the resolution of differences was always stronger than the force for dissolution – at least until a group of men had been together for too long, as was to be demonstrated later. And so:

> *8 January*: Matey seemed depressed, and by dint of some sympathetic listening I think I got him to cheer up a little. The sympathy was genuine enough. The mood was on me and for the moment I could excuse his quirks as those of a man who thinks his life has not been fortunate.

Relief – this time for John and myself – was approaching.

> *10 January*: And the next Monday had better be better than this or we won't be going ashore – high winds from the south-west piling up a sea and bringing drizzle and misty rain.

On 13 January occurred one of those meteorological episodes experienced with more clarity perhaps on an isolated tower rock than anywhere else. Earlier in the day a fine south-easterly gale had sprung up.

> Foul weather. In the evening between 1905 and 1910, when there was five minutes of dead calm, the wind swung round from east-north-east to south-west [to then resume blowing as hard as before]. And in the four hours from 1500 the temperature rose from 35°F to 45°F.

So for those five minutes we had been in the eye of a depression travelling, as usual, south-west to north-east, accompanied, probably, by a warm front. A sharp rise in temperature after a prolonged cold spell produced an interesting effect within the tower. The 4,700-odd tons of chilled granite would take days rather than hours to move to the new ambient temperature; meantime the moisture in the warm air would precipitate out on the walls and form minor floods on stairways and landings, particularly from the kitchen down, where there was no benefit from the warmth of the Cornish range.

The shipping report for 'sea area Plymouth' spelled out the immediate relief prospects, but the general synopsis that preceded it was more useful in the longer term. The ideal was to have a good blow from the north-west because that effectively 'knocked down' the south-west swell that was the cause of so many aborted reliefs; and this was the usual change of wind direction when a depression passed to the north. Therefore it was good news when 'it suddenly began to blow a 7 or 8 from the north-west which improved tomorrow's prospects considerably'. But not enough.

> 17 *January*: Up 0400 to hear the swell still thumping the tower and relief was
> out of the question, as I said over the R/T at 0830. Otherwise a very fine day
> with much sunshine. In the afternoon the wind went north again and that is
> where it is now, at 2230, with much less swell. In the evening darned socks.

I was experiencing the effects, not merely of pre-relief doldrums, but of what I
later came to identify as the mental running-down that went with prolonged isolation, particularly at a gloomy time of year. 'Felt absurdly depressed and mentally out
of sorts'. I had unwillingly been talked into lending my typewriter to someone ashore:

> The thought of S. and the typewriter keeps going round and round in my
> head. These places are ideal for nursing grievances (cf. Matey and Trinity).

> 18 *January*: An opportunity missed. No swell and a good forecast but it was
> blowing a brisk 5 at 0830 and Matey said No where I think I, with less
> caution, would have said Yes. The rest of the day, with a good landing and
> light breeze, was spent in a post-mortem by Matey. But he might easily have
> been right.

> 19 *January*: The impression is growing on me that we may be here for ever.

> 20 *January*: The impression has become a conviction. At dawn the wind
> became pleasantly brisk and there was no doubt about No Landing at 0830.

> 21 *January*: Up at 0940 to find Matey choleric, partly because he made a
> bloomer over Tuesday's non-relief and partly on account of a sore throat.
> Upstairs to exercise on the gallery. After lunch baked, then began sounding for
> fog at 1540 – the last straw – which continued for twelve hours.

I had an additional reason for hoping the relief would not be delayed for ever.
Regional Announcements on the radio had included references to a future talk by a
lighthouse keeper.

> Suspicious glances at me. Matey said it was probably PK Abrahams. I agreed.
> He spoke to Abrahams in the evening and presumably discovered it was not.

This was the 'radio magazine' one coming home to roost. Already, at the third or
fourth reading, the talk had seemed to me the ultimate in banality, and the experience of sitting through it in the company of a man who was going to take every
phrase as a personal affront was not one that I looked forward to.

> 23 *January*: Debacle! Up 0400. By 0830 I had decided that there *was* a
> landing and *would be* a better one – and decided it without much difficulty. To
> chronicle the painful details briefly, the tug came out, by which time a quite
> moderate northerly wind had made a fearful mess of the sea just off the
> landing. So she went back. Disappointing.

> 24 *January*: The day, God be praised! Fine weather, no snags. Climbed aboard
> at perhaps 1230 – always vague about time on relief days. John and I arrived

at Blights in high spirits at about 1340. They were closed so to the Seamen's hostel to book beds for our return, have a cup of tea and so forth. Luxury. Left a box of chocolates for Sylvia at the hostel. Home by 2230.

And home in time to hear the *Window on the West* broadcast the following day, which was decidedly less harrowing than listening to it in the company of PK Rictus.

The broadcast was wretched not because they omitted a paragraph in the middle but because they dropped the last few phrases referring to the walling-up of old keepers.

A sense of proportion was perhaps never my strong suit.

Assistant Keeper Arthur Lane and Principal Keeper the late H.C.T. Horsley. Clearly it is a relief day and a fine one. Both men are in their regimentals which means they are in the double turn and going ashore together. They will be replaced by an Assistant Keeper and a Supernumerary to join the third man who is presumably behind the camera. The ropes are attached to eyebolts right and left but the heaving line, with its weighted end, has yet to be coiled for throwing to the relief whaler as it is rowed in.

8

Fishing and fog charges:
the Eddystone, summer 1955

*T*hus far I had done a nominal six months' duty on the Eddystone, two as stand-in SAK, four as appointed AK. Reality, admittedly in an exceptional two years for weather, was rather different. As against this nominal 25 weeks, acts of God, in unholy alliance with Trinity's archaic relief arrangements, had produced an actual duty period of 31 weeks, Plymouth back to Plymouth. This quite fairly includes the 13 days spent waiting in Plymouth to go off, for as between town and tower in terms of discomfort in winter, the tower was the better place. This pattern was re-established on my return to Plymouth where the relief, due on the Tuesday, was not done until Friday.

At Blights I found a letter from Miss Ann Fox, aged 9, enclosing a handkerchief, a comb, and a picture of herself. I replied to her briefly because I had written more fully the previous November when we received in the relief mail a letter from some children at the Bromsgrove Church of England Primary School, and this had committed me to a visit to the school while on leave. I had noted then: 'Question time could have gone on indefinitely.' The visit was through an accident of geography: the school was conveniently close to my home. Such letters could come from anywhere. I once replied to one from a Japanese skipper who had written to express appreciation of our services. I thought this rather touching. It is one thing to feel appreciation and quite another to put pen to paper and express it – particularly in a second language. Most approaches came from schools. I always enjoyed replying. It was rather repetitive because one wrote what they wanted to hear and they always wanted to hear the same thing: how the light worked; but I knew that the trouble of writing was far outweighed by the excitement of reception at the other end.

As to my other writing, the radio talk:

> I felt greatly cheered in regard to the quality of it when Genghis told me the
> old man threw successive fits throughout the month as fresh offensive facets
> of it occurred to him.

He also told me of the eccentricities of the artist, Kearns – the SAK he had spent the month with. Alas, these are not recorded, which is a pity. It was our eccentricities that kept us going.

> *7 March*: John mentioned that two days ago he lost the cold which he claims
> to have had since a fortnight before he returned.

This is not a random note. I had twice enjoyed the brief holidays offered by the
Common Cold Research Establishment at Salisbury (escaping without a cold on each
occasion) and found the subject interesting. We were extraordinarily free of such
infections. Once past the incubation period of anything that might have been brought
aboard, and provided we were not visited during the month, we did not catch colds.
Perhaps more important, we also escaped influenza which, if it had affected all three
of us, which was likely, would have produced manning difficulties. Indeed, I did not
have an attack of 'flu until I left the Service and when I did it was particularly severe.
Rightly or wrongly I felt I was paying the price of having enjoyed immunity for so
long.

For me it was business as usual.

> In the afternoon wrote in the lantern, and in the evening before lighting-up
> finished writing the radio play; to celebrate which I sang through the score of
> *Rigoletto* for an hour.

I would have done this terrible thing in the Service Room or lantern. Later, when
I was to bring a violin aboard, such isolation was even more essential.

Genghis's relief approached.

> Heard last night that the old man has gone sick, whereat there was general
> rejoicing – the merriment not at his sickness but at his delayed return.

Relief was due on the Saturday.

> Nothing doing. Gale, swell, all the trimmings.

Sunday was the first in overdue and therefore observed as a Trinity Sabbath. Hence,
Monday:

> We missed our opportunity yesterday. John called the tug out [today] and for
> the third time in my limited experience it went back empty. Genghis flashed it
> to go back before ever it arrived.

Yet there was none of the *angst* that had attended overdue at the end of my previous turn. True, I was not going ashore and Genghis may have felt differently, but it
had much to do with it not being spent in the baleful company of Matey. The relief
was done on the Friday, All Fools' Day:

> I haven't known as good a landing since I've been here. A beautiful day. The
> tug arrived late when we were beginning to find plausible various implausible
> reasons why it shouldn't come at all. They rowed right up to the set-off and it
> was a step-on, step-off relief and very quickly over.
>
> *Saturday*: Rather irritable in the evening. I regret the loss of Genghis's
> generous personality.

Assistant Keeper Arthur Lane giving scale to Smeaton's tower. The level at which he is standing would have been the floor of Smeaton's first room. The entrance was lower down, reached by a circular central stairway which was filled in when the upper part of the tower was taken down in 1882.

Matey's stand-in was an SAK, Graham Edwards. 'He tried with eventual success to get the kite flying from the gallery.' Kite-flying was a means to an end, not an end in itself. Two kinds of fishing were possible: from the set-off with rod and line when conditions permitted, and from the gallery when they didn't. The kite was a simple affair of two sticks covered by cloth, but the rigging of it required some finesse if it was to cover the areas of reef most likely to produce a catch. The technique was to pay out the line until the kite was a few feet above the sea when one or more hooks hanging below it would trail through the water. Anything caught would be hauled 140 feet up to the gallery. The result of my colleagues' efforts was that we occasionally had fresh fish, pollack mainly I think – certainly they tended to be of a kind not commonly found on fishmongers' slabs. I was an outsider to the sport. Fishing is supposed to be relaxing. My view is you have to be very relaxed to start with to tolerate such hours of inactivity.

Smeaton's Chair had survived the winter but we thought it could probably do with a little maintenance. 13 April was the day on which Pearn's motor boat paid its first call of the new season:

> She could have come alongside to take letters but [unexpected as she was] we had none. After an early lunch I swam across to the Stump (its first visitor since John and I on November 15th last) presently followed by Graham. We hauled across materials and tools and while he gave the chair a coat of paint I chose a granite block on the far side of the tower and attempted to chisel a logo [was the word known then?] and the date in a commemorative gesture. The granite was infernally hard and I don't know how back in 1758 the masons managed to dress so much of it to such accuracy. We spent about 2½ hours there.

I still do not understand how you dress granite, nor would any layman who had tried to make an impression with an ordinary hammer and chisel on that intractable material.

The fishermen were perhaps becoming embarrassed by their modest catches and where finesse had failed they turned to brute force – to little better effect:

> In the afternoon, off the set-off, we depth-charged fish with fog-charges. Graham went in to recover one, stunned, rock salmon.

The *Satellite* paid us two visits and then it was relief day:

> It promised to be a very good relief in brilliant sunshine, but before we saw the boat a shallow fog came in thickly enough to affect even our view of the Stump. I had abandoned hope when the tug gave a hoot and the relief was effected without much trouble, Genghis coming aboard with the old man. On rowing away we lost both tug and tower for a time. The fog didn't lift till we got into Plymouth Sound with the consequence that I missed my train.

I walked into the house at ten to six the next morning reflecting that had luck gone the other way I might at this hour have still been sharing the row to Plymouth or (just as likely in fog and without a compass) France.

The Corporation had evidently come round to the idea of accepting Sunday as a relief day, though I make no comment on the change.

> For the second time in succession the relief was done on the due date, the old man and the SAK going ashore – the latter having, rather annoyingly, taken the chair down from the Stump at the instigation of the former, who blamed its presence there for the run of bad weather: a variation from blaming the atomic bomb

– one of Matey's themes. I do not say so but I recognise the element of tit-for-tat in the gesture and do not now complain. If I am honest I have to admit part of the motivation of installing the chair in the first place was an awareness of the annoyance it would cause Matey whenever he looked at the Stump and saw it there, an irrational blot on his ordered world. But why had Graham Edwards, who, after all, had been prepared to give it a coat of paint during the month we had shared together, gone along with its removal? Because Matey was there and I wasn't. The chair was a pawn in a month that would otherwise have seen more stress than it did. Its removal performed the function of making Matey feel better. These were games we played.

It was high summer again.

> After tea, on the set-off for a walk, I spotted the fin of a 12-foot shark quite
> close and the others came down and we stunned some fish with fog-charges
> and had them for supper.

Sharks, usually basking sharks, were quite common in these waters and Looe has in recent years become a centre for shark-fishing for sport. Two days later a pair came right in to the set-off. Their curiosity was ill-rewarded:

> The others did their best to stun them with fog-charges, exploded under water,
> but to me, watching from above, it seemed to have no effect whatsoever

– I am happy now to say.

The Looe boats continued their visits and continued to present the usual problem. We revived the fog-charge idea:

> After lunch tested on the set-off a device designed to propel our mail to the
> motor boat. When I fired the Tonite charge, of the quite complicated arrange-
> ment of tins, cylinders within cylinders and so forth only a few slivers of a
> wooden box remained.

We never did succeed in devising a method guaranteed to work in all circumstances.

As in most personal diaries the outer world impinged but rarely. Exceptions were the deaths of 87 people at Le Mans on 11 June, which I shakily translated from a news item on a French station I happened to be listening to in the small hours. (It wasn't for another quarter of a century that I saw the finger of responsibility for Pierre Levegh's accident pointed at one of my school contemporaries, Mike Hawthorn, remembered by me for his blond hair, who became world champion before killing himself in a sprint in a Jaguar along the Hog's Back.) And

> A poor woman is to hang tomorrow. [This was Ruth Ellis.] The other two
> profess to great glee. It is more, I think, than sheer unimaginative callousness.

The 'more' of course was that I had expressed the opposite view.

Otherwise, 26 June, a Sunday:

> A beautiful night. Before three the first light of dawn was showing over

Mail delivery courtesy of Pearn's motor boat from Looe. (How was it taken? I can only guess, by lying out on the four-by-four timber beam that carried the aerial at gallery level – having first, I hope, checked the bracing wires for corrosion! It occurs to me that if I had fallen from this height I would almost certainly have sunk Pearn's boat).

> Plymouth. At 0430 I had a breakfast of bacon and egg, called John, and went
> to bed in broad daylight at 0515. Slept till 0945. Up at 1050 and went down
> on to the set-off to greet the two boats from Looe.

This entry illustrates the flexibility we exercised in handing over watches – here nominally at 0400, actually more like 0500.

It was on days like this that I experienced that recurring sense of astonishment at being paid for what I was doing. Our situation seemed so immeasurably better than that of the Pearn's trippers who, *mal-de-mer* aside, were going back to a holiday which they might or might not be enjoying, harrassed by their children, racketing around irritably in their cars, doing the sights because they had to be done, and then returning home (with relief?) to another year in factory and office. I would not even agree that we paid for these halcyon days in winter: I think we lived better lives than most even then. Such burdens as there were were self-imposed. I was continuing to busy myself with writing, sometimes easily, more often with miserable difficulty.

Relief day was yet another done to time and we had a visit from the Looe boat before the tug arrived.

> A beautiful day. A girl in the boat wanted to take a photo of us but was too
> shy. She obviously thought us very weird and wonderful. When the boat left
> she kept on waving long after the others had stopped. My heart went out to
> such a hesitant soul.

As a consolation the relief brought 'a very good letter from M.' – the girl I was eventually to marry.

Matey had come aboard with new fishing gear.

> Since he wanted to fish he prescribed virtually a no-work morning, so taking
> the lantern table on to the gallery in the shade I wrote a note home… At
> perhaps 1600 a fine yacht hove to to westward and a rather beery pair, a man
> and a girl, rowed in. Before Matey could quote rules and regulations she was
> aboard, waving a bunch of bananas as a passport, and to the top of the dog-
> steps in no time, presently followed by the man. She was a talkative piece, full
> of personal questions and, I thought, a bit rough. Still, the bananas were
> welcome.

They went back to their yacht with the declared intention of waiting for us to put the light in, then shouted their disbelief when we told them we had. The explanation of course was that not until they came into the focal plane of the lens some two or three miles away would they get any impression of the beam at all. The passengers on the Looe boat, which made a rare evening visit a few days later to the same end, must have been similarly disappointed.

Racing pigeons were frequent and messy visitors. They would squat in the window spaces and were reluctant to leave:

> The boat took away our three resident pigeons which I had caught and put
> into a box.

There was the usual 'duty' correspondence.

> On middle watch replied to a Kentish schoolboy who wrote enquiring after
> particulars of the lighthouse and hoping his letter would help to relieve our
> boredom. ... In the afternoon washed some clothes and wrote to Master
> Richards of Ilkeston, in reply to a 20-word request for particulars.

Pearn made the occasional miscalculation, for which his passengers cannot have
been grateful.

> Up 0415, and soon after me, the wind which thereafter blew a 5 all day and is
> still doing so now at 2258. To our surprise both boats came out from Looe,
> taking the devil of a thumping as they drove into the easterly swell. Pearn's
> turned back immediately it got here and the other one even before that.

Anxiety about the relief was justified but by only one day. It was one of those step-
aboard reliefs, with the sea so obligingly quiet that the whaler was able to tie up to the
dog-steps, and I was home by late evening.

The date was Wednesday, 27 August, and for four weeks and a day, until the next
relief (weather permitting) on Thursday 25 September, I was free to renew acquaintances, spend my back-pay, and read through an accumulation of 56 daily newspapers
for in-depth coverage of a world that for upwards of 2 months had passed me by. I
sometimes wonder whether it was the thought of that waiting pile of broadsheets
that, in part, gave me the pre-relief glooms when I was on the lighthouse, and perhaps contributed to a certain lightening of mood, towards the end of my leave, at the
prospect of leaving the unread arrears behind.

9

Over-population, lunacy and appendicitis:
the Eddystone, autumn and winter 1955–6

My next spell on the Eddystone was to prove eventful. Each event in its own way was welcome, which is not to say that they were all necessarily convenient at the time; but if variety is the spice of ordinary life it is the stuff of life itself to the lightkeeper.

When I returned to the Eddystone on 25 August it was to another of those step-aboard reliefs. (Why do I remember them as a rarity? Yet I am convinced they were.)

> For the rest of the day unpacked and listened to the inevitable tale from Genghis of an uncomfortable month with the old man.

> 26 August: Went down to meet the boat from Looe. This being the Genghis regime we had some of them aboard and up the tower. Swam to the Stump to see whether my chiselling of the 13th April was still visible. It is. ... As yesterday I went for a swim before lunch. Very nice in and the water is very clear after so many weeks of calm weather. In the evening for a walk on the set-off, talking to Genghis about my random number producer and about the two-stroke reaction propulsion boat engine I thought up last time off.

Genghis used to get a lot of this, and yet it was to be another two years before he came actively to detest me. As I think I have commented, he was a generous fellow.

> 30 August: The boat came out in the morning and we stunned a few fish for her with fog-charges.

Pearn and his passengers gathered as many fish as they could as they floated to the surface. It may seem that we were rather prodigal with the Corporation's fog-charges in directions of which they would certainly not have approved. It did indeed require a little squaring of the books but not to any gross extent. When we made our relief returns we included barograph records of our fog sounding – the needle responded to the explosions with a blip in the trace every five minutes. This was not for any accounting purposes but for production as evidence of visibility, or lack of it, in a maritime court should occasion arise. In theory we could have simulated consumption of charges by making blips manually, but it would have been a tedious exercise and I don't recall that it was ever necessary: we carried a stock of many hundreds of

The Smeaton and Douglass towers with reef. It needed an exceptionally low tide to expose as much rock as is seen here, and to make the SE reef accessible. An unidentified keeper is contemplating the gap in the reef that produced the difficulty.

charges and strict accounting would not have been practicable. We were paid 2d. per hour Fog Signal allowance while sounding, and before depreciation made this a non-sense it was regarded as 'baccy money'. In those circumstances it might have been worth unscrupulous keepers claiming to have sounded for fog when they had not done so, and Matey told me of one station where this practice, carried out to excess, produced such an embarrassing surplus of charges that the keepers were obliged to dump them. Unfortunately they floated away to strand themselves, all too conspicu-ously, on a nearby reef, providing some deservedly anxious days until a high tide obligingly carried them off.

> After lunch went out on to the gallery with the sea as close to flat calm as it is ever likely to be. Presently swam out to the south-east rocks where I have not been before, then across to the Stump and finally back to the tower.

The month had already got off to a cracking start.

Then came a nasty surprise:

> 31 August: A jolt in the morning in the news over the R/T that two mechanics and two masons were arriving by *Satellite* this afternoon. And, by God, they did! I sat on the gallery until she loomed out of the haze at about 1500.

> Besides the men she deposited a great deal of tackle – ropes, cradle, tools, cement. Our gloom preceding their arrival can be imagined; the reality was, as always, kinder. All four seemed agreeable. We talked a great deal – or rather they did – then we had tea at 1830 and they did afterwards. With seven aboard we have to have our meals in two sessions.

Our consternation was understandable. On a lighthouse designed with minimum comfort for three, four was acceptable, five a crowd, but *seven*! The Eddystone, after all, was no more than a series of vertically stacked rooms, each measuring a few feet in diameter. Two of the visitors, of course, could occupy the spare upper bunks in the bedroom. The others had to go to ground in more makeshift circumstances, one in the Low Light room behind the glare of the Argands, the fourth in the winchroom. I retreated to wherever they weren't and consoled myself by beginning an article 'On Being Seven'. Fortunately it was uncomfortable for them too, and they could be counted on to do what they had to do and get away as quickly as possible.

> Up 0430. Morning watch was a little complicated by the guests, who rose from 0815 onwards and inhabited the kitchen thereafter.

My diary does not mention it but I remember that on a morning when the visitor in the winchroom showed a disinclination to rise I took him first a mug of tea, then ten minutes after that a mug of cocoa, then after another ten minutes a mug of coffee. On each occasion he roused himself with embarrassment and swallowed the drink, then presently appeared in the kitchen looking decidedly queasy. I waved his gratitude aside, assuring him it was all part of the lighthouse service.

Pearn and his motor boats were not our only visitors. The RAF had a flight of Vampire fighter aircraft stationed at Exeter, and it was probably to provide a practice target for radar operators that an aircraft would fly out to the Eddystone at low level, then turn and climb to prhaps 3,000 feet to somewhere over Dartmoor before diving down over Plymouth to repeat the procedure. We had a grandstand seat for this private, if rather repetitive, airshow, and occasionally I would climb on to the roof, taking care not to slip on the dome of the cupola and impale myself on the spike of the wind vane, and wave my appreciation as the plane went past at lantern level about a quarter of a mile away.

I rashly took it into my head to think they might like to have some photographs of themselves banking round the tower below horizon level. Unfortunately my invitation to an approaching pilot by Aldis lamp to 'Send for photos' was misunderstood. I had probably overestimated the ability of a pilot travelling at 300 knots and 150 feet to read Morse, even supposing RAF pilots nowadays are acquainted with Morse.

It was embarrassing presently to have an RAF launch come out of Plymouth, make a circuit round us, and then go back, recognising that nothing was amiss. Fortunately we had the Looe boat and to forestall consequences I wrote to the RAF at Plymouth, explaining and apologising, and enclosing some prints. I thought I had by now learned to identify individual pilots by their different techniques.

> Just after lunch a Vampire made low sweeps. It was the more genial of the two, *not* the one I signalled to on Thursday, and it occurred to me he was giving us the opportunity of repeating the Aldis message. It was not a risk I was prepared to take. We simply waved.

The following day I felt that my letter had been received.

> Earlyish on a bright morning a Vampire gave us a couple of really fast runs – fumes pouring out quite impressively.

Mail continued to come and go with its usual unpredictability.

> The boat came out but there was a bit of a wash on and she couldn't come in close enough. I therefore swam out a few yards with a rope. However, we were at cross purposes, there was a certain amount of confusion and we succeeded in getting mail aboard without despatching it.

The predicament that immediately concerned me was being with six other people in accommodation designed for three.

> The mechanics say they may have to stay here over the relief, confound it.

I also had rheumatism again. The 'screws' (as it was known in the Service: I do not know whether the nicely judged term has wider currency) does not rate highly as a sympathy getter, I suppose because it does not kill. It is even rather comical in its effect on the victim. And if it comes it also goes. Nonetheless it can be extraordinarily incapacitating. One learns to choose one's muscles with care. In a bad spell it would take me minutes to bend down through the lens pedestal door in order to climb up inside and prick out the burners. Genghis was a fellow sufferer and he had had a bad dose of rheumatism when he was stationed on one of the Lundy lights, where it seriously interfered with his love life (the sex act, as I was myself to discover in due course, was incompatible with a severe attack of rheumatism and could produce appalling suffering – and hilarity). Having heard bee stings recommended as a palliative he found a bee (or more likely a hive: Genghis tended to do nothing by halves) and irritated it into doing its stuff. The following morning he was surprised to wake up free of rheumatism but apparently quite blind. Fortunately first impressions were exaggerated. He evidently had an allergy to bee stings and his face had puffed up overnight so that his eyes disappeared. After that he decided to live with his rheumatism.

If I had the screws, Genghis now had other problems:

> Before Genghis went to bed we made a combined assault on a tooth that has been troubling him – filling, not extraction.

I am unsure what we filled it with. I have some recollection that a dentist had provided me with an emergency pack of amalgam and some basic instructions. Surprisingly, there is no further mention of toothache.

> *11 September*: The kitchen filled nearly all morning with smoking men.

This was an enforced observance of the Sabbath. But things might have been worse.

> 13 *September*: At 0600 Tony had to give a no-go to Rame for Reynold's tug which is to bring out someone else – who, no one quite knows. Eight of us – ye Gods!

Fortunately he was never to arrive.

> Just before lunch harangued Genghis on Jung's 'collective unconscious' and all that it helps to explain in the way of telepathy etc. [Poor fellow.]

> In the evening a large three-masted schooner came up from the south-west. We flashed 'What ship?' and she replied 'Russian ship *Serov*', which was a surprise.

I hope I had the wit to flash 'Good sailing' rather than the more usual 'Bon voyage' which by introducing a third language would have done nothing to arrest the downward spiral in international relations. The following day the very attractive motor vessel *Venus* resumed her series of weekly Plymouth–Madeira sailings – the first since dragging her moorings and going aground in the Sound in January's storm.

> We flashed her 'Bon voyage' – acknowledged, and 'Mind the rocks' – unacknowledged.

Our evenings in the kitchen had become convivial and the atmosphere was at times reminiscent of a Wild West saloon without the bar – once accepted that the saloon was the size of a large cupboard and contained six people, one of whom probably had to stand on someone else's shoulders to make room for me to enter.

> Wrote a letter in the lantern, interrupting it to go downstairs and walk in on an exhibition of party tricks by a mechanic. The highlight of the evening was a game of draughts between the mason and his mate in which neither was having any success in taking the other. Someone presently pointed out that one of them was playing in the black squares, the other in the white!

Catching the party spirit, Tony Coleman had earlier travelled down the stairs from the lantern on his backside. Imitatively, the following day a mason or mechanic fell down the same flight, to my surprise 'surviving with nothing worse than bruises and possibly a broken toe'.

It had seemed a long month, but it came to an end, and to time. However,

> too much of yesterday's swell remained to make the relief comfortable, and though the men were exchanged the materials remained behind. Genghis and Tony went ashore, Matey and SAK Allvin came aboard. Dick Allvin had been guaranteed agreeable by Tony and proves to be an extrovert/introvert, if that is a meaningful classification. To me it means that he talks, but not all the time. Spent some time showing him the ropes. To bed between clean sheets at 2115.

It Was Fun While It Lasted

I am obliged to refer again to our aerial entertainers for what one particular performance led to.

> After lunch *our* Vampire came past. I went on to the gallery and he did the usual. I stood astride the weather-vane for his final run and took a photo. This pilot's technique is quite distinctive – and satisfying.

I wish now I had written to tell them how much I enjoyed their performances, particularly that of the one who flew with such *élan*. I remember that it was in the mood of exhilaration produced by this display that I went down to the kitchen and discovered the Lane Effect. (Anyone not interested in science should skip the next couple of paragraphs.) In the absence of fresh milk the common practice was to add a spoonful of condensed milk to our tea. The flavour was different but just as acceptable when one got used to it; and because of its sugar content condensed milk could be exposed indefinitely without going 'off'. Indeed, I have gone ashore for a month, returned, blown the dust from the surface of a half-used tin and resumed its use. What I now noticed, as I withdrew a spoonful for transfer to the teacup, was the similarity of the ring left by a bursting bubble on the surface of the milk to the rim of a lunar crater.

The observation was to me what Newton's apple had been to him. Suddenly a number of things fell into place. It has to be remembered that in those pre-Apollo – indeed, pre-Sputnik – days moon-theorists tended to be divided broadly into two schools, the Magma and the Cheese. Was the appearance of the moon's surface the result of action by the one, or did it consist of the other? A case could be made for either but intuitively I had always favoured cheese. Now I saw in a sudden flash of insight that the moon must be a good deal younger than was generally supposed. *Ultimately* it would be cheese, yes (my intuition had been sound enough there) but for the present it was at the half-way stage of condensed milk!

I am ashamed to say that my first thought was as egocentric as that of any comet hunter, or any contributor of a seminal paper to *Nature*: I wanted to establish right of first discovery. Within the hour I had drafted and prepared for despatch what was probably the only Letter to the Editor to be sent to the London *Times* from the Eddystone. I still recall the opening: 'Sir, May I draw your attention to the moon? Observations recently made here suggest very strongly that it consists, not of cheese, but of condensed milk, sweetened...' I was very pleased with it. My letter did not appear, of course. Without vetting by a peer group of other lunatics I had not expected it to; but it would go on file. I was happy enough to receive in due course the editor's formal postcard acknowledgement of my communication. Meantime I looked to the future. In due course someone with an impeccably unpronounceable name would write a paper for *Nature,* and if academic integrity counted for anything my name would be there in the title: *The Moon Post Lane* – something like that. From here it was but a small step to recognising that I would have to send a copy to the Superintendent at Penzance with a covering letter explaining that as my investigations would necessarily be conducted in the Service's time I would keep him advised of developments.

All good fun but something more serious was now brewing.

> *Wednesday 28 September*: Dick Allvin has been suffering from an upset stomach.

> *Thursday 29 September*: Dick has been enjoying often acute stomach-ache which has taken the gilt off living for him.

> *Friday 30 September*: In the morning with Dick cleaned paint-brushes on the set-off. He went to bed before lunch for the rest of the day and this evening Matey is wondering whether to send a message via Rame tomorrow morning asking for him to be taken ashore. Lit up after tea (Dick being still abed) then went downstairs to console the old man who is tormented by unpalatable alternatives i.e. to send Dick ashore or not to send him, with risks both ways, *from* Trinity and *to* Dick. He temporises by getting into a worry about minor issues that in the circumstances are irrelevant. Thus he was concerned at the question of watches as recorded in the Journal – what would 'they' say if Dick signed for watches he had not actually kept (as when I did his lighting-up). To my suggestion that they'd probably take the sensible view that it was the man and not the books that mattered he replied with the refrain 'Ah, but you don't know Trinity as I do'. I had heard this so often that rashly (but who does not sometimes put a foot wrong in such circumstances) I suggested that his suspicions were exaggerated; that there was room for more mutual trust than he showed. He replied that he had very little trust in anyone – I myself had got him into serious trouble a year ago.

No doubt this was a reference to the 'stopped lens' episode of the previous winter which had almost certainly produced no repercussions whatsoever. I went to bed.

Three hours later, when Matey called me at midnight:

> My remarks had evidently rankled, for when he came down from his final wind-up he at once said he didn't see how the question of exaggeration had arisen in a discussion about a sick man.

He was right of course. It had arisen because I had raised it and I should not have done.

> It made him wonder who was mentally sick, him or me. He had been told it was me.

This was interesting. Of course he did not have the benefit of knowing that my letter to the *Times* (copied to the District Superintendent) had been despatched via the Looe boat the previous day. That would have resolved the issue for him.

> Evidently Matey does at least suspect we find his mental quirks odd. 'I know what goes on behind my back'. 'I assure you you're mistaken. Nothing goes on behind your back'. 'Oh yes it does. "They" tell me'.

At the end of my watch

> I called Dick at 0430. He came down to the kitchen for a rice pudding I had
> made but as soon as he got up the pain returned and he went back to bed.

I was grateful the pain had returned before and not after the pudding. I did not want yet another confirmation of the awfulness of my cooking. (By this time I felt my puddings were pretty reliable – unlike Genghis's, of which I had had to write that 'G. gave us for afters one of the most appalling rice puddings I have ever tasted'.) I stayed up till 0600 when I called Matey before turning in myself. This fortunately clinched the matter and at 0930 Matey asked for a boat and a replacement.

Meantime we had been looking into a book with a title like *The Ship's Captain's Medical Compendium* which the Corporation issued to each rock station. In recent years I have tried and failed to find this excellent work. Perhaps it is no longer in print. In simple text, with colour illustrations, it covered every condition known to man, both pre-mortem and post-mortem. In the latter class it even included, surprisingly, instructions on how to age a corpse. I went up to the bedroom with the book open in my hand and asked Dick to show me his navel. I explained that if we found it had turned green it meant he had already been dead three weeks. Leaving him to be amused at my pleasantry I went back downstairs to Matey, who I think would have felt happier about the whole thing if Allvin *had* obligingly expired. It was going to be much less easy to justify to Trinity the sending ashore of a man with stomach-ache. My own view was that it would be unfair to Allvin, a pleasant-seeming fellow with perhaps dependant relatives ashore, to delay action until this circumstance had come about.

At 1200 Rame Head told us Craig Jevons, ex-Penlee Point, would be out later in the day.

> We had lunch, put down the ropes – a beautiful afternoon – and were helping
> Dick to pack when at 1400 Rame came on again to say that the boat
> wouldn't be out till tomorrow. We took up the ropes again. In the evening I lit
> up, then sang in the lantern before finally walking on the gallery and handing
> over to Matey at 2015. To bed at 2100 and read Dick parts of Flecker's
> *Hassan*, which was new to him. He was pleasantly appreciative. In fact he is so
> miserable with boredom and pain that I think he would have been grateful if I
> had done no more than recite the alphabet.
>
> *Sunday*: To make our two-handed watches even longer the clocks went back
> tonight. So Matey called me at 0410 old time or 0310 GMT. It seemed a long
> watch to putting out at 0625. Gave a weather report at 0600. 'Wind north 1.
> No swell, calm sea, perfect landing.' It was all over by 1300. Craig Jevons
> seems to be non-vicious, non-criminal, non-cretinous and friendly, so the
> remainder of the month should be quiet.

If the weather had been other than it was, Dick would still have been got ashore, up to certain limits by Plymouth lifeboat, after that more dramatically from the gallery by helicopter. In both cases he would have arrived in some sort of style. As it was he stepped on to the quay from the tug to find nothing prepared for his reception. I believe the dock gatekeeper phoned for a taxi to take him to hospital where he was operated on four days later for appendicitis. But it has always been the Corporation's policy to encourage initiative in its keepers.

From here on this turn could only be marked by anti-climax. The unknown engineer, who had at one time threatened to make us eight, still hovered in Plymouth.

> 11 October: Was this the third or the fourth time I have called the tug out to no effect? At 0830 I told Rame there was a landing then but wouldn't guarantee there would be one at midday. Perhaps the engineer would like to take a chance? He did and there wasn't.

We were later told he had gone back to Penzance in disgust and we heard no more from him.

Thereafter there are entries of the kind: 'Somewhat in the doldrums in the evening with nothing literary under way', reflecting the usual downhill mood of the second month, not eased by co-habitation with Matey.

> 17 October: At 2215 Hodges at Rame asked to speak to Matey. I explained that he had gone to bed and could I take a message? It seemed his mother had just died. I scribbled a note, and having woken Matey, held the lamp for him to read it. Having got the gist he made irritable noises indicative of 'Well, what can I do about it?' implying I had wasted his time, and went back to sleep.

Relief day was

> A missed opportunity. Right up to 0830 I was doubtful what to say, so in the upshot I said no. It turned out a perfect landing at the time the boat would have arrived.

Fortunately there were no such doubts the following day.

I arrived back from leave to find *Satellite* working on station and we transferred to her tender for the run in. I have no recollection of this but I will have been impressed by the solidity of the tender's powered approach to the set-off compared with that of our rowing-boat. This was where the Wolf had the advantage of us – but then she needed it.

The coincidence of relief and a *Satellite* visit was luckily rare. It was certainly inconvenient. The men going ashore would be wearing their 'best' so it was particularly bad luck that we were landing coal. 'Found Genghis in a rather disgruntled mood. I hardly recognised him through the coal-dust'. I went aboard with SAK Bilton, and Hammet, a mechanic who had arrived to work on the lightning conductor, which had become unpinned from the granite below the set-off. This was cold and slightly risky work and we took turns to watch over him in case an unexpected sea came round and swept him away. He was a pleasant fellow, quiet, unassuming and compliant and he would have been missed.

I was always aware that my preoccupations did not make me a good companion. I felt guilty about it but it was a fact that I could neither think nor write in company. I had to get away to write at the table in the lantern, or to walk the gallery or set-off for long periods, sorting my ideas out. When I did talk, as to Genghis, it was one-way traffic and rarely indulged, for two reasons. First, I could not see how he could be interested by such specialised preoccupations as engrossed me. Second, I knew from experience (and I remember Henry Moore's comment to this effect) that talking vitiates action; it saps the will to do. I might add also my awareness that any society's cohesiveness depends in part on the exclusion of non-conformists. One could only go out on a limb so far. In theory I wished there had been such a thing as a one-man station. In practice I would not have liked it because even parasitically one needs company.

It could have been a reaction to my detachment, or on the other hand to entirely personal problems of his own (one never knew) that produced an uncharacteristic outburst from Genghis.

> *12 December:* This evening G. suddenly rounded on me and tore me into
> several tiny pieces. I had suggested to Bilton and the mechanic that they
> should try using the carpet as a backrest. I hadn't expected any such reaction.

The disappointments in a diary are the things that are not explained. I don't recall that we had any carpet. Carpets go with comfort and comfort is not something that anyone could possibly associate with the Eddystone. The following morning:

> When I called Genghis for watch he apologised to me for giving last night's
> castigation before an audience (Bilton and Hammet, who I am sure would not
> have missed it for worlds). It can't be easy to apologise to a man who hauls
> you out of bed at 0445 in the morning. Characteristic of him.

> *21 December:* Relief day that should have been. Genghis called the tug out.
> There was a swell then which unfortunately did not decrease and by the time
> the tug got near it was romping formidably round the tower. Miserable and
> raining too. G. flashed them to go back, adding 'Merry Christmas' for finality.

It was the end of his hopes of Christmas ashore, confirmed the following day by a gale warning. We put in an early request to Penzance for permission to 'broach reserve provisions' and then 'found some of the flour stale and no good for bread'.

> *Christmas Eve:* Listening in on 181 metres we heard the Superintendent, on
> the *Satellite*, telling Wolf (now about twelve days overdue) that a helicopter
> from Culdrose was leaving Penzance with a parcel for them and that it should
> arrive at about 1105. There was then silence till 1135 when Wolf said it
> hadn't arrived yet. Consternation! It was eventually learned via Culdrose that
> the pilot hadn't been able to find the Wolf and had gone back to Land's End

before making a second attempt. The pilot requested Wolf via Land's End Radio to exhibit her light. At the second attempt she 'found' and after making four or five passes the Christmas goods were landed on the gallery.

Christmas Day 1956: This is probably the most austere I have ever spent. I passed the morning polishing the brasswork in the lantern.

 A surprising occupation for Christmas Day perhaps. It was the Monday morning watchman's job but I preferred to get it over with the previous day. In mid-morning, delayed by the ghastly carol-singing of the western rocks, a reporter of the *Western Morning News* talked to us by arrangement from Rame Head. He seemed a sharp fellow and Genghis dealt with him with a sensible discretion.

My lunch was my usual soup with, unusually, boiled and baked potatoes. And for afters, steamed fruit pudding and custard. Likewise for the others but tinned steak instead of soup. After lunch we listened to the rather good round-the-world hook-up – with a scientific bias – and then the Queen in a speech as full of safe platitudes as ever. For tea we had fruit, jelly and evaporated milk – almost the last of the frills. Wrote this in the Service Room, sitting by the R/T set, by the light of my paraffin lamp and the heat of the Tilley radiator, before and after listening to Mendelssohn's *Octet*, for which I adjourned to the bedroom to listen on my one-valver with earphones.

It may be wondered why Christmas Day this year is described as austere, with no mention of the parcels such as we had received in earlier years. The explanation is that we hadn't had them. The school in Dumfriess and the ladies in Redhill knew about the vagaries of our relief cycle and posted, as they thought, well in advance, but they had been caught out and their parcels had arrived at Blights after our previous relief on 22 November.

Boxing Day: Cook – with the present state of our provisions not a difficult task. Still gales and no prospects.

27 December: Storm still. Actually there hasn't been a landing here now for something like three weeks.

28 December: Wind still west-sou'-west 6–7 and no promise of abatement. After a long interval I am enjoying a recurrence of the screws.

29 December: At 0830 passed a message home via Rame Head: 'Happy New Year. All is well. Looking forward to hearing from you.' [I made it my practice to leave with the coastguards a number of stamped addressed postcards, useful on these occasions.] No landing. But during the day the wind moderated and went nor'-west in the evening instead of sou'-west as had been predicted. This is a favourable trend provided it isn't overdone. But at the moment, 2348, it is blowing nor'-west 8 or 9 – harder than at any time this winter so far.

There was a shipping forecast at midnight and I added gloomily: 'Forecast for tomorrow west to nor'-west 8 or 9, locally 10'.

> *30 December*: A near miss but in fact it wasn't an opportunity wasted. So it is as well the SAK said No without consulting Genghis who would probably have said Yes. A brisk, bright day ensued and in the evening, with a promise of the wind staying nor'-west and moderating, there was tentative hope in the air.

> *New Year's Day*: Relief day – but not for the Wolf. Genghis said Yes at 0830 and though the wind freshened and there were some anxious moments the tug was determined to do the job. And so we are launched on the second month. Genghis and Bilton went ashore with the mechanic and Matey and Craig came aboard, the former breathing his subdued brand of fire and slaughter in my direction – this time probably in reaction to the Lunar Cheese letter. No doubt we shall be back to the usual nervous cooing shortly'.

Incoming mail was, of course, the great pleasure of the half-time relief and after so long there was a great deal of it. I list the items, including

> Two unexpected missives: from the *Sunday Times* returning my 'On Being Seven' which I sent them some time ago, with an individual note saying that probably the only reason for its rejection was its length – a sop, that bit, perhaps; and from Kenneth Hudson, BBC Bristol, suggesting I might like to write a talk on 'The Keeper' and enclosing as an example of what he wants the typescript of a talk on Howard Spring – which by chance I had heard. A nice letter but a difficult proposition. Howard Spring is an urbane, civilised man and therefore a talk on him can be relatively truthful without doing violence to listeners' sensibilities. If a similar level of verisimilitude were to be applied to, say, Genghis (e.g. his solution to the Cyprus – and practically every other – problem: 'Shoot the bastards') the talk would have the matrons of the Home Service reaching for the largest pens in their armouries.

And if I could not have written about Genghis, could I any more readily have written about Matey? My diary reference to his hostility is, in recollection, under-stated. He arrived, as the phrase has it, spoiling for a fight. He must have found my letter to *The Times* baffling, and the Superintendent's reaction to it incomprehensible in Trinity terms – the Trinity he had joined and had served and suffered so much of his life in. I knew of the Superintendent's reaction because I had had a letter from him on the November relief, thanking me gravely for my communication and asking to be kept informed of the progress of my investigations. I rather wonder now whether it did not persuade him that if anyone could survive Matey's company, I could. There were times when I myself doubted it.

> Called Matey at midnight and talked until 0100 when gratefully to bed. The chit-chat had never really become easy and in an unusual way I found the usual Trinitalia particularly repellent.

There was a flare-up at lunch. I mentioned that I had altered the setting of the lens clock governor in the night. I had evidently timed the rotation of the lens and found it running either fast or slow.

> At once 'I am Principal Keeper here', threats of Three Page reports to be written and so forth. I withdrew to write this up to date in the lantern. If he gets it off his chest now perhaps the rest of the month will be quieter.

I have much sympathy for Matey. He must have seen me as an unpredicatble catherine wheel, shooting off sparks in all directions. At least in part it was the classic clash between traditional Trinity man and the post-war *disengagé*.

> *5 January*: A return to the state of speaking terms means that I have to stay up chatting for sixty minutes after I've called him. He talks, I listen. Grim.

> *6 January*: Down to a quite affable and intelligent conversation with Matey until 2200 when I came, not to blows, but to bed.

> *8 January*: Began the day at midnight with quite an intelligent chat with Matey. He *is* capable of talking sense when the bees in his bonnet quieten down for a while. [At least we were both trying.]

> *12 January*: Before I went to bed at 2205 Matey was in a merry and most communicative mood. His face shed twenty years as he talked – for the moment entirely boyish.

Was I becoming Kent to his Lear? Inevitably there were relapses:

> On calling Matey we sat for half an hour without uttering one word. Simply, I could think of nothing, but I sensed that he interpreted my silence less charitably. But eventually we got going and I didn't until 0510.

> *16 January*: Unusually I failed to rise when Craig called me at 0405 until he did so again at 0440. And while my intellect was still clouded with sleep I dropped the bedroom window can, unfortunately *after* I had filled it. Thereafter the day improved, thanks in great part to the beautiful weather.

Then Matey and I found ourselves in unexpected collaboration. The Stuart Turner charging engine was rated to run at 1,500 r.p.m. but without a revolution counter we seemed to have no way of checking the speed until I made the happy discovery that the drive to the oil pump was in the ratio 40 : 1. This made checking against a watch possible, to reveal that the engine was doing a mere 700 r.p.m. Matey shortened the spring to the governor, then I shortened it further to produce 1,050 r.p.m.

> The generator was now putting in 20 amps – the maximum – even at the end of the charge. The batteries were bubbling away as they have not this many a weary year.

I mention this because I detested this engine, not in itself (on the contrary, I recorded an enjoyable afternoon spent cleaning out the exhaust of the Stuart Turner and there was no irony intended) but for what it stood for, which was keeping a listening watch every two hours during the day, and being able to be *got at*. It represented a downward step from the purity of the acetylene lamp winking from the winchroom door to Penlee Point or the Breakwater, communication which must have been so often happily interrupted by the weather. We ran the engine for only a few hours every five or six days; now we could run it more briefly and the tower would revert sooner to mechanical silence. I did not know my good fortune, though I had begun to suspect it. Quite soon they were to rip out the old lens and replace it with something a fraction of the size, substituting a bulb fed by a generator which would thud all night in the basement, and there would be a radio beacon, and TV for entertainment, and a helicopter pad on the roof guaranteeing instant accessibility... And with all that one might just as well be in a job ashore.

It is in this sense that I feel I was enjoying the Eddystone in its last good days. There *were* mechanical noises – the hiss of the burners in the lantern, the muted rattle of the lens clock governor, the geriatric groaning of the lens, the hourly clatter at wind-up of the back-stop ratchet – but they were nineteenth-century noises. The rest was nature's contribution, the sussuration or roar of the wind according to its temper, the flashing phosphorescence of a gently breaking summer night's sea, the thump and retreating hiss of Atlantic swells. This had been the lightkeeper's world for two centuries, and I was experiencing the last of it. There had been a price paid in terms of social claustrophobia but I now think it was worth it. I am sorry I did not always think so at the time.

We had had our Christmas dinner after all, but in January; and I spent an afternoon writing a thank-you letter to the boys of Crawfordton House, Dumfriesshire.

> *22 January* – a Sunday: Matey came down to lunch in a grey humour. Solution: absent thee from felicity awhile – which I did as soon as possible, retiring to my bunk to read the excellent *Brat Farrar*.

> *28 January*: The day started miserably, sounding for fog from 0420 to 0700 and then again from 0800, handing over to Matey at 0900. Mess, soot (the chimney developed a hole), dampness and a sense of things not well which did not disappear until the sun began to show and I had cleaned up the kitchen.

Mood was as vulnerable to gloomy weather at sea as it is ashore.

> *29 January*: Relief day that should have been, and a chance missed, though probably Craig was justified in giving No Landing at 0830. Shortly afterwards the wind went nor'-nor'-west from south-west and at 1230 or so, near low water, the conditions were good enough for a relief. Now (1557) there is a thumping great swell coming in, but the wind is still west by north so we live in hopes.

> *30 January*: On 0000–0400 during which nothing seemed likely until about 0340 when the wind, from being west by south, suddenly went nor'-west.

The magnificent 1882 double lens of Douglass's tower. The small white objects which may perhaps just be discerned on each Hood burner platform are 35 mm autoform mantles which in use would be on top of the burners, the upper one of which is here partly hidden by the chimney. This lens was damaged beyond restoration in the early 1980s while in the care of Southampton's civic authorities.

And Matey gave a favourable report. In the event it proved a very fine thing. When the tug arrived, somewhat before low water, there was still a noisy swell breaking, but nothing really dangerous. Matey was by now in his customary state of the jumps. I suggested we flash them to hang on for half an hour. 'It won't make any difference.'

I was less disposed to be pessimistic. It was now all but February. I had been aboard since 22 November. Enough was enough. I persisted.

> Petulantly[Matey]: 'It all devolves on me. I've got to run upstairs. No one else can send Morse.' 'I can', I said with alacrity, and did: 'Wait half hour.' Genghis acknowledged with a wave and they went fishing. After ten minutes the absence of threat in the swell was too obvious to be ignored. I suggested we call them in. Matey assented, busying himself with something irrelevant. 'O.K. No force. Come in'. And they came, not liking the look of the white water and rowing poorly through the northerly chop. The final hurdle was getting them the heaving line against the wind. Both Matey and I threw wildly before he threw one close enough for them to hook out of the water. Thereafter we wound energetically and at length, thank God, I was in the boat and rather disbelieving it. And in fact we had a surprisingly smooth trip in and I showed no inclination to part with my breakfast.

As tended to happen when relief was delayed I missed my train, arriving home at dawn.

> Phoned M., on night duty at the hospital, but she was at the time (she told me later) laying out a corpse and so could not come to the phone. It was snowing heavily.

This sort of weather was encountered on leave, not on the lighthouse.

While I was on leave I visited a breaker's yard and bought myself an old bulb motor horn. Vaguely, I thought it might come in useful.

10

The motor horn story:
the Eddystone, spring and summer 1956

I returned to the Eddystone on the last day of February. Company for my first month was to be Genghis and a tall, lanky, bird-faced, talkative Supernumerary called Carl Prout. The tug left the quay at 1000 and it quickly became clear that a break in the weather was imminent.

> I soon brought up my breakfast but only had two bouts and felt well enough between times. Prout and I relieved Matey and Craig. According to Genghis they had had a very quiet month socially.

It was a phrase that meant different things aboard and ashore.

I have said I thought I might find a use for the motor horn. It is a common belief that lighthouses supplement the role of coastguard lookout stations. This is true only in a general sense. On one occasion we were surprised to hear on the BBC regional news that a dismasted yacht had been drifting somewhere near the Eddystone for a couple of days before it was noticed, not by us, and taken into port. Very likely it was a small yacht and not particularly near, but it illustrates the truth that tower rocks do not make good observation points. Surrounded by sea they may be, but they provide a poor lookout. The viewing angle from each window is small and the windows on each floor cover different areas which fall short of overlapping. Even the lantern provides an all-round view only if you are prepared to walk round the obstruction of the central lens, taking care not to fall down the stairs. True, I was later to call out the Plymouth lifeboat, but the circumstances then rather supported the argument. I might add at this point that lighthouses also provide little opportunity for amateur astronomy in spite of an unobstructed sky. This was only not true on some summer nights on the Eddystone when it was comfortable to sit on the roof of the lantern and so be above the sweeping beams of the light.

The first use I saw for the motor horn was for overcoming these limitations of view. Successive blasts up and down the stairs and out of the two opposed kitchen windows should be enough to alert the cook's colleagues, wherever they happened to be, to the imminent appearance on the table of something distantly related to food.

But then I found myself telling Carl Prout that this was only one of a number of such devices being issued experimentally to rock stations up and down the coast. I really do not know why I told him this, other than that he was so eager to learn. I think the presence of such an enquiring mind awakened in me an obligation to respond. It was not a thirst for knowledge that I was accustomed to in my colleagues. When I had read aloud to them passages from Dr Magnus Pyke's digestive tract they had been a poor audience. Prout was a refreshing change and I felt he should be encouraged.

Presently I was able to show him a message which I had 'received' from Rame Head on one of our twice-daily radio tests. It set it all out quite clearly. Each station had been allocated an MHCS (Motor Horn Call Sign). The Eddystone's was two short blasts which until further notice were to conclude every transmission, whether to Rame Head or the *Satellite*.

Prout wanted to know why. I nodded my approval of his alertness. Who could say why the administration of Trinity thought up the things they did? However, perhaps in this case we could make a sensible guess. As he would notice when he presently came to conduct the late evening radio test with Rame, static, particularly after dark, made voice communication difficult and there was an obvious advantage in a single clear motor horn blast –

'A *double* clear blast', he corrected me.

'Quite so.'

– if it at least identified a station in distress in difficult circumstances. He nodded briskly. It all made perfect sense to him.

It was odd to see history repeating itself.

> Carl Prout decided not to go to bed before I called him at midnight, which I found distressing as it confined me to the lantern where I read Gwyn Thomas's *Point of Order* – not one of his best.

This solecism of deciding not to go to bed was exactly the one I had committed with Matey before my own first middle watch as an SAK. You really do not lightly tamper with established lighthouse routine. Three nights later a second withdrawal to the lantern was enough to persuade Carl that the middle watchman did not assail the privacy of the man with 'all night in' (i.e. the one who went off watch at midnight).

> At 2130 upstairs to the lantern to think about the application of an idea to have the lens operate a contact to flash a light in the kitchen to save us the trouble of looking out of the window at the mirror. Then wrote the concluding words of the current story, and while I was lost in this Carl suddenly came round the lens out of the gloom, giving me a fearful fright, to say he was going to bed and that I now had the kitchen. I explained that we usually swore, coughed or said 'Ahem' upon entering the Service Room to give the man in the lantern fair warning of the approach of something perhaps even

more ghastly than Carl. So in the vacated kitchen I washed some underclothes
before going to bed at 0030 tomorrow.

(Sudden apparitions in an ordered world are always uncomfortably startling. A
keeper on Beachy Head is said to have once opened the kitchen door to go and wind-
up in the small hours and found to his horror a set of footprints, still wet, on the
landing outside the door. Now that *was* something to turn one's hair white overnight!
He received an explanation the next day when the caller returned. Beachy Head is
accessible at low water and some reveller had thought he would pay a nocturnal visit,
then decided at the last moment that his appearance might provide too much of a
shock to the keeper.)

Carl was now performing nicely.

To bed at 2145 and was woken briefly by C. honking at Rame at the end of
his evening call. It was done without comment and apparently elicited none.

Genghis or I would have introduced Carl to the coastguard when we showed him
how to conduct the evening and morning calls and Hodges and his colleague evidently accepted that they had an odd SAK 'out there' who for some reason chose to
honk at them with a motor horn instead of signing off with the more usual 'Good
night'.

Obviously this story was something that was going to run and it was worth taking
a bit of trouble over it.

Sunday 4 March: Up at about 0945. Cup of tea and a biscuit, then upstairs
on a beautiful morning – a really warm, bright, sunny day. I mounted the horn
in a wooden box to improve its tone and sent out an experimental transmission, monitored by Genghis on the kitchen set, to determine the best position
for the horn in relation to the hand-set. It turned out that the general resonance in the Service Room provided a quite sufficient signal without such
elaboration.

I was meanwhile busy on the prototype of the lens indicator light.

Made a simple contact with a single-screw fitting. The negative to the R/T set
and Earth are being used to avoid the need for any additional wiring between
lantern and kitchen.

This was an acknowledgement that the arrangement was not one that would have
been approved of and it was important that evidence of it should be instantly remov-
able in the event of the unexpected arrival of authority. This may seem an unlikely
happening on a rock lighthouse but occasionally *Satellite* turned up without giving
radio notice and when it did we had little time to spare for anything but getting the
ropes down.

5 March: We noticed this morning that when Carl spoke to Rame he concluded by blowing the horn but without transmitting. Perhaps he's beginning
to think there's something a little odd about this horn business.

He may well have done but we were quick to set him back on the right path. We ourselves were careful to conclude all our conversations with Rame in the manner prescribed in Circular TH/MHCS/27/64 of 1.3.56. Carl, in his bunk, heard the convincing whirr of the rotary converter on 'transmit' but did not know that we were switching crystals at the last moment so that the MHCS went nowhere. Rame Head received them only from Carl. Rame had begun to probe a little but we did not respond and they were too tactful to press. If our temporary keeper's behaviour was a little odd it was our problem, not theirs.

I now proceeded to make it theirs, going down to the kitchen from my 0930 chat with a grave face to relay a most serious development. It seemed that at the end of last night's test, which had been conducted by Carl, the coastguard on duty, newly appointed to the position, had suffered a stroke and was now completely paralysed down one side. He was still able to speak, but could send and receive only half a sentence at a time, a handicap that could mean the end of his career. He had, as usual, wife and children. I was sorry to have to tell Carl that the catastrophe was being blamed on his final blast of the MHCS, about which the man had not been warned. In a pause to let all this sink in Genghis and I sat and looked at Carl with sympathy and concern. It wasn't something we would have cared to have on our conscience. It is to his credit that he was horrified. 'Good heavens, what shall I do?'

'Well, obviously', I said, 'what is happening is that you're holding the handset too close to the mouth of the horn and peaking on your anode. It's a matter of technique. All that's needed is a slight modification.'

And after breakfast I took him up to the Service Room and showed him how. He wanted to call up Rame Head to apologise but I said better not. Indeed, from the Corporation's point of view any reference to it could be construed as an admission of liability for the man's attack. If this came to court –

'To *court?*'

It could happen, I assured him; it had been known, though the last occasion on which a keeper had been shot –

'*Shot?*!'

– fired in such circumstances had been some time in the late 1930s.

And so on and so forth. I supervised his next two or three exchanges with Rame Head until I could see he had regained his confidence, then left him to blast quietly away at whoever might care to listen.

It was all grist to the literary mill and I at once began to cast the motor horn business as a story for radio. I was probably too close to the topic at the time and I only made a success of it a quarter of a century later when it was read as a BBC Morning Story by the comedian, Bob Monkhouse. So:

> After an unsuccessful attempt to resume the motor horn piece I wrote my first piece of pornographic fiction. Lately (the last three or four days) I have been

> caught up in an erotic mental whirlpool. I therefore gave myself my literary
> head and by the time I called Carl at 0100 had composed most of 'an episode
> of considerable obscenity' [a quote from Flecker's *Hassan*, not my diary].

> In the morning I limed one of the drinking water tanks with Genghis, then
> stayed inside the tank for an operatic session, taking advantage of the fine
> acoustics.

Genghis would not have remained for this and may have been tempted to replace
the manhole cover when he left.

> In the afternoon to the lantern as usual and in about ninety minutes completed
> my obscene episode and then threw it overboard.

I did this less because I was dismayed at what I had written (a man's sexual fantasies,
rather more than a woman's I suspect, have always seemed to me the eroticism of the
madhouse and not worth wasting concern on) than because I would have been embarrassed had my colleagues chanced on it. I wasn't greatly bothered by the sexual
drive during my two months on and when I was I relieved it in the usual way. I had by
now discovered the pleasure of sex *à deux*, but in the absence of women sex was
merely an annoying distraction from literary and mechanical enterprises. Incidentally, it may be thought that the Service would attract homosexuals. I believe I heard
of two. I probably spent a month with one and found his company neither more nor
less disagreeable than anyone else's.

I think it was a difficult month for Genghis, in the company of colleagues each of
whom was a lunatic in his particular way. In spite of my exceptionally benign and
agreeable temperament I was myself finding Carl something of a trial. There are
references to the kitchen radio: 'Added a little to my letter to M. to a blaring radio.'
'Carl, curse him, stayed up to listen to Top Twenty but I bore it with angelic calm.'
When we were lunatic together Genghis's sufferings must have been extreme.

> I retired to the lantern to write out a revised version of 'The Keeper'. Then had
> an operatic fit lasting about ten minutes and on the way down to the kitchen
> heard Genghis, unusually already abed, murmur 'for pity's sake'. He had gone
> there at about 2030 with a headache given him by an unceasing output of
> Radio Luxembourg at full volume, and with it an incessant stream of laughs,
> exclamations and questions from Carl. The latter is totally dependent on
> outside stimulation to keep him happy. I myself am never at ease with him. We
> rub together as smoothly as two sheets of glass paper'.

'The Keeper' was an attempt to oblige Kenneth Hudson. 'Frankly I see every
reason why this should not be done, and as I am doing it, the first phrase of the talk is
"This is a talk that cannot be given." Genghis was the subject; and it never was.

Genghis and I did our best to provide the stimulation Carl needed. I presently
called him for watch at midnight in a state of suppressed excitement with a message
supposedly passed to me by Rame at the 2215 test. It seemed that *Satellite*, after her

initial experience of his Motor Horn Call Signs, was now interested in receiving more formalised transmissions for purposes of calibration. We were therefore required to broadcast our MHCS at 15-second intervals from 0345 to 0350 GMT this very morning on 2,182 MHz – the international Call and Distress frequency. I had chosen a time that would not greatly disturb Genghis, who Carl was to call at 0400 anyway. As for me, it was my 'all night in' and I hadn't the least objection to being roused temporarily by the sound of my fellow-lunatic discharging motor-horn noises into the heedless ether.

But when he presently let rip, was the ether entirely heedless? 2,182 MHz is the frequency to which any ship keeping radio watch listens when it has no business of its own to transact. Certainly Niton Radio and Land's End Radio would be listening and, despite our low power, one or other of those Post Office communications stations should have heard something.

'Have a listen at this, George. What do you think we have here? Does it sound to you like what it sounds to me?' ...

When Carl came down to breakfast next morning we were quietly congratulatory. Ours was the reserve of those who envy another his success. Captain Moat of the *Satellite* had been more fulsome.

'Heartiest congratulations entire ship's company to keepers of Eddystone' was the message Genghis had 'received' at 0930 via Rame. 'MHCS transmission complete success, received strength nine.'

I touched Carl on the shoulder, unable to hide my envy. Did he know what this meant? It rarely fell to the lot of a Supernumerary Assistant Keeper to make an impact so early in his career. From this point on, if he cared to stay in the Service, the Corporation's world was his oyster. Principal Keeper at thirty, District Superintendent at fifty, the youngest Elder Brother ever at eighty-five...

There remained only one hurdle, his Supernumerary's Certificate, Administration, part viii. As he was aware, his record book had spaces for a number of such certificates of competence – Radio-Telephone, Fog Signal and so forth. A recent addition had been Administration, and in my opinion it was a long overdue category. One never knew when one would be required to take command of a lighthouse. There had been too many cases where a young keeper, left alone following an altercation in which his two colleagues had pushed each other overboard, had proved himself quite unable to do something as simple as indent for a broom handle or put together a requisition for oil.

I could see Carl's initial euphoria disappearing as I spoke and I did my best to reassure him. All Trinity wanted was some three or four hundred words in his own hand on some aspect of lighthouse administration, and *Great heavens!* – here I brought my fist down on the kitchen table as at a sudden insight – why hadn't I thought of it before? He really did have the luck of an SAK. The MHCS Experimental Programme could hardly have come at a better time; it was tailor-made for the purpose.

All he had to do was summarise the scheme as he had experienced it so far, taking care to be thoroughly objective (which meant including a reference to his victim's stroke – it was part of the price someone else paid for progress and wouldn't be held against him) and perhaps making a few comments on how he saw the project developing in the future. I spoke with an enthusiasm which I presently saw I was failing to communicate. I thought I could guess at what the problem might be.

'Ah, you're worried about the actual writing. Don't be. I'll do it for you. Luckily writing's a bit of a hobby of mine. I'll knock it up in a jiffy and then you can copy it out and put your autograph –'

'Autograph?'

'I was anticipating – signature at the bottom and they won't know a thing. It's often done like this. We AKs don't like to see a promising SAK's chances blighted by a little problem with words'.

> *11 March*: On 0000–0400 (actually nearly 0500) during which I put together a nicely laid-out report under the headings Authorisation, General, Work Done, Effectiveness and Recommendations. The unfortunate matter of the stroke was not shirked, and a suggestion was made that consideration be given to the addition of snaredrum and alto saxophone to the repertoire of transmitting instruments. In the afternoon I made a fair copy, attaching a brief accompanying letter from Carl to the Superintendent, begging to submit the report with a view to securing his SAK's Certificate, Administration, part viii. Genghis, having read it all through, was quite agreeable to getting Carl to copy it out… The evening by comparison was rather wasted.

> *12 March*: Came down to tea to find Genghis had persuaded Carl to write out the report, Carl's only complaint being a grumbled 'A bit long, isn't it?' I thought this a fairly mild reaction, bearing in mind the gibberish it contained…

> *17 March*: [Middle watch saw] the climax of a short and sharp session of the screws. So no work done. Instead I had a stand-up bath which made me feel better.

I suppose we were enjoying one of our recurrent rainwater shortages.

> *24 March*: At 2215 Rame passed over the relief list. Craig is coming aboard and Carl is staying another fortnight until relieved by the old man – presumably sick. Meantime I will be in charge.

The 'fortnight' was distinctly odd, coming as it did as an extra relief half-way through a standard month.

> A sad blow for Carl. How he will survive a fortnight of Craig's fishing and my preference for the lantern I do not know. I suggested to Genghis that we should not give him the news until tomorrow to avoid the inconvenience of

having him hang himself on middle watch, for which I am now about to call him (0008 tomorrow).

25 March: Genghis told Carl at lunch. He took it very well, partly, no doubt, because for a time he thought we were having him on.

Alas, we had over-cooked the motor-horn business. Evidently Carl had begun to have cold feet.

26 March: During middle watch wrote out in an unnaturally large hand the 'Report on the Installation of Motor Horn Signalling Apparatus at Tower Rock Lighthouses' and Carl's accompanying letter. It is a disappointment that I am having to do this myself, but on Friday evening, when Genghis asked him if he had completed the report, he told us in so many words to go and chase ourselves. So that's that. My angle, and it is one that I will explain in a letter I will slip into Carl's pocket at the relief, is that he is his own worst enemy and that I have been obliged to do good by stealth in submitting the report in his name in his own interest … Downstairs at 2055. Carl told us about cows. To bed 2200.

The half-way relief was upon us, and how agreeably the time had flown.

28 March: Well, no landing. By morning the breeze had strengthened to 5 and later it increased further to an easterly 6.

29 March: An opportunity missed. When I went to bed at 0430 conditions were still impossible, but by 0800 they had improved so much that Genghis (called by Carl) with difficulty decided to say no. Conditions in fact went on improving and in the evening the wind died right away and there was a flat calm.

Would the Shipping Forecast have predicted this improvement? Possibly, but so much depended on timing and, as I have said, our arrangements were appropriate to running a railway, not a lighthouse relief. Not only were we tied to a particular time, mid-morning, but the relief was completed by rowed boat – in the mid-1950s!

I had a high regard for Met. Office forecasts. When they were wrong it was usually in the timing; and this was crucial. Sometimes a delay occurred in the slotting of a gale warning between radio programmes so that it would be broadcast when we had already been enjoying a full gale for two hours. And the Met. office was concerned with the behaviour of air masses; it said nothing about sea conditions. We might have enjoyed light airs for several days but still a ruinous swell could continue to roll in from very different weather far out in the Atlantic.

30 March: In a very material sense the relief brought me bad news. An annoying error, probably by Blights, has resulted in them sending me no condensed milk, bacon, margarine, sugar, flour, tea and some soups. My message via Rame had asked them to repeat the first month's order with the

exception of some named additions and alterations - the latter being the above items in *increased* quantities. For alteration they had read deletion.

Such a mistake could be appallingly inconvenient to a degree difficult to conceive by those for whom the remedy is an easy return visit to a corner shop. Fortunately

> It seems the old man will be coming up by *Satellite*. Whether he does that or whether he comes via Plymouth I should be able to get away a request for some of the items to be brought off then.

I was the victim of only one other such error, and a more disastrous one, when I was on Skokholm, of which in due time.

With so much foolery at other times, we seem to have let April Fool's Day pass:

> 1 April : Oiled and lit up, then sang. Incidentally next month should be additionally musical. I am bringing back a clarinet for Genghis and a violin for myself. Craig plays the mouth-organ but we are not all three here together.

Evidently I had despatched Carl's 'report' on the relief.

> 4 April: By the 0930 test Nicholls confirmed that he had already phoned Penzance about my missing provisions. I heard him say to Carl, who was conducting it: 'By the way, that is Mr Prout, isn't it?' – which I invested with a significance it may or may not have possessed, imagining an enquiry by Penzance office: Had they noticed any horn-blowing? – and so on.

Carl continued to surprise us:

> 2 April: To our amazement he went to bed at 2100 to see whether it would make the middle watch pass more quickly for him than it has done of late.

He was still giving Rame two blasts with the horn when he signed off. So did Craig and I, though with the quick switch of crystals that meant our blasts went nowhere.

That I had some private doubt about the reception likely to have been accorded to the Prout report is evident from the entry for 11 April, when *Satellite* duly came bringing Rictus and a ton of coal.

> The complete lack of any immediate recrimination over the Report was explained in the evening when Craig, his eyes twinkling with the delight natural to any human being who imparts bad news, repeated what the old man had told him in confidence: that he thought I was for the high jump, though the Superintendent had not said so positively. I had to think it likely. Goodman will no doubt have to assume that this, taken with the Lunar Cheese letter, represents a pattern of behaviour that is likely to be repeated in the future. And there he is no doubt right. The news, even though I was prepared for it, made me realise just how well, all things considered, this job suits me. As I exercised on the gallery on a beautiful evening the idea of working in some uncongenial occupation from nine to five for a wretched two weeks' holiday a year seemed repellent. On the other hand it could be for the best after all.

Except as a journalist one can't make a living from writing.

Carl seemed very happy to leave. Originally *Satellite* was going to take him back to Penzance, to his dismay, but someone evidently managed to sway the Captain on his behalf for she went into Plymouth first before going westward. Perhaps they felt sorry for the poor fellow.

> Earlier I had told him that if there was any query about the 'horn signals' he was to quote me as the responsibility was mine. He asked innocently why there should be any queries and, referring to his night test transmission, said 'They got us all right, didn't they?' He evidently thought I was indulging in an academic quibble [or possibly trying to steal the thunder of his success].

If the relief thus brought some anxieties it also brought some good news.

> Matey has at last got his shift. When I came eighteeen months ago he was saying that he thought he would be going at the end of the month. And at last it has happened. That and the thought of my sacking is no doubt what made him look so happy when he came aboard yesterday.

Yet, as always, a workable *modus vivendi* established itself.

> 20 April: Cook. Putting out is now at about 0515 which means the morning trim is finished by about 0600. Thereafter after breakfast and the 0700 news I nowadays have a doze over the table in the kitchen.

This cat-nap enabled me to survive until midnight without turning in after lunch.

> In the afternoon of a fine sunny day I concluded the revision of the current piece in the lantern and just before tea made up some bread while the other two slept on the set-off in the hot sunshine. After tea on a calm evening went down on to the set-off for 45 minutes' walk (about 2½ to 3 miles I should think).

I would have been developing those right side calf muscles within that Trinity twill.

> Spent the evening in the kitchen, the three of us reminiscing. Had a bath and a change of clothes from 2300. To bed at 0100.

Not really such a bad life.

With such diverse preoccupations the arrival of relief day was hardly noticed.

> 28 April: Relief day, but wasn't. When I went to bed at 0500 the wind was a moderate 4 and conditions looked quite promising. But by 0830 it had freshened to a 5 and Matey said No Landing – rightly.

> 29 April: Relief day. When I got up at 0400 the wind was still about 3–4 but it gradually moderated and at 0830 it was about a 2 and the sea was practically flat calm. In fact it was a step-aboard relief, done without panic or pandemonium at about 1230, and we were in Plymouth by perhaps 1415.

'We' were the old man and myself who were replaced by Genghis and an SAK Whiting, replacing the named Darraugh who had thrown his hand in. When Matey phoned the Superintendent at the dock gates he was told Goodman wanted me to phone him at 1100 tomorrow, which made me feel my fate was in the balance. By taxi to the station with Matey where I left him after forgetting to settle for my share of the taxi. Dropped an apologetic p.c. when I realised I'd done so. Our final handshake was probably quite warm. With luck we wouldn't be seeing each other again.

My phone call the following day brought relief of a different kind.

Goodman was most agreeable. All he said was that in future he wanted me to sign my efforts with my own name, and he finished up with a random remark or two about Matey's move. So I am still working for Trinity. I find that I have a little more than £150 in the bank.

The next turn could hardly be other than an anti-climactic two months. The relief was done to time.

I was woken at 0215 by a rainstorm and out here at the 'stone it was apparently blowing hard. But around dawn conditions improved markedly, the wind dropped and we went out of harbour on a fine morning. 'We' were the new PK, John Masters, previously at Flatholm and never before at the Eddystone, suitably grizzled, about him a suggestion of a negro elder, and Bert Thurman who is very West Country and eighty per cent incomprehensible. He is coming out to do the dog-steps. [These were the dog-steps below the set-off. Despite being of gun-metal they were eroded by the sea and needed replacing every quarter-century or so.] John and I replaced Craig and SAK Whiting. Genghis remained aboard.

While on leave I had bought a micro-switch with which I now upgraded the lens warning system from Mk I to II. It took a little time to get the kitchen end right. At first we had it operating a telephone relay but the clicking proved too aggressive. I describe what I call

a most attractive solution which would be fail-safe. The telephone relay magnet would be mounted somewhere high up on one wall. To it would normally be attached an armature held on a piece of string. Should the current to the magnet fail the armature will at once sail across the room and through the provisions cupboard window

– the crash of breaking glass alerting the keeper on watch to the stopping of the lens. I don't say whether I put this to the new PK for his approval. If I did he seems to have turned it down. I settled on the less interesting solution of a red lamp winking on the wall as the lens drive teeth tripped the micro-switch twice a second or so.

I had brought my violin with me together with an album of *100 Melodies*. The clarinet I had intended to provide for Genghis had been lent to someone and then sat on by the borrower and irredeemably ruined.

> 5 June: In the evening fiddled for a while, scraping out popular tunes from my book of popular tunes. This is less satisfactory than *ad libbing*, because with my eyes on the music I tend to turn professional and play two strings at once. Also I am not very keen on popular tunes.

I restricted this activity to the Service Room and lantern, not because I was asked to but because I knew I would be asked to if I didn't. It was always an atrocious noise.

The Looe boats were calling and once again we bent our minds to the problem presented by mail. This was the month we made use of the northern reef where I hadn't been before.

> I swam out with the codline tied to one ankle, then pulled in another length of line with spanners, shackle, wire, and so forth, which Genghis paid out from the set-off. The free end of the cable was attached to the R/T aerial stanchion outside the Low Light room landing window perhaps 80 feet up, so that it slants down at about 30° to the water.

The idea was to slide a hook down the wire to hang just above water-level for the mail switch. Like every other attempted solution to the problem it proved flawed. It worked satisfactorily just once, then:

> 4 July: Having attached the mail to the hook Pearn, too busy with everything, failed to get it clear and it fouled the stays to his mast. He was unable to get way off in time and the wire parted at the rocks. He still had the mail and having got the tangle cleared threw it overboard wrapped in a newspaper. From the Argand window I hauled in as quickly as possible and though caught by a swell the letters were barely wetted.

All this pother was great entertainment for the passengers and good business for Pearn when they took the story back to their lodgings. I suggested we might work it up into a formalised routine with Genghis leaping twenty feet into the boiling surf to recover a letter from a loved one while I blew him back on to the set-off with the well-timed detonation of a dozen or so underwater fog-charges. The passengers would really have gone for that. Genghis liked the idea but wanted the roles reversed. I would do a much better leap and he had always wanted to detonate a few fog-charges under me. It was a point on which we were unable to agree and the idea came to nothing.

> 13 June: Spent most of the afternoon reading the speech by Khrushchev attacking Stalin. Most interesting – and cheering. The newly awakened possibility of dying of old age seems to have resulted in an improvement of my psychological tone.

> 15 June: A letter couched in very brisk and business-like tones. Did I remember the old Cookery talk? He would like to record it as soon as possible. I'm going to say simply Yes.

Kenneth Hudson was still pegging away.

> *26 June*: A perfect relief on a beautiful day. Genghis left us, Craig came in his place. Taking advantage of the conditions the tug skipper and one other came aboard for a look around. Also a youth with a camera and a fear of heights.

Displayed, no doubt, in difficulty in climbing the dog-steps to the entrance.

We were having a magnificent summer.

> *24 June*: We are at present enjoying the finest spell of calm weather that I can remember. An absolutely flat sea. Occasional, temporary winds up to strength two. This, allied to lighting-up at 2115 and putting out eight hours later, makes for marvellous days. Up at 0930. Didn't have breakfast, just a cup of tea. Then down and had a most refreshing swim. Used the lifebelt – not as comfortable as the jacket.

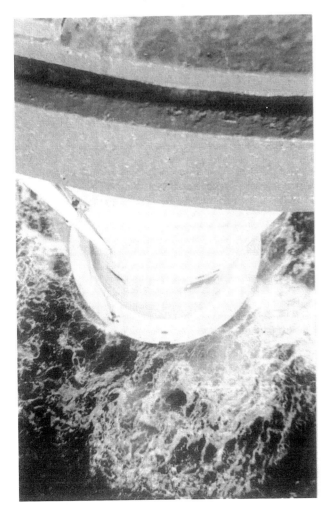

A vertical view from the gallery.

I may have seemed over-cautious but I vividly anticipated the unpleasantness of drifting away to drown two hours or so later – though I always indulged the curious fancy that in such circumstances I would head for the coast and might even arrive there. I was not naturally a good swimmer and it was only later at another lighthouse that I discovered the security and mobility conferred by snorkel and flippers, when getting the head under water provides positive buoyancy. We had a Schermuly rocket and line but we never practised with it and my request to my colleagues was that, in the event of my drifting away, they should not waste time with the rocket. Instead, they should throw the lantern table over the gallery rail as something for me to hang on to.

On 29 June I received a letter from dear old Kenneth Hudson: 'Splendid. In agreement throughout. Shall we say Wednesday 15 May for the recording. Kindest encouragement meanwhile.' I had pegged away at the talk, not liking it, but hacking it into a shape that I thought would prove acceptable to the listening public while not proving false to the reality of the Service.

We had had some trouble with a seeping paraffin tank and the depot wanted a description of its shape. I gave the matter some thought and decided it was that of a segment of a centreless cheese. This was technically accurate but I wished later I hadn't bothered. *Satellite* was calling from Penzance and communication was not easy. Radio conditions were bad and the reply had to go through Wolf and then be repeated, collecting errors on the way. 'Segment', for example was lost; and 'centreless' gave a good deal of trouble.

> Willis on the *Satellite* mumbled something about not having been to High School. The episode left my nerves badly jangled and I spent the evening on a lengthy illustrated letter to a pupil of a school near Wellington, Shropshire.

This was in fact the beginning of an interesting venture.

> 30 *June*: Am stagnating at the moment, having nothing in hand or mind. Oh for a Mozartian flow of ideas!

But the same day:

> This evening there occurred to me the solution of the problem associated with the transmitting barometer discussed on 28 April.

This did not represent stagnation for it was an idea of some elegance which later produced a correspondence with the NRDC (a government research and development body). Ultimately it wasn't found any application but I still think of it with pleasure. Two days later I switched to the other side.

> 2 *July*: Copied out part of my letter to M. in which I tried to imagine the scene in the two airliners that have recently crashed in the Grand Canyon with the loss of 128 lives. Believe I have in it the basis of a short story.

I had. It was a morbid *tour de force* which won a prize in the annual Seafarers'

Competition and subsequently appeared in the now defunct railway bookstall magazine *Argosy*. The real competition, though, seemed to be between the two interests:

> *6 July:* On 0000–0400 during which I fully intended making a fair copy of the aircraft piece. But as I was winding up for the first time in the watch I began to think about the idea of 30 June in its application to temperature measurement.

> *8 July:* Craig sounded throughout his watch and John continued from 0400 until he called me at 0830. I continued then till 1600, Craig to 2000 and John to midnight when at last a clearance came. A general irritability was engendered by this, the longest continuous spell of fog that I can recall here – about 42 hours. I find it impossible to read a book, even, when sounding.

This is not surprising, nor is the irritability. Fog was depressing. For the man on watch it meant firing a charge every five minutes, and going outside on to the gallery to reload every ten. From time to time there would be trips down to the paraffin store to collect further boxes of charges, for of course we got through a dozen every hour. The granite walls ran moisture. Beyond that fog disrupted the whole lighthouse routine. Calling a man for watch required nice timing; a dash down, shaking him into wakefulness on the way, making the tea and returning to the lantern as the fog clock pinged to indicate the next firing. Other than its usefulness to shipping there was just one entry on the credit side. 'Cleaned out the chimney bend, effectively filled by our recent banging.' The fog gone, 'at once our psychological tone improved'. Perhaps more than ashore, mood walked with the weather.

On 16 July we had a caller.

> Not a mechanic to stay as we had thought, but an engineer to visit. This discovery was made in the nick of time, and while he inspected our leaking fuel tank Craig and I dismantled our giveaway wiring in lantern and kitchen. This test showed just how quickly this could be done. It took, I would think, under two minutes.

I was pleased because I had had this eventuality in mind. The distinction here is that a mechanic would have come to do a particular job and he wouldn't have cared what tricks we got up to. An engineer was likely to be from London and caution was sensible.

> The visitor stayed perhaps two hours and hinted at several large changes to be made in the future, notably electrification and everything arising therefrom – electric light, electric horn, electric winch and so on. It leaves me undecided whether these are the good days or whether they will be better later on.

Now I have no such doubts. It was the end of the good life.

In the mail was a letter from the Director of Education, Salop, saying thanks for the letter sent to Trevor Thickens of Lawley County School. Quite glowing. It unsettled me for the afternoon. I couldn't win. It was the letter I had written to settle me after I had been unsettled by my unfortunate exchange with *Satellite* over the paraffin tanks. What I really needed was a one-man lighthouse without a radio, and no boats, and a couple of days ashore once a year to stretch my legs.

> **18 July**: Wrote to Miss Sarah Perkins of Intake Junior Mixed School, Sidney Road, Doncaster who wrote to ask what makes the light work.

Poor child. I will almost certainly have included a full description of the Hood burner. I had also found myself corresponding with a lady in Edinburgh who wanted me to supply her with interior photographs of the tower. I'm pretty sure this didn't come to anything (and I'm sorry now it didn't) but she had written again to ask what qualities were required in lightkeepers. I concluded my reply:

> As to your query regarding the psychological type of the lighthouse keeper the answer is, no particular type: there are probably as many hearty extroverts as mute introverts. Whence the adaptability then to this 'odd' job? Again, the job isn't odd, or rather it is less 'odd' than many more conventional occupations in that it contains far fewer occasions of stress and demands for adjustment. For that reason the threshold of temperamental incompatibility is raised. The normal triggers of irritability – distinctive mannerisms, tics etc. in a colleague – cannot operate in the absence of explosive in the breech. Only the man who would not be happy anywhere is likely to find the job uncongenial, and the sooner he leaves the better for his colleagues.

By chance a few minutes after I had drafted the letter John heard from the Wolf that Carl Prout, of the motor horn episode, had left the job. I ought to have had an uneasy conscience about Carl. I had taken advantage of his naivete, but I doubt whether his decision to leave the Service had been much influenced by my foolery. He was one of that small number of birds of passage that figured in the SAK intake.

I still did my duty reading of the Sunday 'heavies' that were winched aboard with my mail at the half-time relief. Occasionally the stimulus provoked a response. I was impressed enough by the gossamer quality of 'Readers' Queries' in the *Sunday Times* to send in one of my own: 'I am seeking evidence to confirm that the *Bacchae* of Euripides was Virginian. If true it would imply that nearly a millennium before Columbus there existed a thriving barter trade between Hellas and the plantations of the Deep South. I wonder if any of your readers…etc.'

> In the afternoon wrote this on the gallery whereto, for the first time this year, I have taken the lantern table. A light air and the sun not as bright as it might be.
>
> **22 July**: Cook, and not particularly inclined for it. The prospect of going home has made me dissatisfied with my simple lot. However I did manage a good rice pudding. A fine, hot day. From the gallery watched a yacht anchored beneath us and in the evening read an *Observer* they rowed over and gave us.
>
> **25 July**: Relief day and an unanxious one. The wind, from when I got up at 0400, was never more than a 2 from the north-west. After speaking to Rame I sent greetings to Matey Rictus at St Anthony – no doubt he was listening.

11

A visitor and an injured bird:

the Eddystone and the Plymouth Breakwater

*D*uring my leave I toured the West Country with M. with a motor cycle combination. We began at Looe, from where we went out on the Eddystone run, experiencing it through the other end of the telescope, so to speak. I brought up my breakfast, I believe the only passenger to do so. I had expected I would but it was rather ridiculous all the same. 'Pearn let us ride gratis, but I gave Nibs, who took us out, ten shillings for past services.' We timed our run to take us through Bristol on 20 August for the recording. I had a copy of *Lighthouse Cookery* with me but had not been able to bring myself to look at it.

> 18 August: Out of a sense of duty I presently took out the talk and began to read it with a detestation that showed in my voice and added some amusement to an otherwise uninspired rendering. Then M. made the interesting suggestion that I should take out my teeth.

Some years earlier I had had a typical young man's motor-cycle accident and was taken for recovery to the Royal Hospital, Wolverhampton. It was my misfortune that Dr Josef Mengele should have been passing through on his way to Paraguay at the time. There were facial fractures that he neglected and that quickly set themselves out of line. The consequences therefore presently extended to rather more than the loss of some front teeth. I was sent to Wordsley which was then, and perhaps still is, a sort of medical breaker's yard where they specialised in body rebuilds. A surgeon surveyed me with only moderate interest. 'And what did you look like before?' he asked. It was a reasonable question but a difficult one to answer. I remembered that my face had been long rather than wide. 'Like a horse', I said. At which point he stopped looking bored and fished a copy of Tattersall's *Guide to the Turf* from the bottom drawer of his desk. 'And which particular horse do you fancy?' he asked. We went through them and decided on Acanthus who I think had won the Derby the previous year. I came round from the operation feeling rather worse than I had when I recovered consciousness after the accident. Technically, though, it was rated a complete success, so much so that the hospital staff formed a syndicate to enter me for the Cesarewitch the following year. Fortunately, as I now think, I went lame in training and scratched.

All this is by the way but explains why I was thereafter the possessor of detachable incisors.

> I was immediately attracted by the idea of walking in on Hudson *sans* teeth and beginning to read the piece so, and with a gross Birmingham whine. M. was satisfactorily convulsed and I finished the 'rehearsal' in a better frame of mind.

It was thus without teeth that I presented myself at Whiteladies Road two days later. Hudson, with the unflappability they breed into BBC producers, made light of my deficiency; certain things, he assured me, could be put right with the mike. This I doubted. I did a trial reading, with as little enjoyment as ever, then confessed I had my teeth in my pocket but had been practising the script without them and with the addition of a Birmingham accent...

'That's fine. It sounds perfectly all right.'

'I haven't used the accent yet', I said lamely.

I read a phrase or two, slipping with surprising ease into vile Brummigem. Hudson was delighted.

'Pure Goonery', he said. 'Let's try it with a less amenable passage.'

We did and he was still delighted. I told him I'd much prefer to do it that way. Finally I recorded it, first *sans* teeth in Brummy, then straight in English. The former was the more expressive simply because I had lost any inhibitions in a new persona; it was my own persona I wasn't comfortable with. Alas, when it came to the broadcast it was the straight one they used.

> 23 August: Relief day. We left the Sound in bright sunshine but about five miles out both tower and coastline vanished in a scurry of rain and when we finally arrived it was a wet relief. John (PK) and self went aboard; Craig and 'Mad' Kearns went ashore; Genghis remained.

In what respect Kearns was 'mad' is not recorded. We never shared a month, a matter of regret to me, but twice passed each other on the rope. Later he was appointed to the Wolf.

Once again it was visiting time for the committee of Elder Brethren on the *Patricia*.

> 24 August: My morning watch, inevitably. [It was the day following the relief.] Up 0400 and so to the usual familiar routine: fill up Argands [Low Lights] and Tilley [our kitchen lamp], dust in lantern, clean out and light fire, wipe oil off rollers, put out, change vapouriser, lower curtains etc. Breakfast. At 0645 I spoke to *Patricia* giving an unfavourable conditions report, so that she is now proceeding westward and may call on us on the way back.

She had been baulked the previous Wednesday when there was again no landing and in fact she never did get to us this year, though she managed the Wolf after several attempts – an unusual reversal of our fortunes. The weather was decidedly end-of-seasonish.

31 August: Both Looe boats came but it was blowing briskly from the north-east and they turned back just short of us. We were surprised to see them at all in such conditions. Down on the set-off both Genghis and I got wetted by an unexpected sea – unusual on the entrance side of the tower. [Later:] The wind has built up the heaviest north-east swell I have seen here.

2 September: The weather remained squally throughout the day and at tea-time the beginnings of a waterspout were observed a mile or so to the south – an elongated patch of white water swirling up a few feet into the air.

It was the only time I ever saw anything of the kind.

5 September: To bed soon after calling John for lack of anything to say to him.

There was a bigger problem here than I had had with Matey. John had no hobbies, he read no books, and neither of us seemed able to find any common ground. This was bad.

At 2130 he called Rame Head, without success, and mentioned his failure to Craig when he called him at midnight. Of course the test time is 0930 in the morning but 2215 in the evening [an appointment John had by now kept many times]. And in his morning trim he left a number of things undone.

The reserve between us was mutual and it was not to decrease, but at some time we must have talked because he told me how he had come to join the Service. In the thirties he had been working on the road being laid across the shingle at Dungeness. He had noticed the keepers there, in their uniforms, with their job security, their living wage, their expectation of a pension, and had thought them greatly to be envied. In the labour market of the fifties it was a job I had been able to walk into, but in the Depression years of the thirties he had applied and had had to wait two or three years for a vacancy. I felt guilty that this pleasant man, who seemed to have so few resources to fit him for our isolation, had to be afflicted with my company.

However, relief of a kind was at hand.

2 October: At 0950 *Satellite* called us to to say she was coming up to Plymouth tonight and tomorrow would bring out a Mr Snell, a friend of the Deputy Master, who would stay with us a fortnight to gain material for a paper on the architecture of lighthouses. What it will seem to provide him with is information about *a* lighthouse which he could more easily have gleaned from books and drawings.

We felt disquiet. To what degree would we have to modify any unorthodoxies in our routine, bearing in mind that reports might be carried ashore? As a seeming omen of what was to come

a circus of five Naval helicopters flew past out of Plymouth at gallery height. Even got a whiff of exhaust fumes.

> *3 October*: Up about 0845 for a hasty breakfast, got the ropes down and *Satellite* arrived from Plymouth at about 1000. Conditions were good so in three boatloads she gave us not only Snell but paraffin, water and thirty hundredweight of coal, during the winding of which I perspired freely and wore a hole in my hand. She was gone by 1445 or so – for the winter we hope. Snell stood revealed (as the old-time novelists would have said) as a man in perhaps his early to middle twenties, apparently a student architect, with for a grandfather a former head of Lloyds, and for an uncle the head of Stuart Turner Engines, and for a friend (as previously noted) the Deputy Master of Trinity House.

As this was the entry for his day of arrival it can be seen that he lost no time in presenting his credentials.

> We still do not know to what extent we are going to have to put on a show. Me, I feel a bit depressed about it all, the fact of having four at table, the presence of someone who is not attuned to our ways… Only one letter for me from Blights: an offer from Miss I.I. Shotter to send us carols, bless her dear old heart.

This was the lady to whom I had written earlier, thanking her for sending us a book of community songs. In my acknowledgement I decided not to mention that we now numbered four, in order not to provoke her to the sending of an anthology of madrigals.

The following day before lunch we learned that besides the grandfather, the uncle and the friend already mentioned Snell has a brother who contributes to the *Observer*. I retreated to the lantern to 'continue with copying out the story *N.S.B.* (*None So Blind*, which may eventually require re-titling *N.B.G.* – *No Bloody Good*), an activity interrupted by Snell coming up to admire a squall and staying to have a chat'. However, at a superficial level there was some reassurance:

> I fixed up the lens indicator light after an assurance from Snell that he wouldn't speak of such things when he got ashore. Continued with my reading of the often amusing *One's Company* by Peter Fleming [and no doubt wishing it was]. Snell went to bed soon after midnight after we had watched the m.v. *Venus* go past on her way to Plymouth, inward bound from Madeira. Not exactly an awe-inspiring sight but I feel obliged to show Snell everything there is to show him while he is still so conscientiously responsive. Even my bread the other day was 'marvellous'. It's never been called that before.
>
> *6 October*: The afternoon was spent helping Snell to make measurements of the set-off and in the entrance room (required for his 'paper'). The measurements we took could have been more easily derived from drawings at Trinity House.

In the afternoon a light aircraft, presumed to contain a promised friend of Snell (not the Deputy Master: it seems he has another one) made a couple of circuits of us before disappearing towards Plymouth. Snell was in bed as it happened but missed nothing. This day's revelation was that he has flown in the Comet 4 on one of its demonstrations at Farnborough and has had dinner with Audrey Hepburn and her husband and found them very pleasant people. I will have ground my teeth in silent rage at this. I had seen *Roman Holiday* three times having conceived a passion for Miss Hepburn. I wrote, disagreeably:

> Snell, I fear, has no sense of humour by which I mean, as one always does, that he hasn't mine. I can make Craig laugh, though he has no great liking for me, but Snell's heavy jowls remain unshaken. At twenty-five he is already well covered and his development into a *pyknik*-type professional man is a foregone conclusion. He is fond of food and has a light tea in order to enjoy a large supper in which Continental influences are apparent. Last Friday's concoction was additionally flavoured by a mishap when he decanted a mass of spaghetti into the sink, not once but twice – whereupon I could no longer pretend that my amusement was at the comedian on the radio: the comedian at the sink had stolen his thunder.

How invaluable a diary is for venting spleen!

Reserve is difficult to maintain on a lighthouse. The honeymoon period of formal pleasantries was coming to an end. If I found myself in dispute, not with Snell but with Craig, it is still possible that it was the presence of Snell that unbalanced a formerly accommodating trio.

> *10 October*: At lunch we had an impassioned exchange of compliments. I examplified Craig as one of the type on whom the thin veneer of civilisaton does *not* depend. He declared my lack of preoccupation with sex to be a bit odd. I on the contrary regarded it as the expression of a fundamental normality. He, no doubt thinking, in a baffled way, of my long hours spent *in absentía*, said that if civilisation depended on me it would have stood still. And there, I think, the mutual flattery ceased. In the evening we cooed prettily.

Probably there is some tidying-up in this record: I can't believe we made our points so elegantly.

The previous day I had found a distressed bird in the roof gutter.

> Fed the bird all day. He has 1) a broken neck; 2) a broken tail; 3) concussion. But he survives on condensed milk and his general condition improves. Wrote this in the lantern at 1932 with him dozing on my left hand, presently to give him his evening feed.

> *11 October*: My relations with Snell are not at present entirely happy. I called him, by request, at 0700 this morning. It was ten to nine, after a breakfast involving about seven saucepans, two frying pans and a coffee-pot that he cleared out of the kitchen – and I am not naturally at my best at that time of morning. I like to enjoy a solitary breakfast in well-tuned silence. Company, whether of mechanics or colleagues, disturbs the smoothness of the psychic

> rhythm. Apart from the basic offence of making a fourth in a *ménage à trois* he is overtly critical of my bird management. It should, for example, not be brutally picked up but coaxed on to the finger, thus. Nor should it be placed for the night in the 'stuffy' two-foot cube of my seat locker, which is also too dark. Presumably this type of bird is accustomed to some novel 24-hour daylight scheme.
>
> *12/13 October*: The bird is now completely recovered. Another beautiful day. Flat calm, hardly any wind. I'm toying with the idea of swimming across to the Stump on morning watch tomorrow before the others are up and painting an anti-Snell slogan on the top. Just before 1700 a friend of Snell made a promised visit in an Auster aircraft but did nothing spectacular.

How many more friends did the man have? I found nothing there to justify such popularity.

There was worse to come. A day or two later four Shackletons of Coastal Command made a low pass while we were all on the gallery, then came round for another run-in. This really was too much! I persuaded Craig and John to retire with me into the lantern, leaving Snell to take the salute. I think it was this episode that made me understand why the French and Russian revolutions had been accompanied by so much bloodshed. When I considered the expenditure of public money that had gone into organising this particular tribute to a relatively junior member of the Establishment, even supposing it to be tied in with some sort of navigational exercise, it became clear that Socialism would never arrive in Britain without an equivalent bloodbath. These people were simply too deeply entrenched to be got out by any lesser means.

I now had three uncompleted enterprises in hand: the electrode immersion heater, the distant reading barometer/wind speed indicator, and the reaction propelled pendulum.

> *14 October*: Up 0400 and sounded for fog from 0705 to 0820 when I stopped with some surprise for I had taken it for granted we were in for a merry week-end of banging. In fact a very fine day ensued. After lunch I searched the lantern for Charlie [the bird] without success and as an afterthought opened the door of the weight-tube two floors below. There he was, smothered in oil from the lens clock chains. I took off what I could with meths but he still looked a sorry sight and is obviously unhappy about being in such a condition. I read a book in my bunk in the afternoon but sleep was made impossible by Charlie hopping restlessly up and down me, even in my hair. For supper Snell made a compost of spaghetti with something foreign on top. Rather liked it. Very filling. After the test with Rame at 2215 we went out on the gallery in a stiff but warm breeze and chatted.
>
> *15 October*: To bed at 0100 and to sleep – a drunken one. Awoke to a condition approximating to a hangover; the result, I think to myself, of Snell's culinary jamboree last night.

16 October: I should have recorded yesterday, if only for the sense of loss that it gave me, that Charlie died at about noon. It is on my conscience that I did not try and feed him at breakfast. Then he hopped around the breakfast table and on to us and seemed very lively, despite his being greased up to the eyebrows. But when, after lunch, I took him up some cornflakes and condensed milk, he was on his back by the ladder in the lantern, already stiff, where I had seen him dozing earlier in the morning. I felt the loss because in the six days I have had him he has established himself as a personality, struggling in my hand against my attempts to feed him, trotting round the inner perimeter of the lantern as if he really thought he was getting somewhere, brushing himself up with such vigour as to fall over. I was looking forward to taking him ashore if he had survived. Very probably it was the lens clock oil that really killed him. Finished the day with a disagreeable conversation with Snell. He suggested that lighthouse keeping is not a particularly good job.

I think there will have been little common ground between us in defining what 'a good job' is. So obviously a 'career man' himself he may have felt aggrieved that I had somehow, and rather disgracefully, bucked the system.

I left him with his over-full stomach, his big, flabby body and his irritation at my pretensions and went to bed.

The impression I get from my diary overall is that I didn't much like Snell.

20 October: Relief day, but wasn't. Up 0400 and it was blowing a 6 from the west with a heavy swell. During the day the wind moderated. It is now west-nor'-west 4, the forecast is not impossible and Craig is ready to say Yes tomorrow. The amount of white water below there makes me dubious. We shall see… No time to write more as I have to shave my beard off and do some ironing.

21 October: Relief day. Conditions improved during the night and at 0830 there was sufficient cause to say that at 1230 there would be a landing and Craig did so. (Hinchcliff at Rame overslept and didn't come up till 0845.) After 1100 there was no need to doubt. Genghis came aboard with an SAK Marriott, I went ashore with John. With us went Snell who, true to form, stayed well clear of the winch-handles while we were winding, thereby earning a chilliness from me which I allowed to persist throughout our insincere farewells at Millbay. Ever an opportunist, he has made an unwelcome offer to drive John to the Lizard [where John is in married quarters] which he wants to 'look over'; unwelcome because John thinks, probably rightly, that in return for this favour he will be expected to put him up for the night. I made a rapid exit from the other gate of the docks and took a taxi direct to the station where I left my luggage before returning to the Hoe to re-read my correspondence and watch Genghis put the light in at about 1710, my mood, as is customary when I come ashore, one of gloom rather than elation.

I didn't even cheer up when at Bristol I found myself 'in the company of the Glorious, and very noisy, Gloucesters, freshly home from Korea'. Was I becoming institutionalised, like some recidivist old lag? No, it wasn't lighthouse addiction. What my mood expressed, rather, was a simple regret at exchanging productive simplicity for the often negative turmoil of social commerce ashore. People have always seemed to me to take up an awful lot of one's time, and mostly to very little purpose.

A death in the family at this point produced an interruption in the relief cycle. When the likely course of events became clear I wrote to Penzance. Goodman proposed I transfer temporarily to Plymouth Breakwater light from where I could be extricated less expensively if the need arose; I would have to bear the cost of the relief. As it came out the Eddystone relief was done on the Thursday, delayed from Monday. The funeral had taken place two days earlier. The following Monday, therefore, I went aboard the Breakwater to pass the time until I could be slotted back into the Eddystone reliefs.

I was to be on the Breakwater for only two weeks and my problem now is the one that confronted me in giving accounts of my stays at the Bishop (two days) and Longships (one month): the period was too short to have left a distinct impression forty years later. I must therefore again rely on my diary entries.

> 26 November: To Blights at about 0830. Reynolds said he would do the trip for two or three pounds instead of the usual nine.

This was at the intercession of Captain Goodman. The figure of £9 suggests that the fee paid to Reynolds for the Eddystone relief was some £40 or £50.

> At 1300 down to the quay and went out with the skipper of one of the tugs in a very small launch. Had a rather sloppy passage across the harbour and as we came up to the light there was no sign of life until we shouted, when Dee [with whom I had first gone out to the Eddystone as an SAK] came out on to the breakwater to ask what we were there for. It seems the Supernumerary, Fox, had been told he was to stay the month and he was quite unprepared for going ashore. Dee went over to the fort [on the breakwater] to telephone while I went up the tower with Don, a slight Scot with a broad brogue. There seems to be no room at all for personal gear. The light is a 50 mm burner with a rotating shutter, spring-driven, requiring 23 turns a night! [I must surely have intended to write 'an hour'.] Kitchen watch is kept, the light being observed in the reflection from a window in the fort a few hundred yards away beside the breakwater. Dee returned to say that there had been a slip-up in the office; that Fox was going and I staying. So Fox, delighted, hastily packed his stuff and left, passage paid. Unlike the Eddystone [which had the Low Light room] this tower contains only one habitable room, so here I shall have to do all this sort of thing [the diary].

I had so often passed the Breakwater Light and thought how limited the accommodation must be. This impression was not mistaken.

> *27 November:* The breakwater is about a mile long and not particularly
> comfortable walking – but at least the walking is not circular as elsewhere!
> The tower is perhaps 75 feet high. A few awkward steps lead up to the
> entrance. The staircase is of stone. The first floor is the paraffin store, the
> second the kitchen with two large windows, the third the bedroom and the
> fourth the combined Service Room and lantern. Nevertheless there is more
> actual living room than I expected.

But surely not much more. I suspect that the Breakwater was one of those towers that
were built for a crew of two, and three made a tight fit.

> *30 November:* Wrote a note home in some difficulty and with resulting
> incoherence on account of the wireless. [There was nowhere here that I could
> go to get away from it.] Mac broached a bottle of whisky to celebrate St
> Andrew's Day. To bed in the fume-laden bedroom at 2200.

Memory does not tell me whether the fumes were from Mac sleeping off his whisky
or from the burner, hissing one floor above.

Mac had been a merchant seaman and told me a number of anecdotes which,
foolishly, I did not record and of which I recall only one. As helmsman he had once
got into hot water when his skipper, in an uncertain temper, lurched on to the bridge,
consulted the compass and let out a roar of rage.

'Ye blo-ody fuel! Ye're sailing north. Turn west – west! D'ye want to run us ashore?'

He was not to be reasoned with so Mac turned west and headed out into the
Atlantic for a couple of hours until his skipper had sobered up sufficiently to have it
explained to him that while he was passed out in his bunk his ship had passed out of
the Mediterranean and Liverpool now indeed lay 'up there'.

I find this story easier to believe now than I did at the time, for some years later I
was in Bermuda when something similar occurred in a vessel tied up to the quay at St
George's. The ship had put in for repairs and one night the captain gave the order for
steam to be raised. This was not sensible because the boilers had been drained. This
was pointed out but he would have none of it. The burners were lit, the engine-room
caught fire and the town brigade was called to extinguish the blaze. After a further
delay the ship sailed with a new captain. Mac was insistent, as he sipped his Scotch,
that most skippers drank.

Socially Dee and Mac were exciting company. It will be remembered that there
had been set-tos between Dee and PK Matey Rictus on my first visit to the Eddystone
as an SAK. Now he and Mac generated a similar voltage and I found myself, as a
visitor, filling the role of pig in the middle, particularly in the matter of their cigarette
butts. They both smoked, usually half a cigarette at a time, the remaining half being
put aside for later. I say put aside but in fact they were always hidden, for in this
matter neither trusted the other, and I found myself coming upon laid-by halves and
quarters in some unlikely places which were so many and varied that it must have
taxed the memory of both to keep track of them. It is this, I think, that produced the

problem at one breakfast when Dee, with Mac present, accused me of having taken one of his cigarette ends. Both of them knew the question was absurd as I didn't smoke. How we went on from there I do not now know, but I hope I strung it out sufficiently to give a good run to all three of us.

The Breakwater seemed too easy a lighthouse to be entirely real. Semi-automated it would have made an admirable station for one man. Visiting workmen came and went on the breakwater (I watched a 60-ton block being added to the defences on the seaward side: an impressive operation) and took away mail. Jack Beale, of the Plymouth lifeboat, came once a week with mail as well as papers and bread. The relief produced no problems.

> 10 December: At tea Mac ate a haggis. Having learned what was in it I declined his offer of a fragment. At the time of writing (2234) the wind is blowing quite hard and anything up to a gale is promised for tomorrow. But here this apparently means no more than that it may not be possible to do the relief at all states of the tide. Tomorrow, for example, we may have to wait until after lunch.

> 11 December: The sea was coming over the breakwater when the tug came out at ten so we had to defer the relief until the afternoon. But stepping into the boat at 1445 I was at North Road station at 1530 in plenty of time to catch the 1545 train to Bristol.

I did not return to the Breakwater Lighthouse. I look back on it as a pleasant interlude away from the station that was 'home'.

12
Unsettled moods:
the Eddystone, Christmas 1956 and spring 1957

*T*hrough a misunderstanding I went down to Plymouth a day early.

> *20 December:* To Blight's at 0830 to find that relief is tomorrow – as I had supposed until the tug men said otherwise when I came off the Breakwater. Not very distressed by the discovery.

It may seem surprising that this could happen – that we were not formally notified by Penzance office of the due date. In fact it was not necessary; reliefs, now that Sundays were included, succeeded each other invariably at intervals of one month and one day and the District Office left us alone during our month ashore. They had even stopped telling me to get myself vaccinated against smallpox.

An old diary is a constant reminder of the selectiveness of memory. I had been convinced that though I had witnessed several aborted reliefs from the tower I had never done so from the tug. I was mistaken.

> *21 December:* It has happened to me at last! We went out and came back again, the relief undone. In Plymouth, both before and after, it would have seemed a perfect day for a relief. But once we got out into the Sound the freshness of the easterly wind was felt and we had a rough trip out. Craig felt bad: I was less afflicted but brought up my breakfast nevertheless. One of two schoolgirls aboard was also having a thin time. Once arrived there the sea round the tower looked a mess. The three on the set-off made no encouraging signs and finally old John waved us home. The return trip was better as were riding with the swell, and we got back to Blights at about 1415. Presently I gathered the ingredients of a cold meal together and ate it in my room at the Seamen's hostel.

Was I about to break my sequence of Christmas Days aboard? No.

> *22 December:* Relief day. And done. A much quieter sea, though still with some fairly big ones coming round the tower. But I took two tablets instead of one and hung on to my breakfast, as did Craig. And so we got aboard, and Genghis and Cochrane went ashore, Genghis looking very happy, Cochrane, with a separated wife and four children, less so. Old John remained aboard. He too looked happy. It seemed to be a good day for most people.

> *Christmas Eve*: Cook. Putting-out now is not until 0822 or so. But it was a beautiful morning and in fact a beautiful day. At 0830 we passed a list of shifts to the Breakwater. The Bishop relief should have been done yesterday, but wasn't, but was done today.

The Breakwater didn't have a radio-telephone but, like us, did have a 'trawler band' on its domestic set and so was able to listen to our transmissions. The 'shifts' were personal movements of which we had learned, probably by way of the Wolf. They were grist to lighthouse table-talk.

This was to be my fourth lighthouse Christmas and my third on the Eddystone.

> *Christmas Day, 1956*: Quite a merry day. The wind had developed into a full south-easterly gale during the night and it continued at near storm force before suddenly going nor'-west in the evening. Craig did an excellent lunch of chicken, peas, baked and boiled potatoes and gravy, preceded by tomato soup. None of us had any room for pudding. Before lunch we had been drinking whisky and beer. Afterwards we listened to the programme preceding the Queen's speech while the gale roared without. Craig went to bed and old John and I sat and thought until teatime at 1800. At 1845 Radio Luxembourg broadcast 'Eddystone Rock', a programme of rock and roll tunes, for fifteen minutes. Craig and I then made music – mouth-organ and fiddle – before I listened to a reading of Thurber's story *The Night the Bed Fell on Father*. Talked and concluded the smoking of father's cigar, begun after lunch. Thus was our Christmas Day.

The consumption of alcohol was, I suppose an irregularity, though one in which we were eclipsed by the Irish lights who, almost traditionally, produced a bucolic hulla-balloo throughout every Christmas Day on the radio. I don't recall that any of us ever brought drink aboard for regular consumption, I suppose because drinking is essentially a social activity and one that needed a wider society than ours.

The weather was now becoming interesting. It had been splendidly appropriate on Christmas Day, and subsequently:

> *29 December*: Yet another gale blowing up from a deep depression whose winds have already damaged the 50,000 ton *Liberté* sufficiently to cause her to return to Le Havre.

> *30 December*: Gale still WSW, freshening if anything, and from the open Low Light room landing window I have been watching the seas run up the Stump – and one or two up to this very window.

> *31 December*: Whilst writing the previous entry yesterday with the tower being shaken periodically by the heavy swell I conceived a possible solution to the seismograph problem at which I've worried from time to time...

Over the next few days I produced a rig which, anchored to the lantern floor, produced significant indications, though it was too crude to provide quantitative measurements. I have always thought it would have been interesting to measure how and to what degree the tower moved in a storm. Granite will be elastic, like every other material. What was the amplitude of the displacement in the lantern and did the tower have a harmonic period? I wish I had thought then to beg or borrow the appropriate equipment; I was in the ideal situation for such a study. I doubt whether officialdom had ever carried it out.

Throughout the year on fine and not so fine days the reef had an almost daily visitor from Plymouth, a small boat crewed by two fishermen who came out to lay and lift lobster-pots. If they have not been mentioned before it is because they made virtually no impact on us. They ignored us; we ignored them. On a radio test I once asked Jack Beale of Plymouth lifeboat about them.

> He was able to tell us that the boat *Sweet Home* is skippered by Charlie
> Clapper and that his mate's name was Lilliecrap. It didn't sound very likely but
> I did not think it proper to query such names over the air.

A less frequent visitor was a larger crabber which made the trip from a French port. I was told, with what truth I do not know, that her deckhands were the Gallic equivalent of our Borstal boys, working out their sentences.

I had arrived to merrymaking and laughter, but below the surface relationships were beginning to crumble. Genghis and I had served together at St Anthony and now we had been together on the Eddystone. We had very little left to say to each other. Craig I rubbed along with. As to old John, it seemed I could find nothing at all to say to him, nor he to me. We spoke, but the exchanges had become odd. He would make a remark. I would respond with what I hoped was some appropriately progressive addition. His next remark, however, would advance, not from mine, but from whatever it was he had last said, and so we would go on, I fluting an errant obbligato to what was essentially his monologue. I recognised it as a 'game' (Berne had yet to publish his *Games People Play* but Stephen Potter had identified such procedures humorously in his *Lifemanship* books) and now I would label it Conversational Block, a variant of Berne's General Motors. I saw no way out but to retire to my bunk to read *Scoop*; and also to work at the idea for the seismograph, about which there are several pages in the diary.

Perhaps to slot me back into my turn with old John I was to go ashore, exceptionally, after one month.

> 10 *January*: A most beautiful, spring-like day. After lighting-up spent the
> evening singing in the lantern, being in vocal mood. At 1650 we got,
> unrequested, our relief list via Wolf: old John and I are going ashore, Genghis
> and an SAK Lines coming aboard. [He didn't.] Glad – but as usual, disturbed
> – to be going ashore.

There had been the usual correspondence to be dealt with: letters to a Mrs Fisher who had sent us some magazines; to a Mrs Tobias, in Dublin, and to a Mrs Sanderson for sending us magazines and a book respectively; to Mrs L .M. Smith, my particular correspondent from the Redhill Women's Institute, who sent the Christmas parcel; and to the boys of Crawfordton house similarly. (I doubt whether theirs was the whisky we drank on Christmas Day, although it is a Scots school...) And to the persistent Miss J. S. a 'farrago of nonsense which I hope will discourage her'.

> *19 January:* After lunch down to the set-off for, I think, the first time this month, while Craig tried to do some fishing. One of the lowest tides we've seen, due probably to the strong easterly winds of the last day or so.

Not to be able to get down on to the set-off was a common experience in the winter months. It was at such exceptionally low tides as the one referred to that we were able to see the undercut in the reef on which the Smeaton's and the two previous towers were erected, and which was nominally the occasion for building the present fourth tower elsewhere. I say nominally because I have always suspected that Douglass simply wanted to build himself a splendid lighthouse before he retired. I know the urge. Years after I left the Service I built an Eddystone replica to a scale of one inch to the foot, with a rotating optic. At 4,668 tons Douglass has the edge but my couple of tons of reinforced concrete is going to prove a serious embarrassment to whoever tries to remove it when I am dead. It is reinforced internally with steel rods. I recommend the use of a thermic lance.

> *Sunday 20 January:* Relief day – and was. The forecast was 0–2 strengthening to 5 later in the day, so I spent a rather anxious four hours up to 0830 when I gave the OK to Rame Head. In fact the relief was quite comfortably done by about 1330. John and self went ashore, Genghis and John Kearns came aboard. Amongst my mail was a copy of *The Seafarer*, the magazine of the Seafarers' Society, containing my gloomy story *Inquest* without a single perceptible correction. I didn't mind reading it – which is an unusual reaction to my own stuff.

Perhaps I was jumping to conclusions, but I couldn't regard an unexpected letter from my old *bête noire*, Matey Rictus, as a coincidence. He had no reason to write to me but

> He often spoke of the connections he had with the right people, and it could be that with the printing of this story I now come into that category.

Less satisfactory was a letter from the Met. Office saying that the distant reading sensor I had sent them had been damaged in transit, that they thought it would work well enough for temperature and humidity, but that they lacked the staff for its development and were referring the matter to the Air Ministry's appropriate department for decision. I had not been happy anyway about their request that I should send the instrument for assessment. The principle behind the device was essentially simple, as is often the case. Any competent engineer would have grasped it at once from a descriptive paragraph and would have been able to decide whether it was of interest to him or not. I would not have minded if it had been turned down by such. I felt I was dealing with technical illiterates and I was probably right.

I returned on 18 February:

> Relief day, as was obvious from early morning. At the Eddystone we have
> lately been very fortunate. After the last one [on which I had gone ashore]
> there was a period of three weeks, it seems, without a landing, and today's
> was the first comfortable opportunity, though it could have been done yester-
> day at low water, apparently. A smooth trip out in the *Alexandria* with old
> John in bright sunshine, and by 1240 the boat was on its way back with SAK
> Kearns (now appointed to the *Wolf*) and Genghis.

I was discovering the difference between pure and applied thought. It was su-
premely enjoyable to spend hours worrying away at some problem in the abstract; it
could also be fun knocking up a model that might or might not work. A different
matter entirely was trying to sell ideas to sceptical businessmen who put questions
you had not anticipated to which you had to provide instant answers which were
much less adequate than the ones you thought of ten minutes after the interview was
ended. Also marriage was in the offing. No sensible man or woman can welcome this
prospect with unreserved rapture. One may suspect that the outcome will be an improvement in the quality of life, but until the fact is established by experience the
condition of doubt is a sensible precaution. (The following forty years with the same
woman were to provide increasing reassurance.)

Such is the interdependence of mind and body that I went on board with a developing sore throat, and finished the next day mentally drafting a letter to Bertrand
Russell, no doubt inviting him to agree that the world was in a desperate condition
and asking him what he recommended we do about it.

It is quite surprising to what a low state one can be driven by a combination of
failed commerce, impending marriage and a streptococcal infection.

The transistor had now reached the market-place and I had bought a small receiver kit for three pounds seven shillings to replace my one-valver. Results were not
immediately satisfactory. I spent a couple of days putting it together and installing it
in a veneered box which Genghis made. Early transistors were of variable quality
and I found myself listening through a background of waterfall noise. I presently
discovered (how, I can't imagine) that this could be persuaded to abate if I warmed a
particular transistor over the flame from a paraffin lamp. It was a curious way to run
a radio.

> 4 March: Over the R/T came news of injuries on the *Wolf* involving two of the
> three keepers, one of them shaken and very shocked, the other progressing
> nicely. Davis being very canny about whys and wherefores.

Davis was presumably the PK or the Keeper-in-Charge. His reticence over the air
was understandable but disappointing.

The openness of radio transmissions meant that there could be exchange of gossip
of only the most superficial kind. A real grapevine hardly existed. We had no cause to
visit the depot at Penzance and, even if we had, who would we have met? The relief

days of the different stations were dictated by the weather and rarely coincided. Hard information came by word of mouth with the arrival of a newly appointed keeper from elsewhere, and by then it could be months old. I once went ashore with old John to hear him telephone the Superintendent and be told by him that a man had had to be taken off the Bishop Rock, 'mad'. It was an interesting story which, alas, we were to hear no more about. This might seem to confirm the popular impression that every lighthouse keeper lives on the knife-edge of sanity, but I would insist that any-one who goes mad in the relatively stress-free environment of a lighthouse was prob-ably half-mad before he got there.

I seemed to be cheering up.

> 7 March: In the morning cleaned the lens steel-work with Genghis… Mean-while in an inverted jam-jar on the gallery I was brewing a hellish concoction of two parts of hydrogen and one of oxygen, and with one-fifth part of a jam-jar collected I detonated it with my HT coil. The energy of the explosion was sufficient to throw the jar out of the bowl. I was suitably satisfied with this result. With bigger jam-jars, bigger bangs. I used the R/T batteries for the electrolysis. The idea of detonating a 5-gallon drumful of H_2 and O, collected over a period of days via a wind-driven generator, is very attractive.

> 16 March: At 2215 I woke from a horrible dream, a vague nightmare which lingered into wakefulness. Some momentary lesion, perhaps, in the brain. Horrible. It suggested to me the acute misery of contemplating with the sane part of one's mind the disintegration of another part – presumably the lot of some unfortunate people.

My colleagues had never been reassured by my tendency to nightmares, which seemed an extension of what they regarded as a waking eccentricity. Such episodes were presumably anxious in origin. The worst were as usual of an indescribable horror. The lesser could be enlivened with humour:

> I was in hospital, masquerading as a patient. Nearby a group of surgeons were going through the operation scene from Thurber's *Walter Mitty* ('sock-stretcher' etc.). I watched with the absorption such scenes always command. 'Is all that sock-stretcher stuff technically right?' I asked at the end of the performance. 'Of course', said a Grand Man. 'Thurber was a stickler for realism.' Later, still in hospital, a nurse got into my bed and prepared to go to sleep. 'Isn't it a bit unusual, this?' I asked her uneasily. 'I mean – patient and nurse in the same bed.' 'Oh, it's in the regulations', she said cheerfully; 'intensive care'.

As marriage was in the offing I can only guess at what a Freudian psychologist would make of such dreams.

The ordinary anxieties of relief day were on us again. We had been fortunate with the previous two reliefs; we were not to be fortunate now.

> 19 March: Called Genghis at 0110. He seemed in the mood for a talk and presently we embarked on a woolly theosophical/psychological discussion

which took us up to 0220 when I went to bed with prospects for relief not looking bright. And at 0830 old John said No without hesitation.

20 March: On 0000–0400, a middle watch which I largely wasted reading science-fiction stories which Genghis had carelessly left lying around: my middle watches seem ill-spent nowadays. The wind had risen to something near a gale, with heavy rain, and relief was out of the question. But I am writing this on the lantern table at about 1148 in sunshine so hot that it is making me feel a little ill. The sea is still a mass of whitecaps, and Genghis, who has his share of the mental wear and tear of relief-time, is as morose as his considerate disposition allows him to be.

21 March: A missed opportunity of a sort, in that I said No at 0830 and there was a landing from – *landing be damned*! I've just been out on to the gallery in response to sea-noise and watched an express-train go past the spot where the boat would have sat, had she been so unfortunate as to row in. But a day of beautiful sunshine so I cannot take this overdue too seriously even though it is delaying the next relief… My test at 2215 to Rame Head went: 'Right, here it is, Mr Nicholls. Wind SSE, force 3, good landing, and we look forward to seeing them between midnight and one o'clock. Over to you.' Pause, then a hesitant Nicholls: 'Er – would you mind coming again, Mr Lane? I got your weather but – surely – ?' I reassured him.

My correspondence with Lawley County Primary School and its Head, Mr Lineton, led me to write to Plymouth Library to ask whether they would be prepared to let me borrow their copy of Smeaton's account of the building of his tower. We were now approaching the bicentenary of the laying of the first stone and it occurred to me it would be interesting to make an abstract of the Journal and send it to the school. An outline drawing pinned up and progressively filled in over the succeeding three years would certainly convey an idea of the difficulty of construction.

22 March saw no relief and the 23rd was a bright day but with a bigger swell than ever. Routine work went on.

In the morning sprayed the glazing, greased the fog-jib and oiled the lens.

24 March: Relief day – and about the most difficult I remember here. At 0715 I had decided No. An hour later it looked marginally better and at 0830 I decided Yes, adding to my message that they should stand well away from the tower on account of occasional SW breakers. Thereafter there was anxiety until the moment the boat cast off and pulled away. It was a beautiful morning as far as sunshine was concerned, and brilliantly clear. They didn't arrive until about 1230 when the tide had turned and they had missed the best of it, and they rowed in most reluctantly, shouting imprecations. Certainly it can't have looked good from the boat. But we did it, and with the mid-day forecast promising only deterioration, were glad to have pulled it off. Genghis went ashore and Craig arrived. Thereafter unpacked provisions, had a rice pudding, and adjourned to the lantern until teatime with my mail.

28 March: A day dominated by fog. Cleaned the windows down the tower, then from 1140 to 1555, with a break for lunch [when a colleague took over] I sounded. And at 2000 John began again, to hand over to me at midnight. A wasted day, as they so often are when upset by fog.

29 March: Following the pattern, a wasted middle watch. Sounded till 0115, then an uncertain two hours' respite before resuming at 0315 to hand over to Craig at about 0430.

Sounding in the small hours was indeed a miserable business. The lantern dripped, inside and out, with moisture. If the fog was thick, one stopped the lens and the beams, unnaturally still, punched out over the sea like umbrella-spokes for a couple of hundred yards.

We finally finished at 1000 and thereafter the morning became quite bright, and with its brightening so did our spirits. The French liner *Flandre* has just gone by into Plymouth at speed, no doubt making up time after the fog.

2 April: A beautiful day so after lunch ambulated on the set-off for a while under the watchful eye of a seal on the rocks below the Stump. Then with old John chased a bird out of the lantern. To do this we both had to clamber around the top of the lens in order to drive it down to the floor fifteen feet below. I then dropped my pullover strategically behind it and it flew out of the door, no doubt feeling itself well rid of two maniacal monkeys. At 2250, just as *Satellite* called us from Falmouth to say she had put in there because of fog and would be coming this way tomorrow, fog overcame *us*, and I sounded till midnight or so when I handed over to Craig. (John eventually finished at 0730 tomorrow.)

3 April: Heard John talking to *Satellite* at 0500 and again at 0645. They called us at 0845 and the launch came in at perhaps ten o'clock, intending to land coal. Conditions were never as bad as when we did the relief but she was discouraged by the admittedly large swells and went back. The tender then steamed off to rendezvous with the *Beacon* in Torbay. Writing this in the lantern I am fairly acutely aware of the onset of a bout of rheumatism in my left leg... Had just written the above when *Satellite* called us again to say that her rendezvous with *Beacon* was cancelled, that she was returning to Plymouth today in order to leave for dry dock tomorrow night, and what were conditions like now? Replied, unavoidably, good. So in the afternoon she landed 22 bags of coal. Hard work on the winch which I normally enjoy, but with my 'screws'...

Physically we were softened by lack of exercise, then found ourselves doing heart-pounding work on the winch. Two days later I comment on tiredness, adding 'I don't think I've yet got over Wednesday's exertions.'

15 April: A station of crocks. Old John has a bad back (lifted the Valor stove awkwardly) and my 'screws' are giving me hell – unquestionably the worst

ERRATA

p.28 : The Longships light was eclipsing, not occulting;

p.44 : For Devon read Cornwall throughout;

p.181 : The Gardner engines were four-strokes.

In an otherwise factual book two minor excursions into fiction should be admitted. With one remembered exception Trinity House uniform trouser legs were of matching length; and, on p.110, there was no Coastal Command Shackleton flypast tribute to Snell.

session ever. At 2000, having with some difficulty persuaded John, lit up for him. He has ideas about needing to keep his back mobile but I can't see that the contortions required to climb into the lens will do him any good.

This may seem like a noble offer. No doubt I was expiating a sense of guilt at being such poor company for the old boy. However, there was a practical appreciation, too, that I could always choose alternative muscles whereas he had only one back.

16 April: John only pretends he isn't incapacitated and doesn't fool us. Weatherwise today surpasses Sunday. This *is* summer. I am writing this on the gallery at about 1240 and finding the sun almost unpleasantly hot, though it would be foolish to admit as much out loud. But for last month's overdue it would be relief day tomorrow.

17 April: Up 0415. A brilliant start to a day that was presently marred by cloud. It was a belt of cloud on the horizon at sun-up that foiled a hope that I might see the Arend(?) comet which should be visible near the sun at dawn.

19 April: In the morning sprayed the glazing while *Mayflower II* could be seen moving up the coast from Start Point to Plymouth under tow. A Miles Gemini (press probably) came round us and I gave it the customary wave from astride the wind vane. [*Mayflower II* was the replica of the vessel in which the Plymouth Brethren sailed to America.]

20 April: At 1730 *Mayflower* emerged from Plymouth under tow and with an escort of boats, yachts and three planes. Hopes of a closer view came to nothing when, no more than four miles out, she slipped her tow, hoisted sail, and in conditions of flat calm slipped back east along the coast until with nightfall we lost her. At midnight there wasn't a movement of air on the gallery...

21 April: Up 0930. *Mayflower* had worked her way to westwards of us during the night and was still in view about ten miles to the West at 1400 and later. After lunch listened to some messages from her to Land's End radio.

22 April: On middle watch am writing this at 0222 with relief assured insofar as relief can ever be assured. Light, northerly wind.

The confidence was not misplaced. It was one of those rare, unmemorable reliefs about which there is nothing to be said, the usual switch taking place, Genghis and SAK Lines replacing old John and myself.

13
Strained tempers:
the final spell at the Eddystone

I was developing an unsought role as a lightkeeper correspondent. Thus the Superintendent had sent me the address of a Japanese lightkeeper so that I presently found myself writing to Mr Akiyoshi Arai, c/o the Meshima Lighthouse Office. And now I collected from Plymouth library their copy of Smeaton's massive volume from which I was to make the extracts for Lawley School. This seemed very trusting of the library, though apparently the volume is not as rare as I then thought it was.

> 21 May: Relief day. A beautiful morning on the Hoe. Drake's Island shrouded in mist, not a breath of air. [There had to be a catch.] At Blights learned that the Superintendent is coming off with us for his annual visit. On the tug had the inevitable difficult conversation with Captain Goodman. [I will have provided the difficulties.] It was a fine trip. Genghis and company put down the ropes at the last minute as we were rowing in, for they had been dashing round brightening the place up for the Superintendent.

And, no doubt, removing our various modifications.

The following day I began typing extracts from Smeaton's *Journal*. His account is in diary form so it was not difficult to make daily abstracts. Fortunately, too, the seasonal visits of the Looe boats were starting, so my drafts could go ashore at regular intervals for typing and duplicating by the library staff before being forwarded to Lawley School and perhaps elsewhere. In practical terms I was unlikely to be still on the Eddystone for the bicentenary of its completion in four years' time. In fact my time there was already beginning to run out, though I did not know it.

> 24 May: At about 2100, in a spanking NE wind, three yachts came out of Plymouth, and one had just gone by when her mainsail ripped right up the centre and straggled out in the breeze.

Without doubt we had just witnessed a rather expensive incident.

I note that during this month we occupied ourselves painting the interior granite, large areas of which had remained virgin since the tower was built. It did something to lighten the gloom on the spiral stairway.

27 May: It is as well we came off last Tuesday as we have not had relief conditions since.

28 May: To bed at 2215 after Genghis and I had discussed our relatives.

I am irritated now by my sloth as a diarist. What did we say about them? Nothing to their credit, I'll be bound, and therefore the more worth recording.

29 May: While down on the set-off I hailed a Plymouth fisherman with three aboard and he came in to the set-off – high tide luckily – and took away the Smeaton extracts for Plymouth library and to Mr Lineton, and the air-letter to Mr Arai.

I canot recall a single other occasion on which a visitor so obliged. On the other hand I can't recall an occasion when we asked. It would not have been sensible for a stranger to have come in at other than high water; the danger of fouling the propeller was very real.

Now that, for the first time, I had my typewriter aboard, I began to bring order to old John's station records, starting with headings for the Reserve Provision Book and going on to the Oil Consumption Sheets and so forth; all executed, I am sure, with my meticulous, lunatic neatness. When it came to deciding what to put in the columns, however: 'down to do some Station Fuel calculations with old John, who proved as bad at arithmetic as I am'. I produced one set of figures, he another. I recall us collapsing into laughter at a shared incompetence.

The Looe boats were now enlivening our mornings with their visits. We were still preoccupied with the problem of how best to collect mail in less than the best conditions.

6 June: Repeated the experiment we tried last night of heaving a weight out into the gut [the channel separating our tower and the Stump] on the end of a codline. When the line is tightened from the gallery it rises almost vertically from the water so that the Looe boat in dirty weather can heave the weight out, attach the mail to the hook on the weight, and the latter will bring the mail inboard when released by the boat. This is the latest of many ideas and seems very promising but in this form it does not of course provide for despatch. Genghis, however, has something in the way of a net in mind.

Pearn was a gallant trier. All our ideas ultimately foundered on the need for him to do everything himself, his passengers being too incapacitated by fright, sea-sickness or inexperience to provide useful help.

6 June: A frigate [oddly enough I remember it as a submarine] hove to, then put down a launch which came in with the captain, some officers, and a number of ratings. There was a certain amount of slop on the water but they all got aboard and went up the tower. Genghis and I stayed on the set-off while John showed them round. They voiced favourable opinions.[Needless to say, they were that day's postmen.] To bed at 2215 after Genghis had done some reminiscing.

Ah, Genghis, what did you tell me? Genghis's reminiscences were rarely nasty, occasionally brutish, but never short.

The literary mill was grinding away.

> 9 June: On 0000–0400 – nominally; but I put out at five-fifteen and called John at six – he had in fact just got up to see if I had fallen downstairs. To bed then, having managed a full five hours' typing. Up at 1100 and resumed in the lantern. Finished *Full Moon* just after lunch, in 24 hours. About 7,000 words I should think… [And then decided I didn't like it!] A poor Whitsun so far as Whitsun is concerned. Quite a swell accompanying the wind from the SW, and rainstorms over the coast.

> 11 June: The Looe boat again. I learned that there had been an item on the BBC Midland News ref. the Smeaton diary project, referring simply to a keeper (thank God!). Presumably a discussion with Lineton and the boy Thickens who started it all. Also there came the first batch of Diary entries from Plymouth Library. Very well done too. Each one on a separate leaf and very clearly duplicated. With them was a letter from the Librarian with some questions to which he would like an answer. I wrote one in something over 2,000 words on the old topic of what makes the light work.

> 12 June: The bicentenary of the laying of the first stone of Smeaton's tower.

Inevitably I regarded it as an historic date. Apparently no one else did, and I am fairly certain it passed quite unobserved ashore. It was a neglect which was an indirect commentary on the way Plymouth, as it had grown in size, had grown away also from the interest it had previously shown in its own lighthouse. In the afternoon I attempted my own act of commemoration by swimming there, an attempt which, when halfway, I decided not to press home, 'there being quite a rise and fall on in spite of the oily sea'.

> Genghis is like a fused bomb this month. I mentioned that he was and he said that sometimes he gets so crazy with boredom he could blow his top off. Not usual with him. It is explained, I think, by the fact that he has put in for a shift and is unsettled by the prospect of the move.

The perspective of forty years is not enough to provide a confident alternative to that perhaps trite assumption. That I was not myself bored was no consolation at the time. As usual I felt his boredom was at least partly my fault; but this was my particular response. There were besides generalities at work of which I have already written. I mean that Genghis and I, and to a lesser extent John, had now been together up to, and beyond, the point at which three males could sustain each other. The relationships were stale and it was time for the infusion of a new personality.

I think I have commented on the absence of the low temperatures of the kind experienced ashore. Now:

> June 15: The fine spell continues. The temperature at 1800 was 71°F. I never remember it being higher.

Ashore it almost certainly was. The sea exercised a moderating effect at both ends of the scale.

> *18 June:* Middle watch 0000–0400. I carried on with the Journal in the lantern, with my shirt off. A very warm night, therefore, and a warm day to follow. There was a nasty incident at breakfast which it will take me some time to forget. John came downstairs in a hurry for the telescope, saying he thought there was a body in the water. The three of us went up on to the gallery. Just beyond the eastern rocks was floating what seemed to be a white helmet of the bone-dome type, with something broader lying under it in the water. The sea was absolutely calm. John said that when it had been nearer he had seen outspread arms and goggles. It slowly drifted away eastward on the tide. I suggested we might signal PH79 [our regular lobster fisherman] which was then coming up about three quarters of a mile away.

I was unable to persuade him. They did pass quite near whatever it was but failed to see it. What lends credence to the sighting is that I believe a Royal Navy Gannet had been lost somewhere to westward a few days previously.

> *19 June:* Relief day. Not as good as the days that have preceded it. A lot of cloud, warm still but with a 4 easterly breeze which was springing up as I was giving the OK to Rame at 0830. Yet the relief was comfortable enough. Genghis went ashore (he hopes for the last time) and Craig came aboard. There were two letters from Lineton (one of them offering to have the girls knit socks!) and in the same context a letter to John from Goodman passing on a query from Trinity House as to why in the *Wellington Journal* of such and such a date a boy records a definite invitation from the Eddystone keepers to visit the place. Lineton sends me this paper and I can see that it is the usual flapdoodle and, there's no doubt, Trevor Thickens' comment is there. As I had expected, I find nothing in the single letter I wrote the boy a year ago that he could have construed as an invitation.

I typed a letter of explanation for the Superintendent, then found I was obliged to write it into the Report Book in triplicate – another of the famous 'Three Page reports'. I could not resist referring to the letter I wrote to the East Cowes Superintendent in similar circumstances three years ago, asking permission to horsewhip an editor. Needless to say, apart from an amused acknowledgement, that was the last I heard of the matter. In his role as District Superintendent for the news-prone western rocks Captain Goodman was accustomed to the ways of the press.

> *20 June:* Not a very satisfactory day, nor are they likely to be until the Elder Brethren have been, on the advanced date of Monday next.

The visit produced the state of nerves associated with any Commanding Officer's inspection in the armed forces, particularly so in old John, as PK.

> After tea John and Craig worried the winch rope. [It would not do to deposit an Elder Brother in the Channel – though I was told that in a curious mishap

one of them had once arrived on a lighthouse upside down.] I hung around until I could see that I was getting on John's nerves, then went upstairs to clean out the lantern gratings.

23 June: After tea with John I made sure I knew where the distress rockets are. We also rigged the Schermuly pistol up to the point of pulling the trigger. We did it in, I suppose, three minutes, which is the time one conventionally gives a man to drown.

The experiment was probably my initiative. We had never done it before. The episode of the 'airman' still haunted me.

25 June: Cook. A most beautiful day, particularly in the morning. The *Patricia* called at 0930 at the Rame test to say that the Elder Brethren will probably be here Thursday morning. Read papers on the gallery while the others breakfasted. With today's Looe boat came the latest batch of duplicated slips of Smeaton's Journal, and also the first of the letters I wrote the children about this lens. After lunch to bed and sleep. My routine nowadays is to sleep in the afternoon when cook [which was the usual custom, because the morning watchman who rose at 0400 and then had the 2000 watch would not be going to bed until the following midnight] and then work from 2200 until I call John at between one and two instead of midnight. Needless to say he doesn't object, particularly as I usually work in the lantern [i.e. keeping 'lantern watch'; not uncomfortable in the summer months]. I did this tonight, calling him at 0115 tomorrow after three hours' work on the Journal, revising what I had already done for the year 1758. A beautiful night following a beautiful day. To bed at 0200.

27 June: John called us at 0700 to say Patricia was coming out of Plymouth to us. The EBs came aboard, not in ideal conditions, at 0915 and were away again by ten. A Chipmunk flew round at 1600. After tea spent ninety minutes on the gallery composing a letter to Lineton – which thereupon blew away in the breeze – four sides! I hadn't the heart to begin again.

It's odd how certain images linger. I still see those pages fluttering irrecoverably down to the sea and remember my impotent exasperation at the wasted effort.

The following day we tested our new recovery device.

The boat came out with a big sea running. The conditions tested our new system to the limit. But Pearn, ever a trier, juggled with the throttles and on his own seized the codline and hauled in the weight, then slipped the bound packet over the hook. When he let go I hauled away on the gallery as fast as I could and they swung into the set-off without dragging in the water – the one questionable element in the technique.

The prize was worth the effort. Amongst the letters were prints of photographs I had taken on my last expedition to the Stump on 1 June.

The photo of the 1757 stone is exceptionally clear but I cannot even begin to decipher the numerals under the weed and molluscs, despite the attempts I made at clearing them away. John suggests I take over some lime as well as a hammer and chisel.

I had only become aware of the existence of the date on that particular stone through my reading of the Journal. Smeaton, with a proper sense of the value of what he was leaving to posterity, dated three stones on his tower: the foundation, 1757; the one above the entrance, 1758; and, I believe, another at the top, now, of course, preserved on Plymouth Hoe. It occurs to me that possibly never since Smeaton had anyone looked at the foundation stone with any awareness of the date buried under the limpets and weed.

29 June: John began to sound for fog at 0430 and thereafter Craig continued for two hours or so. I got up at 0915 when I saw it coming in thick again but by 1015 it had cleared for good and a fine hot day ensued. I spent almost all of it in the lantern stripping down the lantern clock which has been showing signs of debility.

I wonder, could this have been the origin of the dramatic canard of which I later heard that that eccentric Lane 'had stripped the lens clock'? – an altogether vaster enterprise and one which would have required the facilities of an engineering workshop. I suppose this clock, which bore the word 'Eddystone' on its dial, now graces the home of some Elder Brother.

Finished polishing the parts by 1915 and thereafter listened to the radio in the kitchen while cleaning the case.

For years the irritating chore of 'listening out' every two hours in case *Satellite* called had been complicated by the need to climb the lantern stairs and walk round the lens to check the time. I therefore took the opportunity to re-mount the clock above the staircase where it could be seen by an upward glance from the Service Room.

To bed at about 2200 after watching the Ark Royal pass to south'ard on her way back from New York.

3 July: On 0000–0400. Got up to continuous flashes of lightning (well, that's the sort of person I am) which continue as I write at 0148. Fortunately we are getting some rain, too... [The rain did not really arrive until 0245 and, culminating in a hail-storm, it was finished by 0400, but in that time it two-thirds filled our tank.] A considerable disappointment after lunch when, too late, we saw a largeish canoe floating past. Conditions weren't ideal but I'd willingly have had a go at getting it in. What a difference a boat would make here!

How fortunate we did not see it in time. I now recall the canoe as lying in a grey, turbulent sea, and if impetuousness had outweighed prudence I would certainly have drowned.

4 July provided a day of more than usual entertainment, and one which for me began at 0400 and lasted 23 hours.

> After lunch I went across to the Stump in a calm sea but with occasional lumps going by. I took with me a block which I secured to the seventh dog-step. We now had a line extending between the two towers which provides John and Craig with a means of dropping crabpots into the gut. But while there I made use of it to bring across a bucket of lime with which I outlined the shape of the (filled-in) doorway and the numerals 1757 above it.

When I paid a return visit in 1997 after an absence of forty years the lime had gone but the area to which I had applied it could still be identified.

> When I got back the whiteness showed up very well – well enough to come out on a photograph, which is my aim. I was unable to do anything about cleaning up the foundation stone. Craig climbed down the dog-steps in a life-jacket with the idea of coming across but thought better of it – rightly. He is a non-swimmer and conditions were by no means ideal for a sampling of the buoyancy of the jacket. Old John told me later he had been trembling like a leaf. I think that to take even the first steps he did reflected credit on him.

And to decide not to go further, even more! I recall once seeing him, jacketless, dancing on the set-off to evade the thrashing of a six-foot conger eel he had just landed. Fortunately the fates preserved him to become, some years later, PK at the Bishop Rock.

The day was not yet over. I now, to my surprise, found myself responsible for calling out Plymouth lifeboat. During the afternoon an RAF launch from Plymouth and, I think, a Coastal Command Shackleton, had been engaged in some sort of exercise to westward of us, and when I left the kitchen to go up for the 2215 test with Rame I noticed through the landing window a light flashing intermittently in that area. I had no doubt at all of the connection but thought it worth a mention to Rame. I assumed they would find it easy enough to establish whether a marker light was unaccounted for. However, I said I'd listen again at 2300 in case he needed to come back.

I almost forgot the appointment. I had been too sanguine about the efficiency of inter-Service communications. Rame had evidently found out nothing and Plymouth lifeboat had been obliged to put to sea. This was not at all what I had wanted, and I was quite sure it was not what old John would have wanted. Thereafter things became even more expensive. A Shackleton, diverted from a sortie, turned night into day with a brilliant, and useless, drop of flares. Lane had really started something here. The lifeboat was now out of the Sound. Rame and I were in shaky communication on 137 metres, the lifeboat and Rame perhaps on some VHF frequency. This did not make for flexibility but was the kind of inter-service incompatibility that was common then and that was not resolved until some years later. They flashed their light in our direction and requested a bearing. 'I suggested they steer due south and I would give course corrections.' This involved me nipping up the lantern stairs to check their progress, then down again to advise. I wondered if they had reached my own conclusion about the origin of the flashes and were enjoying the trip on a rather nice night.

> Two or three more corrections of course were necessary before they saw it and at 0155 they drew alongside and identified it as a light marker about 3 foot 6 inches long and 9 inches in diameter. There is no doubt they wouldn't have found it without benefit of the direction I was able to give by virtue of the 130 foot elevation of the tower, for the light was flashing intermittently, was lying very low in the water, and was rising and falling a good deal in the swell... I called John at 0225 and retired to bed at 0300.

I told him about the razzmatazz and he asked no questions. Privately he was probably quailing in horror at images of another Three Page report.

> 5 July: A very hot day. Both boats came out from Looe, both with some stimulating feminine talent on board. There was a hefty swell going by and it was not without some difficulty that Pearn eventually secured our line and sent up a basket of cabbage and lettuce.

This was unusually imaginative on someone's part. Our particular lack was fresh food of any kind except, occasionally, fish.

> 7 July: Up 0430. How quickly these Sunday cooks come round. The intervals never seem like three weeks. A brisk morning with quite a hefty swell. No Looe boat. In the afternoon I went to bed – had to after eating most of my plum duff. In the evening typed out some lighting-up time lists which John read out to me.

> 8 July: A calm day. Brasswork in the morning. The Looe boat brought a happy letter from M. Pearn shouted across: 'Does she still love you?'

Perhaps I reminded him that absence etc.

> 9 July: In the evening soon after six an RAF Tiger Moth came out and did a couple of circuits waving. I waved back from atop the wind-vane.

This was the supreme vantage-point and may have looked hairy but was safe enough provided one did not slip on the dome of the roof and impale oneself on the spike.

> In the evening finished the lighting-up tables with John.

When I look back it is such days that I remember with pleasure: varied, relaxed and productive. There were really a great many of them. Fog alone produced real displeasure; storms, excitement and a welcome emphasis of isolation.

> 10 July: Cook, so up 0400 (nominally). Both Looe boats came out on a fine day and stayed some time, cruising around. As usual, I worked in the lantern and it was a beautiful night with a gentle breeze in which one could smell the

land. Nicholls, of Rame Head, said at 2215 that the lifeboat appreciated the
help I'd given them the other night. Embarrassment upset my typing for the
next fifteen minutes.

Off-shore breezes at night were a common feature of fine summer weather but it was
only rarely that we enjoyed the actual smells of land – gorse and heather. In such
conditions moths and butterflies were also carried out, some to flutter against the
glazing, others to continue towards France, never, presumably, to arrive.

> *12 July*: In the afternoon I concluded the record of the construction of the
> lighthouse from the Journal. It only remains to précis Smeaton's references to
> the days immediately following, when the light was exhibited for the first time.
> In the evening old John cut my hair and in a mood of unusual communication
> we looked at the problem of maintaining discipline as leader of a group of
> three. John spoke of it as a most difficult thing. I, from apprehension of my
> future performance, agreed.

This was a moment of rare intimacy with John. As I have made clear, despite considerable good will on both sides we usually had too little to say to each other.

> *13 July*: I concluded the Journal – revision and then finis. Twenty-three
> foolscap sides for the second and third years of construction – single spacing!

> *15 July*: Brasswork in the morning and sprayed the glazing. Then began to
> clean the gallery gutter covers and strip them of paint. Also topped up the
> batteries and started the engine. Continued with the covers all afternoon and
> on finishing them just before 1730 cleaned out the chimney bend and – called
> a halt. But I felt in the mood for this display of energy.

This was for the usual reason that relief was pending and left one too unsettled for
anything else. A couple of days earlier I had noted: 'Spent an idle evening. Taking a
holiday before the strain of leave.' Preoccupation with the weather was another sign.

> *17 July*: An untimely change for the worse in the weather. Heavy driving rain
> for much of the day with fresh sou'-west winds. In the afternoon cleaned out
> my food locker, listed food etc. In the evening read through some *Listeners*
> with prodigal rapidity.

> *18 July*: Relief day - should be. But at the time of writing (0230) it looks
> doubtful. Wind WSW 4 and an untidy sea. Forecast at midnight, SW 4 to 6,
> perhaps 7. Presently I will take off my beard and shave… No landing. Even
> before I called John it had gone SW and it remained fresh throughout the day.

> *19 July*: On 0400. Wrote this 0730 still undecided what to say at 0830.
> Wind now NW and there is certainly a landing, though a messy one. Also a
> SW swell. Will probably say no. 0857: well, I did say no, on a very last-minute
> decision, and immediately felt relieved rather than disappointed. We would
> probably have done it: almost certainly there was a landing. The question is,
> would they have been able to handle the boat in the fresh NW wind? Again,

they probably could have done, but taking both doubts together tipped the balance. The forecast suggests improvement rather than otherwise... It was still unpleasantly choppy when the wind dropped by the necessary margin to guarantee that the landing could have been made with little trouble. A pity...

Frankly, I had missed a chance. I never recall any recrimination on such occasions. We knew the decision-maker felt badly enough about it, without the additional burden of his colleagues' reproaches.

20 July: Rather a messy day so far (1553). Soon after 0800 Craig called John into consultation over the advice to give Rame at 0830. Conditions were very much as yesterday, but with a prospect of strengthening winds. They decided on an equivocal 'There's a landing now and there will be one at mid-day if the wind doesn't freshen.' 'Tugboat' Reynolds didn't like this and we heard from Rame at 1145 that he had phoned Penzance for advice and the Superintendent had said they should not go out. So we looked in vain and were more relieved than disappointed. We've done a relief in more worrying conditions but it wouldn't have been comfortable. In the afternoon John went to bed as well as Craig... [At home] M. had asked for the night off so that we could listen to the Prom together. Alas, the misfortunes of lighthouse keeping. Prospects in the immediate future are not good. Strong NW winds tomorrow (as yesterday and today) with another depression coming up. Odd, the savage momentary stab of satisfaction one gets on hearing that the worst is not going to get better yet awhile. I think we all feel it. In my quieter moments (albeit irritability is very near the surface) I am very content, and will be perfectly so if I can fill the time with some satisfactory writing. I anticipate, with a pleasure which probably won't be realised when I get it, the details of going ashore, of arriving at home, going up to my room, looking at the mail that has not been sent on, seeing M... Interrupted in this panegyric by John who came down to paste the typed slips into the reserve provisions book. I offered to help, then found myself doing the whole thing. To bed at 2115.

21 July: As intended I spent the middle watch writing to the 'Dear Boys and Girls' at Lineton's school about overdue and reliefs. Didn't particularly want to do so, but thought it a topical opportunity not to be missed. Had my last egg for breakfast, then in the lantern morning and afternoon continued and concluded the children's letter. Wrote this 1627. Still blowing about a 6 from the NW and squally to boot. But the forecast for tomorrow is for an improvement. It's a pity we can't be sure the weather predicted will be realised in time: 'Decreasing to NW 2–3'. This, if true, is good. *If* true ...

22 July: Writing this 0815, and if nothing calamitous develops in the next quarter of an hour I shall be able to tell Rame 'Good landing. Wind NNW 3'. Wolf is also hopeful. Bright, too. I hardly dare write it, but this might be quite a nice relief... It was. We stepped off and on, Genghis (again!) and one Richardson coming aboard, old John and I going ashore.

Awaiting me was a pleasant note from the Superintendent.

> The sort of letter I expected from him. He acknowledged my letter on the matter of the *Wellington Journal* and went on: 'I completely agree with the last two lines of your letter; the average journalist or reporter would sell his own mother to make a story of it. Be careful that you do not degenerate into a journalist yourself!' As a further sidelight on Captain Goodman, when John made the usual phone call to him in Blights he at once exploded into complaints that he was inundated with trouble. F. had been brought ashore from the Bishop, mad; the Irishmen were a pack of trouble-mongers, and so on. John's face when he hung up was blissful; he had been able to assure the Superintendent that there was no trouble at *his* station.

It occurred to me afterwards that had I not been present he might have told Goodman that he did have one certified, or certifiable, lunatic in his crew, but that for the moment he was more or less under control.

> While we were in the shop Dee and his wife came in. The pleasure of our renewed acquaintanceship was muted. [I had shared one disagreeable month with him on the Eddystone.] His wife looks horrible, and presently old John said he recognised her as Moona MacNab or some such woman, who he had been out with in his youth – 'but I wasn't caught'.

A fortunate escape I would say. Presently we took a taxi to the station, he to go west to the Lizard, I to go north and home.

Life ashore was becoming increasingly threatening and leave was spent house-hunting. We included in our search a country house, having heard it well spoken of. It turned out to be extravagantly large.

> A lot of other prospective buyers were there. Seemed rather cluttered with tapestry, pictures and other bric-à-brac. Draughty, too, I would think, and expensive to heat. Interesting display of genitalia in the Statuary Room…

We didn't have much difficulty deciding against Chatsworth. And the price wasn't right.

> 20 August: At Blights soon after 0840 and presently met one Dungey and PK Muckler, going off to the Breakwater today. It is the first time I have known our reliefs to coincide. In consequence there was delay in Blights and we were late all along the line. It was a fine day, though we did a certain amount of pitching and tossing and there were a few whitecaps about. My stomach gave no trouble whatsoever, probably because I was talking the whole way to an uncle and two nieces – latterly in particular to one of the nieces, who was quite pretty and with whom the chat was becoming increasingly tête-à-tête as the time approached to leave. I was now, in my early thirties, getting quite good with women.[Though earlier, while on leave, when I had phoned one, I

noted that I had had before me a list of subject-headings in case I ran dry.]
Thereafter she showed herself prominently on the tug, and I on the set-off as
we got in the ropes, and when the tug signalled its farewell we waved vigorously... John and self aboard, Craig and SAK (Dolfuss or some such name)
ashore. Nothing much has changed.

Indeed, nothing much *had* changed. It will be noted that Genghis was still there,
loathing the arrival of too-familiar faces, and probably my face in particular, still
frustrated in his efforts to get away. I did not know it was I who was presently to get
away. With the possible exception of the first, this was the turn that I recall with least
pleasure. Things were breaking down between the four of us appointees, and if my
diary mentions only a couple of occasions of overt discord, there is an impression of
unhappiness conveyed, that can be read between the lines. I was as busy, and therefore as preoccupied, as before. Ten pages are devoted to a synopsis of a novel which
I began, and eventually finished, though like most amateur novels it was too flawed to
find a publisher. And there were short stories, generally better in their conception
than their execution. I sketch the outline of one that I describe as *petit Guignol*. My
comment now is that Maupassant might have made something of it, but that I wasn't
Maupassant.

27 *August*: An absurd little imbroglio with John in the morning. In the anxiety
of wondering whether we'd get the mail away I went down to the set-off
without asking whether he had any, and he followed me down in a justified
huff. However, I took exception to his comment that 'It's always Lane for
himself', as I was at that time engaged in doing his lunch.

Even in the privacy of a diary one perpetrates dishonesties: his comment had too
much truth to be disavowed, and there was no reason why I shouldn't have been
doing his lunch: I was cook!

28 *August*: At about 1000 the Ark Royal came out of Plymouth and presently
there was an interesting skyful of Gannets, Skyraiders and swooping
Seahawks. She went back into Plymouth but re-emerged later in the morning
and just short of us turned west to embark some Gannets – the first time I
have watched aircraft landing-on. In the afternoon six Venoms landed-on in
the distance, after first jettisoning fuel from their tip-tanks. Wyverns also
showed. The naval paddle-tug came out and was annoyed by a low-flying
Shackleton. Quite a full day.

30 *August*: A beautiful day. In the afternoon and evening a breeze impaired its
perfection. Am currently enjoying the most vigorous attack of the screws for
some time – left hip as usual: writing this standing up for comfort's sake.

1 *September*: After supper had an interesting chat with Genghis about
conversational difficulties aboard lighthouses, of which we are often so acutely
aware. It is in exchanges like this that I become momentarily aware of a

glutinous affection for my fellow man. Other people's vulnerabilities always bring out the best in me – when they aren't personally inconvenient that is.

Correspondence went on:

> Down at 1610 and wrote, while listening to the Prom, to Miss Susan Edwards, C10, Class 3a, North Road Junior Modern School, Southall, Middlesex who wanted to know how our light works. [For the umpteenth time!]

> 4 September: On 0000–0400 with the screws at their damnedest. But typed out a good deal of *Full Moon*, not calling Genghis till 0515.

It was swimming weather and I took advantage of it, retrieving the pulley attached to the Stump's dog-steps on the previous turn off. With the equinoctial gales to be followed by winter, most fishing would be done from the gallery with a kite. I never found any correlation between the activity of swimming in a cold sea and rheumatism. The complaint seemed to have its own rules for when it came and went. This was Genghis's experience, too.

> 9 September: These are emotional days. At breakfast we were grinding through a laborious *conversation-à-trois* about gifts offered by breakfast cereal manufacturers when Genghis suddenly snatched the cornflakes packet from hands and exclaimed 'For Christ's sake let that thing alone, will you?' adding: 'Before I spit in your eye'. What was this about? We must hope we see the end of the month without bloodshed. He re-established relations at tea in his usual diplomatic fashion and I, embarrassed, found myself wishing he hadn't. The safety valve is too obviously ready to lift again at any time.

This was a classic men-on-a-lighthouse incident of the kind the layman expects to hear of but which rarely happens: one being driven to distraction by another's trick of speech or mannerism. I do not want to particularise – the more so as I think I was something more than the catalyst. Conjectures, anyway, though they might be interesting to the psychologist, are beside the point. The problem was a general one: three men were confined in a tower doing what was essentially a caretaking job involving simple tasks which, the 24-hour coverage apart, could have comfortably been done by one. Contrast this with, say, a South Pole geophysical station. The conditions would be more severe but the numbers would be greater, each man would have responsibility for a particular area of high-grade work, and the work-load would be heavier. These are factors that make for good morale and we possessed none of them. That *I* was content and would have been willing to stay at the Eddystone indefinitely (or until it was ruined by modernisation) was a social accident, and a constant and genuine source of self-reproach.

> 17 September: After lunch went over to the Stump to disentangle what proved to be a mass of green nylon line (not anything of ours) wrapped around one of the stanchions by some chance. Found it too entangled to dis. The choppiest crossing I've made, for no very apparent reason.

18 September: Relief day and done in beautiful conditions. Just a slight heave on the water but nothing troublesome. Up 0920 and after a fried egg (I forewent the bacon which I can now afford to admit has gone bad) put the ropes down with my shirt off in the warm sunshine. The tug brought Craig, as disgruntled as ever, and also a surprise Trinity House engineer come to look at the fog jib with an eye to the long-promised inside loading scheme. Genghis quickly nipped into the lantern and took down the wiring for the lens switch but the visitor proved amiable and incurious. He stayed about an hour and a half, deciding this and that, and left us a bar of chocolate when he went. Genghis went ashore.

There came a letter from Mr Akiyoshi Arai at Meshima Lighthouse Office, Nagasaki, 'written in something far more interesting than English'.

23 September: Up 0415. The shipping forecast at 0745 was the liveliest I recall, with talk of Force 12 (hurricane) to the westward and possibly 9 for Plymouth as the cyclone which sank the *Pamir* yesterday with 90 hands came up from the Azores. But writing just before 2100 the barometer has not yet begun to drop. In fact it is still rising very slowly. [The *Pamir* was a German training barque.]

24 September: The depression has changed its track so that we have had none of the promised wind. But during the day a really big SW swell began to roll in, and in the evening it gave the tower some hefty thumps. John claimed that one blow sent the spray up to the Service Room.

27 September: The boat paid its first visit since Wednesday week. Mr Pearn at the wheel, grinning through the glass. It brought a batch of letters from the children of Lawley School and a surprise letter from the Ministry of Supply explaining that they didn't think they could use my Infinitesimal Comparator, and why: I had taken this for granted months ago.

28 September: Fish for tea. A thriving industry at present which means that Craig is almost civil.

2 October: Craig caught a lobster. Great jubilation. At 2000, just before they put it in the boiling water, I went up to the lantern, oppressed with morbid reflections [about the appalling fate of lobsters].

5 October: At 0700 heard the electrifying news that the Russians have launched an artificial satellite. Remarkable enough as a fact the details are even more so: height 560 miles instead of the hoped-for 200-300, weight 184 lb against the Americans' planned 22 lb, speed 18,000 miles an hour or 5 miles a second. A broadcast recording of its transmissions almost moved me to tears with the awe of it.

This entry conveys the common wonderment at the time. Meantime our own *Satel-*

lite, with a somewhat slower orbital speed, was busy stocking up the isolated stations for the winter.

9 October: Satellite loomed up out of the haze soon after 0900 without warning and it was a case of quickly up, and down with the ropes. Presently the launch came in with a load of water and tied up, but conditions were so sloppy with a brisk wind from the east that they left with nothing accomplished except an exchange of mail from us and old newspapers from them. The popular papers gave the satellite the full treatment and very idiotic it was. Spent the evening sifting the wheat from the chaff. In the afternoon, though still afflicted with the current malaise of intellectual lassitude, I concocted a collective reply to the children's letters, commenting on something in each of the twelve and concluding with a description of the effect of a heavy ground swell. That seemed partly to redeem the day.

10 October: Greatly improved conditions despite fog from 0600 for a couple of hours. We expected *Satellite* all day out of Plymouth and were relieved when she didn't come. We could have seen the last of her this turn off as she is returning to Penzance tonight and has two reliefs to do next week.

13 October: After lunch old John found the drain blocked while washing up. We were both in a state of muted aggressiveness. I said: 'Leave it. I'll see to it presently' and he snapped 'I'm not fucking useless.' We re-established contact at once and I felt ashamed of having provoked him.

14 October: In the evening, in the kitchen, dismantled and cleaned the fog-interval clock. [This was the clock which rang a bell to indicate the five-minute intervals for firing the fog charges.] Then until I called Craig at 0035 I reassembled and oiled it and got it going again on a temporary basis.

15 October: Old John this morning became the first of us to see the Russian satellite. I had asked him to call me but in the event it moved too quickly for him. He seemed greatly impressed – 'As obvious as the moon and of the same colour'.

16 October: On 0000–0400. Taking over from John I sounded until 0110 but had to resume at 0215 and Craig finally finished at 0530 when the fog turned to rain for 3½ hours with a bright, breezy day to follow. Feel extraordinarily tensed-up for reasons I don't understand. [A few nights earlier I had had another anxiety nightmare.] Prospects for tomorrow's relief now contain an element of doubt. Early tea, as is necessary at present [because of the intrusion of lighting-up] and at 1721 lit up.

Appropriately I was to conclude my time at the Eddystone with an overdue experience as tormented as any.

17 October: Relief day that should have been but wasn't. As had become evident during yesterday the weather was breaking up after the recent fine

> spell, and in fact we were pipped to the post by a matter of hours. The forecast was of winds increasing to strong to gale and the question – with a good landing, no swell, and a 4 from the SW at 0830 – was, how soon would the change for the worse occur? I mentioned this when I spoke to Rame at 0830 and he came back with the message that Reynolds was going to have a try. Conditions were possible till 1030 or so, but if we saw the tug she soon turned back, and by the afternoon it was blowing a full gale.

The postponement gave me the opportunity of making a final improvement in our working conditions. 'An idea has been nagging for some time and a remark of John's has reawakened it.' I may have mentioned that the normal means of detonating the fog charges was by pushing the plunger of a magneto. Immediately above the generator for that, however, was the socket for the Aldis lamp, and the socket led directly to the R/T batteries at 24 volts. The idea was simply to use the contact between hammer and bell of the fog-interval clock to fire a charge. This would mean we could leave the lantern for nearly ten minutes at a time while firing instead of only five. Modifications to the clock were minimal: one screw terminal to the frame of the clock, the other to the bell. Before he went to bed old John spoke very sensibly about it, having noticed what I was up to. He emphasised the need to avoid incriminating attachments, even obscure ones that a Supernumerary might carry tales abroad about. I assured him that I was as much concerned about that as he was. He added that Goodman had told him when he was appointed here that there must be 'no inventions'. He assumed this resulted from a tale carried by his predecessor, Matey Rictus. It was the first time I had heard of this.

> More or less up to midnight I was setting up the necessary wiring in the lantern. To bed 0050 or so with almost no prospects for tomorrow.

And so it was, but it didn't matter. I was operating in the area I enjoyed most.

> 18 October: I tried various resistances in series with a detonator from 5,000 ohms down, and the detonator finally exploded when I put a 3.5 V bulb in the circuit. The effective factor is the extremely short time taken by the detonator to blow itself to pieces, perhaps a hundredth of a second. For that reason the bulb merely comes to moderate brightness, even though in a 24 V circuit. Essentially it is there merely as a fuse. I demonstrated it to John after lunch and he seemed satisfied with it as an easily dismantleable arrangement.

The construction of this bit of jiggery-pokery gave me satisfaction out of all proportion to its possible utility. Whether it was ever used I do not know for we had no fog before the relief. This was the only occasion on which I actually looked forward to a spell of fog!

> 19 October: A chance missed by Craig though on the showing at 0830 he probably made the right decision. Rather annoying as it leaves tomorrow open – a Sunday, and a wretched day to go ashore… After lunch, casting aimlessly around for something to dismantle, my eye lighted on the fog signal exploder

> (now theoretically redundant) and I spent most of the afternoon cleaning and
> greasing it.
>
> 20 October: Having been responsible for the abortive calling-out on Thursday
> I had told John that I would call him into consultation if I was at all doubtful
> this morning. I was. There was a landing at 0830 and had been all night. But
> the forecast was SW 4 to 5 against present conditions of WSW 4. So we had a
> chance, though I felt the margin was insufficient after one abortive calling-out
> already. John's attitude was that we could do no more than give the conditions
> at present and couldn't anticipate what they would be like in four hours' time.
> A perfectly valid view. I therefore gave the present conditions to Rame and
> said that if the wind didn't freshen further there would be a landing when they
> arrived. It did freshen and John flashed them to go back. Nobody's fault. But
> it's the first occasion on which I can recall two baulked reliefs on the same
> overdue.

We cannot have been popular ashore, with the tugboat crew obliged to miss their
Morning Service and Blights having to open to lash up the boxes, and then to open
up again to unpack the returning perishables. John said nothing but I suspect he was
thinking that Trinity wouldn't be too happy either at getting three billings for one
relief from Reynolds. My own view was that if they chose to saddle us with an archaic
tugboat/rowing-boat sequence they must occasionally pay a financial penalty. Never
once, in my time at the Eddystone, did I feel we made an irresponsible decision – that
is, one influenced by wishful thinking. Perhaps John's anxieties were behind another
spat in the evening:

> As John was leaving to go to bed I said to him: 'If you want a second opinion
> in the morning I'll probably be awake', and he jumped to the conclusion I was
> being sarcastic. I had a devil of a job pacifying him. He is, and says he is,
> deeply suspicious of me.

I can only conclude now that I may have sometimes indulged in a style of banter
which left him perplexed.

> 21 October: Nothing doing this morning, with or without my advice. Instead
> of bacon and egg for breakfast and cheese for tea I now have corned beef
> from the reserve provisions for both.
>
> 22 October: Nothing doing again. Wind brisk from the NW. The right direc-
> tion but the wrong strength.
>
> 23 October: Cook again. Determined not to be caught out a third time I said
> No in the light of a forecast of 'W 4–5 gradually becoming 6'. But the 6
> never arrived, there was a flat calm off the landing and in spite of the brisk
> breeze we could have done a comfortable relief. But at the time I think my
> decision, in the light of what had gone before, was the inevitable one.

24 October: Woke at 0545 and didn't go to sleep thereafter. A fine morning
and a fine relief done in unusually quick time. John and I were replaced by
Genghis and S.H. Lines. We were in dock at 1410, in time to have a drink
with the tug skipper.

Thus ended my stay at the Eddystone. Two weeks into my leave I received a letter
from Penzance ordering me to Portland Breakwater. I knew that Genghis had asked
for Portland and now I had got it. This did not seem satisfactory and I believe I
expressed my disquiet to Penzance. They merely confirmed the move. I was left with
the conjecture that Genghis had written to them himself while on leave to the effect
that if he ever found himself on the Eddystone again with AK Lane he would probably kill him, Yours faithfully, G. Khan. That would have done the trick. Trinity were
always very sensitive to the sort of press publicity they got when keepers started mur-
dering each other.

In all I had done fourteen turns on the Eddystone, thirteen of them of two months,
one of one month. Each 'month' consisted of 29 days and was added to by overdue
– which occurred on all but two of the fourteen turns and averaged 6.14 days per
turn. The total of 870 days' duty breaks down as follows: 784 days standard, plus 86
days overdue, of which 17 were spent in Plymouth waiting to go off, and 69 aboard.
Overdue thus represented 9.88% of the total. (I would expect these figures to be
rather worse than comparable figures for the Bishop Rock but decidedly better than
those for the Wolf.)

Reynolds' tugs had completed 41 reliefs. There were in addition seven aborts of
which I viewed one from the tug and six from the tower. This failure rate of 14.6%
may seem high. On the contrary, bearing in mind that they were inshore tugs, that
only one of them was less than fifty years old, that the timing took no account of tide
state, and that the final stage was completed by rowed boat, it was quite modest and
does credit to the judgement of the morning watchmen in being right so often with
such a small operating margin.

14

Literary confusion and messing about on a boat:
Portland Breakwater

The launch for the lighthouse relief was provided by the Navy from the dockyard across the harbour, and it was at 1400 that I presented myself at the dockyard gate having lurched up from Portland Square with a crippling weight of hand luggage. A taxi from Weymouth, rather than the bus, would have been sensible but it didn't occur to me to use one. Taxis for me have always been vehicles for conveyance of the gentry. As I paused at the gate to regain my breath a short, stout, elderly man passed me dressed, I thought, in Trinity uniform. I say 'I thought' because although I, too, was in full Trinity regalia, he gave no hint of acknowledgement, which was odd unless I was mistaken.

I was not mistaken. I had just had my first encounter with Principal Keeper Trotter of the Breakwater light, with whom I was to share the double turn. On the launch, too, I did not appear to exist and when I presently took the initiative with some conventionally bland conversational opening his only response was a grunt and the swivelling of one eye as if astonished at my temerity. This gave me the opportunity of noticing that the other eye appeared to be missing from its socket. I congratulated myself that I was in the company of an eccentric.

I was not to be disappointed. Over a cup of tea ten minutes after arrival Mr Trotter was explaining to me in calm and quite rational tones the reason for his behaviour. It was designed, he said, to confirm the reputation he had throughout the Service of being a holy terror. I had no doubt heard of him as such? I had to confess I had not. Trotter was not a name known to me, with or without frightening connotations. Nor did I find this surprising. As I have said, the lighthouse grapevine operated erratically. Reputations, like gossip, tended to be localised within districts. I suppose Matey Rictus could be said to have had a reputation of the kind claimed by Mr Trotter; but had he been heard of on Portland Breakwater? The Eddystone had been within the province of Penzance, and here we were in East Cowes country.

By way of apology for my ignorance I suggested some such explanation to Trotter but he would have none of it. What I said might be true of ordinary terrors, but terror of the kind he had provided throughout his career was not of a kind to recognise frontiers. He insisted my memory was at fault. I *must* have heard of him. He spelled his name out encouragingly. It seemed to matter so much to him I pretended to hunt through my memory bank though I knew the name Trotter was not there. Helpfully, I listed a few names that *were* known to me: Bailey, Dogger, Wight, Robert Louis Stevenson, the Marquis of Bute. Warming to an interesting problem of identity I asked him how sure he was that his name *was Trotter*. Was it not, perhaps, Spencer, or, say, Prendergast, or how about Corrigan? He began to pump up and down in front of the Rayburn, his hands gripping the rail behind him, his knees flexing, a trick with which I was to become familiar, assuring me that so far I had known him only from his good side; wait till I knew him from his bad side. Those were not his exact words, but what he said rang such a familiar bell that I automatically substituted the threat so often uttered by Lieutenant Dub to the good soldier Schweik, and so often lamentably ignored by him. I had known Mr Trotter now for no more than twenty minutes. It seemed we were in for a lively relationship.

However, I was quickly to discover a down side to the entertainment.

> *18 December:* On 0000–0400. Trotter didn't call me till 0035 and then didn't leave till 0140. …Rose at 0930 or so. For 55 minutes up to 1040 Trotter gave us a dramatised account, with actions, of the death and cremation of his mother. I hope the spate will ease up presently. I'm afraid that at any moment in the middle of one of his recitals I will rise abruptly and retreat into the bedroom, slamming the door behind me. This would be a discourtesy difficult to explain. [In the evening:] listened to the story of a Trotter/policeman encounter until about 2145.

> *19 December:* On 0400–1200. Trotter called me at 0440 and after a slow start cantered away in fine conversational style to depart for bed at 0600! He looks oddly like Will Fyffe [a Scottish actor of the time] when his mouth is closed, which means that such reminders are fleeting. In the evening wrote this, then with Jeff Clements went on a torchlight promenade along the breakwater, with the old man in his workshop making the lights flicker with his electric saw.

Trotter's hobby was woodwork, which he pursued in a building further along the breakwater. I hardly ever saw the inside of this. When he went ashore on leave he locked it behind him, and when he was in there I was discouraged from asking about what he did in the knowledge that he would tell me at excessive length. My diary records the 'Triumphal erection in the kitchen of Trotter's three-compartment soap-cupboard', with a note that the commotion that accompanied it reminded me irresistibly of Jerome's account of Uncle Podger hanging a picture in *Three Men in a Boat*.

What he had decided about me was revealed quite early. He confided to Jeff that he thought I had been a gentleman's gentleman, unfrocked after being found out in some impropriety, and now declined into lightkeeping. I found this a not unattractive conceit and when in due course our watchkeeping sequence changed and it fell to me to call him for watch instead of the other way round, I made it my practice to place the mug of tea on his bedside table with some such phrase as 'Clement morning, Mr

Trotter'; or, 'What will it be today, sir? The soup and fish, or the brown check?' Trotter, on these occasions *sans* teeth and spectacles, one frosted lens of which ordinarily concealed the empty socket, would not be looking his best. It was a colleague who described the appearance of him in bed as being like 'an old skull lying in a bundle of rags'.

I have mentioned Trotter's tendency to dramatise. I do not suppose there can have been a raconteur, on or off the professional stage, who gave of himself so fully. In an exchange involving as many as four characters he was capable of taking all the parts. Like many elderly keepers he mostly rang the changes on the game of ISIS. 'I said to the Superintendent I said' was a variant of the boss/employee confrontation acted out by the underdog in every walk of life. For the lightkeeper it usually involved a visit to the district depot, walking in on the Superintendent in his office, lifting him off the floor, and throwing him back into his chair as a preliminary to a critical discussion. I had previously seen it played at Casquets and the Eddystone. What was different here was that in these encounters Trotter would take both main parts, as well as any subsidiary roles that might figure in the story. He would cower in a chair as the Superintendent for a quavering 'What exactly seems to be the problem, Principal Keeper?', then be up and lowering across the kitchen table as himself to declare what the problem was, then back into the chair as the Superintendent to summon over a mimed telephone the Chief Clerk, then outside the door to knock, back to the chair for a 'Come in', outside the door again to make a shifty entrance: 'You sent for me, Superintendent?' Back to the chair: 'Indeed I did, Ricketts. The Principal Keeper here has been telling me... ' And so on. It's little wonder we had not one chair with a sound set of legs, and a loose table.

Obviously such performances did not happen all the time. At that level they would have taxed the stamina of a young Henry Irving. And if they made extreme demands on Trotter, Jeff and I weren't often able just to sit there. Sometimes we found ourselves caught up in the action. If we didn't move, or mis-read the script and moved in the wrong direction, there would be an impatient 'Tchk, tchk', a toss of the head, and a laboured negotiation of the obstacle that was us, together with sometimes a sigh as from a man burdened with the company of idiots.

At other times things were more pacific. Trotter would take up his stance with his back to the Rayburn, grasping behind him the chromium rail that was a feature of that model and merely pumping up and down in his knees-bend action as he pursued his narrative. Occasionally he would slide his hands to the centre of the rail, place his heels against the stove, and lean forward as though in an attempt to tug it from its alcove. Fortunately he never succeeded though I always half expected to see it move forward with a gush of hot water from fractured pipework. I was told that some hooligan had once greased the centre of the bar so that Trotter found himself launched forward in mid-rhetoric to fall across the broken meats. This I would have liked to see but it was not something that could be done twice.

Jeff, who had been appointed to the station some time earlier and who had heard it all before, passed the time I know not how. He appeared to doze, slumped in his chair, his fingers interlocked comfortably on his stomach, his eyes closed. At first I thought this simulation of sleep a rather daring response to the anecdotes of a man who was the terror of the Service. Surely it was polite at least to pretend an interest and from time to time I would murmur 'Fancy that' or 'You amaze me, Mr Trotter.' But when I did, Trotter would stop and look at me blankly as though surprised to see me there. I believe he had grown accustomed over the years to an inattentive audience, or perhaps he didn't need one. While talking he kept his eye fixed absently on the dockyard buildings on the other side of the harbour. So presently I too learned silence and busied myself with the mental drafting of correspondence, including a death-threat letter to be posted to the Superintendent in East Cowes in a year or two's time when Mr Trotter had become altogether too much.

When I look back over my nine turns on the Breakwater I find it dominated by the image of Mr Trotter, brisk in motion, cantankerous in temperament, unstoppable in narrative flow. I wondered whether he and Matey Rictus had ever been together as AKs in earlier years when they were honing their reputations as terrors. If they had I would have liked to have been the third hand. It would have been a character-forming experience.

But these are merely the highlights of what was really a very agreeable life. Portland harbour was enclosed by three breakwaters. One was connected to the naval dockyard, the other to the approaches to Weymouth. Ours was in the middle, isolated from both by the quarter-mile gap of the two harbour entrances. The lighthouse, situated at its southern end, was of the kind which Chance Brothers, of Smethwick, supplied 'off the shelf' to anywhere in the world where such a navigational light might be needed. The whole thing would be sent c.k.d. (completely knocked down) in crates and reassembled with outsize spanners to its height of 70 feet or so on site. All the purchaser had to do was provide the foundations.

Its appearance was severely functional. External bracing girders from ground to Service Room surrounded first the circular entrance room and then the tube enclosing the spiral staircase. Immediately below the lantern in the Service Room were the paraffin tanks which, unusually, had no separate air tanks. The lens had only recently been modernised and was small and neat, with a weight-driven lens clock that did not, unlike the one on the Eddystone, look as though it had been hammered together by a blacksmith. The fog signal was a bell driven by the lens clock. The extra load imposed when the bell was sounding was provided for by an alternative gearing to ensure lens and bell kept time.

The entire one-mile length of the breakwater was a mess of derelict wartime buildings and those closest to the light had been converted into quite agreeable accommodation, with telephone, mains electricity (by underwater cable across the harbour) and flush lavatory. There was a living room and one single and one double bedrooms. The Rayburn stove in the living room provided hot water. After the Eddystone the living conditions seemed really quite civilised if not exactly comfortable; though pres-

Portland Breakwater light-
house, as supplied in kit form
by Messrs Chance Brothers of
Smethwick.

ently I was to do something to improve our comfort further.

Mail came and went regularly via the dockyard. Once a week the water boat called and topped up our roof tanks. The breakwater provided an opportunity for exercise, and half way along it was a testing station from which Vickers Armstrongs launched torpedoes across Weymouth Bay, though this was too infrequent and unheralded an event to be relied on for entertainment. At eight each weekday morning, elements of the peacetime navy, frigates and submarines mainly, went out through the gap in the breakwater and returned at five, keeping office hours.

A feature of some interest situated just off the dwellings was a concrete caisson, of the kind that had been towed across the Channel on D-day to make the Mulberry

Harbour. There had been more of them, but in the North Sea storm-surge of 1953 that produced the floods in the Home Counties and broke the Dutch dykes, they had been taken away to plug the gaps in the polders.

Soon after I arrived the harbour began to provide an anchorage for oil tankers. They were modern and well-found but their size had become uneconomic with the closing of the Suez canal and the enforced opening of the Cape route from the Middle East. By the time the canal opened again the age of the supertanker had arrived and I assume the fate of these fine ships was to be scrapped.

I was to do nine turns on the Breakwater, all but one of them of the usual two months. It was as true here as of any other lighthouse, that if life on it was interesting it was because we made it so. There was little incentive to go ashore. On New Year's day I did so for the first time and found no profit in it. Portland had little to offer, and Weymouth was as dead in winter as later I was to find it overcrowded in summer. Anywhere else was ruled out by the need to be back at the dockyard for the return boat across the harbour in mid-afternoon. When visits to Weymouth did become interesting it was because I devised an unorthodox way of getting there.

The enemy, of course, was always with us.

10 January: Wild, wild weather.

It was odd, but true, that bad weather was experienced with much more immediacy on the Breakwater than it ever had been on the Eddystone. Our dwellings were effectively at sea-level and the hourly walk to the tower to wind up on a foul night was a matter for oil-skins and a calculated run between successive sheetings of spray. A walk to the far end of the breakwater in a full gale was a stimulating experience.

Mechanical preoccupations had now receded somewhat and I was writing articles which didn't satisfy me much and certainly satisfied no one else: they bounced like cheques from a bankrupt account. Trotter continued to eat into time that I regarded as properly mine.

12 January: The old man stayed talking till 2335 – the latest yet; perhaps because he knew I wanted to get on with something.

That is, he left 25 minutes before I was due to call Jeff at midnight!

At my half-time relief Pete Chainey had replaced Jeff Clements. He too found Trotter somewhat oppressive and I recorded an occasion when he joined me in contriving a little light relief.

2 February: At breakfast Pete and I tossed the shuttlecock of invention back and forth in a brisk volley. Turning our attention, for some reason, to the term 'hollow-ground' as applied to razors we suggested that it dated back to the time when to make a hollow in the ground and take refuge in it was the only way of avoiding the knives attached to the stub-axles of chariot wheels.

'You're telling me something now I never knew before', said Trotter interestedly. Presently we were moving on to discuss Cleopatra's 'affairs' and found we had some difficulty remembering the names of her paramours.

'Of course', I found myself saying, 'the whole sordid story was covered in comtemporary copies of the *News of the Nile*'.

'Really?' said Trotter; 'newspapers in those days?'

'Well, of a kind – '

'Didn't they dig some back numbers up only recently?' Chainey asked.

'I believe so', I said. 'And of course they wrote in heiro– '

'-glyphs', said Trotter. 'On stone, didn't they? A sort of picture-language.'

'Yes. The picture representing a postman, for example, was a truss – '

'A truss? Really? I was with a keeper once, at Bull Point – or was it Hartland? – '

' – hernia being the Egyptian postman's occupational hazard from carrying around those heavy tablets'.

Chainey/Lane, 1: Trotter, 0. But these were hard-won victories.

We fortunately did not have a television, but we did have a radio. Trotter resented it, I think because he found it no sort of a listener and altogether too voluble a talker.

> 8 *February*: At tea I had incautiously mentioned Variety Playhouse as the radio highlight of the evening, which provided Trotter with the cue to get out the station books and complain presently that the radio was too loud. In his irascibility he puts me in mind of an elderly hamster.

There follow four pages of description of a mini-bore steam heating system supplemented with diagrams labelled Cock A, Cock B and so forth. For me now it's just a load of cock, but I'm glad of the evidence it provides that, *maugre* Trotter, some sort of independent mental activity was still possible. 'To bed just before 2100, the old man being in abracadabra mood' – whatever that was.

> 11 *February*: Gale warnings for all sea areas on this, my first relief day here. Do I attract these situations? Trotter told me when we got aboard the boat that it was about the worst relief they had ever done. It was blowing a full gale and embarkation at the usual point, the breakwater knuckle, was ruled out when the stern of the boat was repeatedly blown round by the wind. So we had to take all the gear down to Whitehead's, half-way along the breakwater, where there was flat calm on the seaward side. Trotter grumbled and swore quite horribly at having to leave his monstrous car batteries and umpteen parcels of woodwork behind.

He used to travel with his batteries to keep them charged.

It was an untypical end to my first turn on the Breakwater Light.

On 22 February, by mutual agreement, M. and I got married in what was reputed, on very slender authority, to have been a hunting chapel of King John. I found it all much more enjoyable than expected. The parson had allowed us 'Let all mortal flesh keep silence' as one of the hymns, thereby showing what I believe is the modern flexibility in such matters. (A friend of ours was similarly permitted 'Rock of ages', again for a wedding, for the sufficient reason that she liked it.) I had wanted 'Who is this with garment's gory, triumphing from Bozra's way', to Ton-y-Botel – madly barbaric words to a magnificent tune – but unfortunately it wasn't in *Hymns Ancient and Modern*. My brother did his best with the asthmatic organ, using the stops that didn't come all the way into his lap when he drew them: Bach's *Du Bist Bei Mir* for the warm-up, Purcell's (or, as has now been decided, Clarke's) *Trumpet Voluntary* for the entrance of the bride, and Mozart's *Fantasia in F Minor* for the exit of the happy couple (though now I can't imagine how he managed that tyro piece on that organ). I had myself warmed up the early arrivals by bellowing the *Pro peccatis* from Rossini's *Stabat Mater* and during the service the parson was visibly moved to one side by my contribution to the hullaballoo of 'Praise, my soul, the king of heaven' at the altar rails. Overnight there had fallen the first snow of winter and its detergent whiteness provided the parson, a married man himself, with the motif for his brief admonitory address. Marriage, he told us, was like the snow; first the pristine purity, full of radiant promise and all a-gleam in the God-given sunlight, and then the decline into slush, and grot, with seepage through the welts of all but the best boots. In the vestry afterwards I asked him whether he could recommend a make of boot that we would find marriage-proof. Years later I encountered him in the main street of our local town and reminded him of his words. 'You were spot on about marriage,' I told him. He died not long after, survived, probably, by his wife. That's usually how it is.

Such had to be the doubts of the time. In fact the adventure did not turn out at all badly and after forty years is still on-going.

On my return to Portland Trotter was almost effusive. 'Hello, you', he said, and walked past me to his taxi, from which I later carried his batteries to the launch – evidently he had been across during the month to collect them. There was a letter awaiting me from Dr Hope of the Seafarers' Education Service to say *Argosy* wanted to buy *Malaguena*, which I remember as an exercise in the Steinbeckian mode and almost certainly imitative rubbish. I had written it on the Eddystone. As usual the prospect of being exposed in print filled me with gloom rather than elation. My literary ventures in another direction presently found no favour with Trotter either.

> *28 March*: Uproar, occasioned by the arrival of the second issue of Trinity's house magazine *Flash* [to which I had contributed some deadpan nonsense apparently entitled 'A Useful Nut-rest']. Trotter immediately started dipping into the magazine while I retired to the other end of the breakwater. The withdrawal was well-advised. 'A Useful Nut-rest' was printed in full without a spoiling introduction, indeed exactly as sent in. Initially, Jeff tells me, Trotter was apoplectic, but cooled off somewhat before my return. He said

> aggrievedly: 'If you've any complaints about the running of the station you should make them to me.' I was tempted to plug the advantages of the nut-rest – 'surely a most sensible idea' etc. – but he was so obviously injured that I had to explain, as best I could, that it was a quite legitimate exercise in humour. I couldn't get him to see it.

> 'What are people going to think when they read this? Trotter, they're going to say, must have gone off his rocker, smearing nuts with beeswax.'

I think the mere existence of a magazine like *Flash*, with its acceptance of contributions from the lower orders, represented for Trotter an undermining of the hierarchical Service he had served so in for so long.

Forty years later I have to wonder whether I did not get the Breakwater because it was felt that, as someone who had done time with Matey Rictus, and survived it, I would probably manage to survive Trotter also. Credence is given to this thought by the posting of Genghis from the Eddystone to Sark, a 'nice little number' in the parlance, where we presently heard there had been some kind of rumpus. I think there might have been a similar liveliness at the Breakwater had Genghis got it. He was a good man, but impatient. His solution to problems was to shoot people.

Trotter was evidently passing through a bad patch.

> *7 April*: At 2045 I went into the kitchen from the bedroom to find the old man, unusually, in an uncommunicative mood.

> 'And what sort of night is it like outside?' I ask cheerily.

> He waves a hand towards the window in impatient moroseness.

> 'Obvious, isn't it?'

> I glance out, feigning surprise.

> 'Good heavens – dark!'

> – and waffle on a bit in the rare enjoyment of my own uninterrupted voice'.

> *11 April*: [On a day of some literary confusion] off came the Superintendent, in very pleasant mood, to congratulate me on *Malaguena* which he said he had read in *Argosy*. This is of course news to me: I had not been expecting it to be in until July or August. Moreover the introductory blurb apparently mentions that the story has been sold to the BBC. More news to me – and to Pete and the old man, the latter assuming that the piece the Superintendent was referring to was 'A Useful Nut-rest'.

Totally confused myself I left them in that belief. In fact I don't think the BBC ever did use *Malaguena*. (I very much hope they didn't!) As a communication within the lighthouse service this one arrived no more than usually garbled.

> *19 April*: The old man tapped the barometer, inspected the thermometer, and said we couldn't do anything aloft today.

Probably he felt like getting on with something in his workshop. Such was the admirable flexibility of lighthouse routine.

> In the evening listened on the earphones to *Pagliacci* in English.

I believe I now had a more practicable transistor set, one which it was not necessary to warm over a flame in order to get something more than waterfall noises.

> Pete used the earphones for the first time for Saturday Night Theatre, the old man clearly annoyed and hunting around for some suitable quotation from the rule book that would enable him to prohibit their use.

He probably saw earphones as an impediment to reception of his own transmissions.

> 21 April: On the way back from a walk I found a two-drum home-made boat of the kind I was admiring the other day in Weymouth. With Pete's help I embarked in it but found it almost completely unmanageable and had to come in again.

But it caused me to think that we already had a boat, stowed under covers beside the lighthouse and the crane. True, Trotter insisted it was his, a personal gift from the dockyard Quartermaster, but this I doubted.

> 22 April: In the afternoon cleaned out the boat – 'Oh, what's this?' from Trotter – and in the evening had a row with him, inevitably, about my proposed use of it, then lowered it into the water with the crane and went out with Pete. We circled the newly arrived tanker *British Merit*, then went to the fort and back to the lighthouse where Pete disembarked. I then rowed to C Head along the inside of the breakwater and back along the outside. A flat calm evening and one of the most enjoyable I had had in a long while. The old man, having blown his top, was saccharine when we entered the dwellings. I think we can say that the return of the boat to corporate use is now an established fact.

> 23 April: In the afternoon I drafted a letter to Plymouth Librarian asking whether he intended to continue the Smeaton scheme, and whether he could take any steps towards recovering the Eddystone lens for Plymouth when modernisaton takes place.

If he ever did they were not successful. It would have been better for the survival of that magnificent lens if they had been. Instead, it went for some reason to Southampton, a city which had none of Plymouth's historical connection with the tower. On a visit to Southampton in the late 1960s I saw the lens on the pier, exposed to the elements and already in a sorry state. When I visited again in 1984 it had disappeared and the pier, now derelict after a fire, was closed. When I asked after it at the newly opened Maritime Museum I was shown correspondence and a police photograph. The correspondence had been annotated: 'This is an appalling business.' Either thieves or vandals had got into a yard where the lens was in temporary storage and it had been smashed, either in in an act of vandalism, or for the sake of its non-ferrous metalwork. An Elder Brother had viewed the wreckage and had been obliged to say it was beyond recovery. This was a lens which Trinity had gone to great trouble to disassemble on site, transport ashore and to Southampton, and reassemble there. In 1997 it has proved difficult to get a clear statement as to the whereabouts of the remains, but it is probable that the pedestal and some undamaged panels are still in the possession of Southampton's civic authorities. Paradoxically, financial constraints have now obliged the city to adopt a policy of refusing anything that does not have a direct association with Southampton, so that the lens, or what remains of it, is no longer of any interest to them.

Messing about in a boat continued to provide refreshment and contention. An oar had broken in the course of a voyage to Weymouth and I had learned the trick of paddling from the stern

> *4 May*: Rather a brisk wind all day so didn't go out in the boat till evening. Trotter remarked to Pete that it was the first time he'd seen a man paddling a punt in dark glasses and gloves. Pete explained that before becoming a gentleman's gentleman I had injured my hands in dramatic circumstances in the RAF. Impressed silence. 'You're telling me something now I never knew before' etc.etc. I was wearing the glasses against the sunlight and the gloves against blisters.

A few days earlier I record Pete and Trotter having a fair to moderate exchange of words about this and that, Trotter having got up in a black mood. 'There is a streak of mad irrationality in his arguments which makes discussion impossible.' He could, however, be rational when it suited him.

> *5 May*: According to Trotter some men came over and chopped off the wire of the crane early this morning, but we suspect he will have done it himself to prevent the boat being used next month. For the rest of the day I generally busied myself with preparations for the relief.

> *6 May*: It was blowing a good 5 when I got up at 0445 and continued to do so. The result was yet another relief snatched from the jaws of disaster. [There did seem to be something about me and relief-day weather.] The old man spoke doom from the moment I took him his tea. In the event, of course, he and I simply stepped aboard (Jeff Clements and a Supernumerary Ahrens taking our place) and, lifted to the station on a petrol tanker, I was in Weymouth at 1515.

Even on the Breakwater, relief day was inseparable from an attack of nerves.

15

The games Keepers play:
a farewell to Portland

*B*aulked for the time being of the pleasure of travelling across the surface of the harbour I presently turned to the possibilities of travelling under it. Not a naturally good swimmer I had exercised great caution at the Eddystone, usually taking to the water in a life-jacket. Here there were no life-jackets and I pushed an old ladder ahead of me for extra buoyancy. Thereafter Lane became a familiar sight as he cruised around the harbour.

> 18 June: Another fine, hot day. In good but not perfect conditions swam out
> to the nearest tanker, *Thallepus*, to find only the mate and a caretaker aboard.
> Stayed awhile while they made me a cup of tea.

But this activity only really took off when I bought a snorkel and flippers in Weymouth.

Mr Trotter had meantime had a misfortune which had taken him first to hospital, then home. Going on the scrounge for some varnish he had fallen into the dockyard boat instead of stepping into it. The date was 13 June, and before leaving that morning he had told us it was the anniversary of his losing his eye in the First World War. It seems he had been an observer in an aeroplane and had incautiously looked over the side when over the German trenches. This was one explanation of his loss. Those less charitably inclined ascribed it, with probably no more validity, to a nocturnal encounter. I was never able to make up my mind. Sometimes I thought one thing, sometimes the other.

When I had used the boat to visit Weymouth, paddling it to the next breakwater and walking in from there, he emerged from his workshop on my return in a state of high excitement.

'Bincleves police have been phoning about you', he shouted.

They had phoned, to check my declaration of identity at the gate but, for Trotter, merely to be the subject of such attention implied at least an association with crime. The police seemed always to have been a cause of anxiety to him. In Brighton, for example, they had apparently transmitted messages about him through their helmets, the spike acting as the aerial and the circuitry being accommodated in the crown. This was surprisingly prescient of modern-day communications technology, but why Brighton and why about him we never discovered. He showed his usual irritability when we expressed our doubts.

The following day I gave him cause for further anxiety by 'swimming to Weymouth', as he apoplectically put it. In fact I swam only the quarter-mile gap to the next breakwater, using snorkel and flippers and pushing in front of me a plank to which I had nailed a pole from which hung a waterproof bag in which I packed my clothing and shoes for the walk into Weymouth. This time I was 'known' at Bincleves and Trotter only learned of my departure when I returned in style on a pleasure-boat which landed me at our own steps.

The plank had not been entirely satisfactory. It had been difficult to keep level and the pole had tended to tip and dunk the clothing bag in the water. A week later I substituted a ladder for the plank with more success.

> *6 September*: After breakfast it was blowing 3–4 with a few white horses but I took a preliminary look across the gap to C Head and it didn't seem too bad, though sloppy on the landings. So had a shave, put my library books in my kitbag and went along to the end again. Using the ladder the crossing was no trouble at all, thanks to my mask and snorkel. Certainly I could not have done it without the tube as the slop was breaking over my head all the time. Halfway across, a pleasure-launch came up and asked if I needed help. I suppose it seemed highly unlikely that a man in my apparent situation would *not* be in need of help, but I was able to decline. On C Head I dumped the ladder, dressed and walked into town… Had a good lunch at the 'Criterion' for five shillings, changed my books at the library, then walked along the promenade to the east end to where it left the road. Then back to C Head for the return.

By now Trotter's nerves were in such a state that when, a couple of days later, I simply took a walk to the end of the breakwater, he assumed I had gone to Weymouth again. It was on that occasion blowing a near-gale from the south-east!

In calmer conditions I pottered regularly round the harbour, typically making a round trip of perhaps one and a half miles to a laid-up tanker, the *British Piper*, on which the resident engineer and his wife gave me coffee and we had a chat. When I said, on my return, that I wished I had thought to invite them back Trotter threw up his lunch in horror: 'Against the rules!'

I have a note that on the evening of 15 September we had a discussion about pianos and harpsichords. Generally I did not note the subjects of our conversations; rather, I noted the writing activities that I managed to fit in between such exchanges. Articles, short stories, the occasional play buzzed to and, with rare exceptions, fro. Some of my best ideas occurred to me as I snorkelled about the harbour leaving, like the ideas, very little wake. On one of the days that I chose to set course for Weymouth 'two reporters' (more probably, a reporter and a photographer) from the *Southern Times* came out by boat to find their bird flown. Returning after a smooth crossing I found Trotter in a state of high excitement. Reporters! It was all very irregular; and with nothing in the books to cover it. A couple of days later I called at the newspaper office and cooled their enthusiasm by telling the truth: that my published works numbered precisely five. By coincidence I had just returned to *Punch* the corrected proofs of an article. Perhaps that made it six.

Midnight is never a natural hour for rising, and then to sit for up to ninety minutes under a bombardment of Trotter anecdote is the sort of experience one associates (with some flippancy I agree) with the stress of a noisy night on the Western Front. Occasionally the ennui was felt with more than usual ferocity:

> 3 October: On 0000–0400, a watch which started with a wonderfully illogical expatiation by Trotter of the principles of Principal-Keepership. The theme, of course, was the pump which – God save us! – is to be repaired again this morning.

This will have been the air pump for the IOBs which had been giving trouble and which, having been 'repaired' by Trotter in an extravagant display of Principal-Keepership, continued to do so. I recorded our return to the task more or less verbatim (I can hear that voice now):

> 'We're going to put it together again and then it's going to work. You say I'm cocksure. That's how cocksure I am.'

> 'We put it together again and it didn't work, whereupon Trotter retired for the rest of the day into a brown study from which could be heard the occasional crackle and buzz you get around high voltage insulators in misty weather. The fault proved to be in the tap immediately above the pump which was of the wrong type. This altered the system then worked.

The month ended with a flurry of postings. Chainey was to go to Alderney, and Clements to the Casquets. One of the replacements was to be someone called Robertson, who had been with Trotter on Sark when Trotter was in his heyday as a holy terror. I awaited his arrival with interest as I thought I detected in Trotter's response to the news of his coming something less than a welcoming. He was no longer the man that, by his account, he had been, and there could be old scores to be settled.

The Christmas turn of 1959 was singularly devoid of incident. Several factors contributed. It was now another winter and the weather, though undramatic, did not encourage boating or swimming. I did take one dip, on Christmas Day, just for the hell of it. It was a chilly hell with the sea temperature at 49 °F – as compared with the announced Serpentine temperature of 40 °F in which the octogenarians were doing their usual stuff. Two days earlier Pete had brought back from a visit ashore five small cigars and a flagon of cider each. Thus I passed my sixth and penultimate lighthouse Christmas Day with a ritual puffing at cigars which I didn't much like, and drinking cider which I didn't much enjoy either.

I wrote a good deal. *Punch* nibbled at one piece but finally sent it back; others were returned unnibbled. Such experiences are sometimes, I believe, the precursors to eventual literary acclaim and resounding popular success. Not in my case. Forty years on my life is almost completely unmarked by success in any direction, a circumstance to which I attribute a sound digestion and sleep achieved without the help of tranquillisers.

Otherwise I wrote letters – to bank managers, plumbers, estate agents, moneylenders, solicitors, local authorities: that army of predators who batten on the happy estate of matrimony. Our experience with the plumber was particularly instructive. Engaged in the summer he turned up in winter, installed a stove and hot water tank, and presented his bill. He was one of the very few people M. and I have ever employed to do anything, and also the main reason he has remained the exception. We had a close look at his workmanship and considered the size of his bill and decided he must be greatly in need of friends.

Thus was born the *Friends of Worcestershire Plumbers* whose founder, and only, members dine *à deux* annually on the feast of St Faucet.

The New Year brought a reminder of Genghis, now at Sark.

> I found Trotter this morning smiling odiously at a bit of tittle-tattle he had just heard, to the effect that Genghis had been 'aggressive' at Sark and has been reported.

It was the following morning that I was privileged to be given an insight into the psychology of Principal-Keepership.

> Assisted Trotter in the tower. He discovered a quantity of paraffin in the air receiver and refused to listen to my explanation of how (I am quite certain) it got there. He explained: 'When you take advice from anyone, you have lost power.'

Without advice you are also quite likely to run a ship aground, set off an atomic bomb, or continue to have paraffin in your air receiver. It had occurred to me, not for the first time, that Trotter's tragedy was that he was a First World War general with a two-man army.

I had been looking forward with some anticipation to the coming of Arthur Robertson. Now, in advance of his arrival, he telephoned:

> to exchange a good deal of bad language with his old colleague, Trotter. Amongst gleanings was the interesting news that there has been a further 'incident' at Sark and that in consequence the Principal Keeper has been urged to retire at 62. Yes, the PK retired, not Genghis sacked.

To Trotter, of course, this was quite incomprehensible: the hierarchical world of Trinity was being turned upside down.

It was reassuring to know that our own social difficulties could be merely echoes of even greater rumpuses elsewhere. I sometimes felt I did not make sufficient allowances for Trotter and yet –

9 March: On 0000–0400. Trotter talked for a whole hour in a wild,
unconsecutive way that, as on one or two previous occasions, brought me to
screaming pitch. I felt alert and ready for bright thoughts when I got up, and
now like an old rag. A whole bloody hour of it. I suppose the flow of words
helped to soothe his apprehensions about the coming month. It would be nice
to think one of us got something out of it. Having stood outside in the cool
night air for ten minutes I now feel able to resume about the pendulum…

I went ashore after, unusually, only one month. This will have been a result of the
recent postings and had the happy consequence for me that I would not in future be
in the double turn with Trotter. And so, welcome Dineen and Robertson.

Dineen has the reputation of being quiet and so he remained as we never knew
he was coming till we saw him on the boat. I wrote Robertson a note welcoming him to Trotter's Kingdom of Terror which I managed to pass to him on the
landing.

It was high time some new parameters were introduced into the group sociodynamics
and with them would come, with luck, a new set of Games Keepers Play.

The first game we played on my return was Short Circuit.

The year was brightening up. That for the first time I was spending one of my two
months apart from Trotter may have had something to do with it. And it was that
most uncertain and yet disquieting of seasons, Spring. I recall Arthur Robertson as
not having much patience with routine. Thus he showed me a list 'as long as your
arm', as he described it, of jobs Trotter wanted done in his month ashore, in the
instant before he tore it into pieces and consigned it to the fire. I got the impression
they had not mended many fences in their month together. Had I been in charge I
think I would have given the list the same short shrift. I remember being impressed,
in the early days of our relationship, with Trotter's announcement at tea that we had
a heavy month ahead of us and that tomorrow we would be making a start by 'burning the pots'.

'I have some matches', I had said eagerly, wanting to show willing.

Later I asked the third hand what it meant. He explained that the pots would be
gathered, a little cotton waste and some paraffin put into each, and that one of my
matches would be used to set fire to each. This was 'burning the pots'.

'And then?'

Then nothing; that would be it. The following day we might 'clean the brushes'
and some time after that we could embark on a little leisurely painting if the wind was
in the north and there wasn't an 'r' in the month.

So things were looking up; and presently I was able to make an individual contribution to the improved quality of life in the form of a little in-house entertainment.

For the sake of reliability our main light was provided by paraffin and the usual Hood burner, but in the dwellings, as already mentioned, we had the advantage of a 'mains' power supply provided less certainly by underwater cable from the dockyard. This was split at the fusebox into one circuit for power points in the living room and bedroom, and another for the lighting. It occurred to me that a rather interesting effect would be produced if I wired the power points (of which in fact we used only one, for the domestic radio) in series with the lighting. This I did, taking advantage of the absence of Able and Charlie on a walk along the breakwater. (With the coincidence of three Arthurs on the station this month these pseudonyms were necessary.) The date was 15 April. I hadn't thought of it in time for April the first.

On their return I drew Able's attention to an interesting anomaly that had developed in the electrical supply in his absence. He would observe, I said, that while the lights still functioned, the radio was quite dead. He inspected the fuses and found them sound. This was puzzling. He spent an hour after tea fooling with the fusebox and the switches and at each new approach I would either insert or remove a shorted plug from the socket in the bedroom. When I inserted the plug we had the lights. When I took it out we had the radio. It was all, Able declared, quite baffling. He and Charlie went round the dwelling banging the conduit that carried the cables. In the bedroom I was equally busy removing and replacing the plug so that at one moment we had lights, at another the radio, never both.

When it became dark we had the radio for Harry Secombe but I brought back the lights later. I wanted to write a letter to the Superintendent, East Cowes, saying I had heard rumours that I was to be posted to the Nab Tower and would be glad of his assurance that this was not so as I was thoroughly enjoying myself at Portland Breakwater.

A refinement then occurred to me. I recalled the simple dimmer device occasionally used in amateur theatricals, consisting of a jar filled with salt water in which a rod could be alternately raised and lowered to provide a variable resistance. There was no lack of salt water and a glass jar and a rod were easily found. These I wired to the plug with which I had carried out the earlier manipulations. The socket, as luck would have it, was on the wall above the head of my bed. The glass jar conveniently stood on the floor beneath the bed where I could operate the rod from the sleeping position – though with some minor danger of electrocution.

Able had by now found a table lamp which he plugged into the radio socket so that during the night, whatever the state of play, we would have illumination from one source or the other: that or the ceiling lamp.

By the happy chance of a couple of abortive phone calls that came while Able was using the lavatory I had managed to persuade him that these mysterious electrical malfunctions now included even the telephone. I encouraged this belief when I called him at midnight. I reported that the lights had gone out once, briefly, while I was in the lavatory but that otherwise things had been pretty stable. We chatted desultorily of this and that and then I yawned (it had been a busy day) and went next door to bed. Before I turned in I gave Charlie a push. I had by now put him in the picture. He was not on watch until 0400 but had said he didn't want to miss this.

I waited twenty minutes. There was the sound of the chair being pushed back, then receding footsteps. I gave Able time to get to the lavatory, waited till I heard the distant sound of the chain being pulled, then cautiously withdrew the rod. Beneath the door I saw the crack of light dim and go out. Stumbling footsteps returned, a chair was kicked in the darkness, there was the click of the switch at the radio socket and light, this time from the table lamp, returned under the door. I let Able settle himself then slowly replaced the rod.

There was the sound of a chair being hurriedly pushed back.

'I've got to see this', Charlie whispered. He got up and quietly went into the kitchen where Able was standing, open-mouthed as the saying is, as the table lamp and ceiling light alternately dimmed and lit, each one coming up to full brightness as the other dimmed to nothing.

'Did you ever see the like of it?' he demanded in an amazed whisper out of deference to my own slumbers.

Charlie agreed he had not. I left them to their discussion, and the rod in the bottom of the jar, and turned over to enjoy my 'all night in'.

In the morning Able was in no two minds about it. This was something for the dockyard electricians; certainly it was beyond him. In fact before he got up I had restored the wiring to orthodoxy, only deliberately blowing the lighting fuse as some sort of alibi in what was now a thoroughly confused situation. I tried to persuade him to have a final scout around but he wouldn't hear of it and presently he was on the phone to the dockyard.

'Yes, I know it sounds crazy but it's a fact. When I jump up and down on the roof the lights go out, and when I flush the lavatory the phone rings. What? …No, of course I'm not joking.' He replaced the receiver angrily. 'They'll be out this afternoon. Fools!'

After lunch we persuaded him to have a final go at the lavatory chain. He pulled it and – Hey presto! – everything worked. (I had by now replaced the blown fuse.)

'God dammit!'

After that he was never still, and listening to him jumping up and down on the roof, repeatedly pulling the lavatory chain and thumping the conduit – for the boat was on its way across the harbour and 'How am I going to explain it to them?' – Charlie confided to me his fear that we would drive him out of his mind.

Three electricians came over (the dockyard never did anything by halves) ferried by a boat's crew of three seamen, and they all spent well over an hour mulling over the problem. They clearly found Able's account difficult to credit and I have to admit it sounded improbable enough to me, little though I know about electricity. If opportunity had offered I would have taken one of them aside and hinted at domestic worries.

In fact the truth only dawned on Able when they were all peering into the fuse box and he realised that the arrangement of wires he now saw before him was not the one with which he had become altogether too familiar over the past eighteen hours. He became rather quiet, and after seeing them off on the boat returned to make what the police would describe as 'certain threats'. I had quite a job pacifying him.

'You have an expensive sense of humour', he said. 'Now they're talking about re-wiring the place.'

This was not good news. It meant days, perhaps weeks, of tea-making and general dislocation.

Fortunately it didn't come to that. The electricians did not return and I was left with the regret only that I had not postponed the episode to the following month and Trotter. But I could not count on fooling the electricians a second time.

I did, though, have one entertainment lined up for Trotter. The breakwater build-ings had been virtually stripped at the end of their wartime occupation by the army but I found a mains-voltage alarm bell in working order, probably left behind because its casting had been broken and then crudely repaired. This I wired up to the mains socket in the bedroom via a French striking clock which I had brought off. The ham-mer of the clock now completed a circuit to the alarm bell at each blow. The discor-dancy of the hullaballoo in the dwellings as it tolled the daylight hours was most impressive. I hadn't heard anything as nerve-jangling since those far-off days of the Zeeman String Ensemble. I was sure Trotter would be impressed by it.

He arrived on the half-time relief of 5 May, replacing Able, displaying 'the usual alternation of aggressiveness and bonhomie. Charlie was soon in the toils of conver-sation'. Trotter and I were equally soon back on a war footing. He had never become reconciled to our use of 'his' boat, and after I had gone for a very pleasant paddle round the harbour on a quiet, sunny, early summer evening he asked me whether I knew how quickly that quiet harbour could become a maelstrom of boiling, moun-tainous seas which would drown me and, on the debit side, lose the boat. I told him I did not know it and – here I paused while my clock in the next room rang out the hour of seven, conversation being impossible while it did so – thought it unlikely it would turn that way within the next couple of days.

'And that's enough of that damned row,' he said.

'It's only a clock, Mr Trotter, and clocks must strike.'

I took him into the bedroom and showed it to him, the delicate nineteenth century French movement in my twentieth century perspex case; rather elegant I thought. I drew his attention to the bell, no more than three inches in diameter, and the miniscule hammer adjacent to it.

'Hardly offensive, surely?'

'That makes that noise?' he demanded incredulously.

'What else?' I asked, in the confidence that the wires that led from the clock dropped invisibly to the floor and followed the skirting-board to rise up to the alarm-bell, mounted on the back of a chest of drawers whose timber-work added an impressive resonance to the hullaballoo. 'I think you may have forgotten', I said gently, 'that when we get very old we tend to become more sensitive to certain frequencies'.

'You're telling me something now I never knew before', he said with interest.

I suppose I've been lucky in this knack I've always had of knowing how to calm people down.

Yet at midnight he was back on the war-path.

> *10 May*: Concluded the typing of Chapter IV up to midnight [I had embarked on another novel.]

> 'Nice morning, Mr Trotter.'

> 'Right. You wound up before calling me? Correct?'

> It wasn't. I left him to fume and crash and bang around.

He had accused me of the solecism of winding up the lens clock before I called him for watch rather than after.

It seems to have been a proper sort of summer.

> *2 June*: Relief day, and a fine one. Had a swim in the morning instead of a bath.

Charlie and I were replaced by Mike Dineen and Ron Bolton.

On my return I took over the role of Napoleon from Trotter during his month ashore. The job of Keeper-in-Charge automatically devolved on whoever happened to be the senior Assistant Keeper. I think it had once happened to me at the Eddystone and it was to occur again at Skokholm. On each occasion I swung at once into an entrepreneurial role, looking around for opportunities for making 'improvements' that sometimes irritated my colleagues and that authority would in most cases not have approved of.

> *3 July*: Spent the evening scrounging the materials for a scheme to run the Aldis lamp off the mains.

It was true that we had an Aldis signalling lamp. However, we had no battery for it; and the reason we had no battery was because we had no use for an Aldis lamp. Nonetheless I presently had an array of seven 100-watt bulbs set up in parallel with the mains, passing the three amps necessary to feed the 24-volt bulb of the lamp, together with a socket in the dwelling entrance to facilitate the passing of messages which it was extremely unlikely we would ever need to send. A bonus was the level of illumination in the entrance, which was now spectacular.

Obviously at this time of year we were spending a good deal of time in and on the water, and on one occasion Dineen went out in the boat and amazed me by coming back with eight mackerel. I had not expected this evidence that we could occasionally catch fish whose name we had heard of.

This did not mean I was neglecting my professional responsibilities.

> 17 July: In the evening and up to midnight sign-wrote a board for the paraffin store. It took so long because in the absence of a brush I had to use a piece of string.

(But weren't there paint brushes – the ones we had immersed in paraffin and sat and watched, the morning after the day on which we had 'burned the pots'? Yes, there were, but Trotter would have locked them away in his workshop.)

Altogether it was a month heady with activity.

> 21 July: Gave a second coat of paint to a white line painted on the Oil Store floor and attached a chalk-rest to the bottom of the oil tally board. Then exhausted by my labours I retired to bed.

However, all good things must come to an end.

> 28 July: Relief day. Trotter and Bolton came off. Dineen and Clarke went ashore. Immediately on arriving Trotter threw a paddy over numerous things including the state of the lino which has allegedly been scratched by the nails in my shoes. I am now going around with my feet wrapped in sacking tied on with string. He has yet to see the 'improvements' in the paraffin store and lantern room. He knows about the Aldis lamp but hasn't yet fathomed how I did it. It is all very tiring and I find myself regretting the productive tranquillity of the past month.

> 29 July: Slept poorly and seemed to hear and comprehend every movement of the lunatic on watch next door. Fortunately on calling me at 0400 he went with very few words spoken.

It seemed unlikely I would ever be mentally composed enough to write anything this month. But in the evening:

> I retired to the bath-house – a heavily armoured building with a bath in it, to enable the garrison commander to take his ablutions under fire – and began a story which may or may not come to something.

Sometimes I was able to contrive a counter-attack.

> 6 August: After breakfast along to B Head and swam across to C Head.

It may be remembered that after one of my first excursions on this route to Weymouth the police at Bincleves had phoned Trotter to have my identity confirmed. By now I was well known and came and went without question; but in Weymouth I thought I would cheer Trotter up with a telephone call of my own, doing so in the guise of a sergeant of the dockyard police to say it had been necessary to detain one of his, Trotter's, men. It seemed I had not been cooperative.

'I may say we don't like his manner', I concluded, to clinch the identification.

It had been necessary, I went on, as part of normal procedure, to hand me over to the civil police. I regretted this but it was now out of my hands. If Mr Trotter insisted I would of course do what I could to halt proceedings, but… Trotter hastily disclaimed any wish that I should intervene. He himself knew nothing about me, he said, then added inconsistently:

'If he's been taken into custody I suppose I had better see about getting a relief.'

'Perhaps you should do that, sir,' I said, and hung up.

With my call I had succeeded in combining Trotter's worst expectations with his fondest hopes. He bustled along to Ron.

'He's done it now!'

In his agitation he phoned back to the police at Bincleves, who of course knew nothing about any arrest.

'The bugger's been having me on again,' he said to Ron as much in sorrow as in anger. At Bincleves on the way back a policeman, with another grinning in the background, reproved me for taking their name in vain. I apologised and he said 'Proceed.'

In the evening Trotter said I'd gone too far this time all right: it was the Superintendent for me, now. Poor devil, his face was grey with a sense of injury. 'I made a show of looking at the Situations Vacant in the *Telegraph*.'

As usual we patched things up.

> **9 August:** Trotter said the copper would poison the water.

I had made an electrode heater which boiled water when it didn't blow the fuses, hence Trotter's concern. The armistice was brief.

> **13 August:** Up 0400 to an hour's exchange of pleasantries with Trotter. Out of them came the interesting disclosure that I was moved from the Eddystone because Genghis had threatened to thump me, which confirmed what I had always suspected'.

Apart from the writing, which under Trotter's regime was proving difficult to pursue, I was intensely into boilers.

> **18 August:** Wrote this 0053. In the sketch A is a flame heating the water in the boiler B. Normally the only connection between B and the container above, BB, is internally through the water pipe C and externally through the steam pipe. This ensures that B is kept filled, for water flows down C and the space thereby vacated in BB is taken up with steam admitted via D.

In all there are five pages of it, interrupted briefly with:

> At short notice the Superintendent came after lunch, in good humour. Chatted at great length as usual about this and that. I was able to establish that he knows nothing of an intention to move me at present and I emphasised that I liked it here. Trotter, overhearing this, was quite *furious*.

Then back to the boiler.

It Was Fun While It Lasted

We were grinding towards the end of the turn. Bincleves police were becoming nervous. One policeman begged me to tell him I was making the crossing from C Head by boat as otherwise he would feel 'embarrassed' if I drowned. I agreed to observe this convention in the future. On the way over I had had to shout 'Fore!' to a boat bearing down on me and a surly face looked over the side and shouted something critical of the venture as it passed. It seemed a day for gloomy prognostications.

There is not much mention of reading, but it went on. The visits to Weymouth invariably included the library. I had just finished Maugham's *Of Human Bondage* and now I was wanting and not wanting to continue with Greene's *The End of the Affair*.

> I am fed up with love unrequited, rejected, sundered by death, blighted by doubt. I want to read about love that ends with at least a hope of happiness, if not a promise. [Quite. But of course it sells fewer copies. The diary entry continues without intermission:] My reasoning on page 138 is faulty. The elbow of the syphoning pipe must after all be placed *below* the lip of the outflow...

And so to relief day, consoling myself with the thought that at least nowadays Trotter and I had each other's company for only one month in three.

It was the freedom with which I exploited a particular one of those Trotter-free months that I think determined that this was to be my final turn. If I had survived the episodes of the Short Circuit and the Impersonated Policeman, it was the Three Piece Suite affair that made me, finally, too hot a property for Portland Breakwater.

I have mentioned in regard to the Eddystone that the Corporation's idea of an improvement in the seating accommodation was to substitute canvas-bottomed and backed tubular stacking chairs for the previous unpadded oaken ones. They were an improvement only insofar as, once a day, they were easier for the morning watchman to move when he washed the slate floor. With less excuse in terms of limited space we were little better off at the Breakwater; indeed, we had exactly the same type of chair.

I thought something might be done about this.

> 10 October: Called at an auctioneers' in Weymouth and explained our requirements for a chair for ten shillings and left that sum as a deposit.

I had been thinking in terms of a single armchair, and a wait of a week or two, before something so awful as to be otherwise unsaleable came into the auctioneers' rooms.

They phoned that same afternoon with astonishing news. Of the stuff they had in for sale the following afternoon they thought they could let us have a three-piece suite for our ten shillings. Well, not quite a suite, but anyway two armchairs and a settee. Would they do? I accepted with alacrity, accepting at the same time the problem of how we were to get them from saleroom to lighthouse. The facilities of Whitehead's torpedo testing station half-way down the breakwater might have something to offer. They had a sizeable launch which they used to recover the torpedoes at the end of their run across the bay.

> 2 October: Down to Whitehead's early to get advice about contacting Captain Gunn. Returned there in the afternoon and found him amicably inclined towards collecting the sofa and chairs from Bincleves. On returning to the dwellings I found a message to say we *had* secured the goods and by phone I made arrangements for their carriage from the auctioneers' to the breakwater gates. To bed early to listen to *Famous Trials* and that other famous trial, Brahms' Violin Concerto.

> 3 October: Up 0800 and paddled the boat to C Head, arriving at Bincleves police gate at 0930 just after the furniture van had. The police were very helpful in arranging that the goods should be stowed in a shed until Monday.

The charge for carriage, 15 shillings, was more than I had wanted to pay but the chairs and settee were good stuff, heavy and very old-fahioned, and comfortable. The covers were dirty but sound and the seats did not sag. I looked forward to many seat-warming hours.

> 5 October: Up early in view of the possible arrival of Captain Gunn and the furniture. He came alone at 0840 to discuss procedures and it arrived after lunch.

I remember the wind as being a bit brisk and still have an image of that incongruous cargo on the bow of the launch as she nosed in towards the landing. Not without difficulty we lifted the sofa off by crane; the chairs we man-handled, appreciating for the first time the sheer weight of the brutes. It was enough for the moment to get them up the steps and I went down to Whitehead's to offer Captain Gunn the £1 which Mike Dineen had thought might be appropriate. 'But he returned ten shillings with an astonishment that made me feel foolish at having offered so much.' The total cost of the enterprise had thus been 35 shillings which we shared between the three of us.

Mike had an agreeably solitary disposition and one of his first acts after meeting Trotter had been to establish himself in one of the ruined army buildings, blocking up the odd broken window with cardboard and installing an old stove with a more or less intact flue-pipe which he fed with driftwood. He was now able to burn the packing-case that had been its single item of furniture and instal in its place the sofa. It was too immense to go anywhere else. Thereafter one would hear the sound of his radio, and see the smoke, some emerging from the flue, some around the door, and know that Mike was in residence. From time to time would come the choking cough of the partially asphyxiated.

To our disappointment it proved impossible to find room for either of the chairs in the living room but they did a great deal to relieve the stark functionality of the two bedrooms – though I resolved that the one in Trotter's must be removed before his return. He would be unlikely to approve of an improvement in living conditions that for the past seventy years had been good enough for him.

A further venture of this month was the building out of abandoned breeze-blocks

of a weather-wall 6 foot wide and 7 foot high immediately outside the dwelling entrance. Unfortunately there was no way of scrounging some cement and sand or we
could have made a permanent job of it. As it was it had to be free-standing and it
proved its efficacy as a wind-break by bulging ominously in the next severe gale. I
didn't think Trotter would like it at all.

He arrived on the half-time relief in an unusually pliant mood: perhaps my 'shift'
was in the air again; and he accepted the wall and even the armchairs without froth-
ing, showing acerbity only when I told him, when questioned about their origin, that
they had come from a sale-room in Weymouth. I'm not quite sure why I told him this.
It was not my habit to tell him the truth when a little invention could supply something more interesting.

Luckily I was not believed and Trotter supplied an alternative of his own.

'Don't tell me any of your stories. I know', he affirmed darkly, 'where these chairs
came from'.

And presently, inevitably, he enlarged: they had come from the state-room of the
THV *Beacon*. His mind was clearly made up and I knew he preferred not to be crossed
in argument so I said no more.

Three days later he discovered the settee and demanded to know by whose authority *Beacon* had landed a three-piece suite here. With complete confidence now that I
would not be believed

> I began to explain again that they had come from a sale-room in Weymouth
> but he interrupted to say he wasn't going to listen to any more lies. He
> happened to *know* that they had come off the *Beacon* – that surprised me,
> didn't it? I had to agree it did. I asked him how he had tumbled to it. Later he
> implied to Ron that he had made use of the telephone extension in his bed-
> room to make a few inquiries and had discovered that the suite had belonged
> to a Captain Bennet (of whom I have never heard).

His assertion was implausible in the extreme. The *Beacon* was the district bucket. It
spent its life servicing buoys and sea-marks and, when it was not doing that, supplying
lighthouses in the East Cowes administrative district with coal, paraffin, broom-handles and toilet rolls. It was not possible to think of a state-room and of a Trinity
House Vessel without an interval in which one thought of something else. The ideas
were mutually exclusive.

On 27 October we had an exceptional storm and as on previous such occasions it
was curiously much more impressive at sea level, as we were, than storms had been
on the Eddystone.

> It awakened me before I was due to come on watch at midnight and I went out
> to warn Ron not to pass in front of The Wall in the gusts. (In fact it moved but
> didn't fall.) It blew a nine or perhaps even a ten direct from the SW and spray
> drove continuously against the windows and swept across the route to the

tower in sheets. High water was at 0150 but fortunately it was not a particularly high tide. When I called Trotter at 0400 he came in in a very bad temper. Nothing was right and I left him as soon as possible, advising him not to pass in front of the wall during the gusts 'or it may fall on you and kill you and then all sorts of people will be pleased'.

Of course he knew I was only joking.

I had now reached Chapter VII of my book – whatever it was – and in the meantime was obliging Short, who had succeeded Butters as editor of the house magazine *Flash,* and who now asked for 'a seasonal piece for Christmas'. I saw very few of these pieces as I was presently on the move and distribution was erratic. I believe the magazine improved later but at that time it told keepers very little that they wanted to know and was not highly regarded.

> *1 November:* Much of the afternoon was spent scrounging wire for an idea I have had for connecting up the bedroom electric fire in such a way that in use it will make the lights brighter instead of dimmer.

The following day I applied it with success. Evidently the supply emerged from the harbour waters in three-phase and I had wired the fire to the unused phase. In defence of such activities I would say only that so far as I know they never killed anybody; at least while I was there. If deaths occurred after my departure it can only have been because someone was careless.

> *11 November:* Armistice Day – but not on the breakwater. The Superintendent came at 1400. I saw little of him and when Ron and I did meet him briefly his manner was awkward. Or perhaps he was dazed, having just been closeted with Trotter for the past thirty minutes.

I had been looking forward to the Superintendent's visit as Trotter had undertaken to protest in the most vigorous terms at the dumping of Captain Bennett's derelict furniture.

'And the boiler-plates', I had reminded him.

'Boiler-plates?'

Yes, apparently the *Beacon* had left some boiler-plates at the Casquets, part of a condenser at the Nab Tower, and a steam pump at the Hanois. Indeed, I continued indignantly, if she continued this shedding of bits of herself at every lighthouse in the parish, it was difficult to see where it was all going to end. It only needed the careless discarding of a sea-cock and we would all begin to feel the pinch. A shortage of broom-handles would be the least of it.

I forget how long Trotter allowed me to carry on like this or how much of it he conveyed to the Superintendent, but I think I managed to persuade him of the gravity of the issue; and that may have been why, at this visit, he insisted on the protocol that he alone should have Jock Sharman's ear when he called. He had, besides, already made it plain he wasn't happy at the way in which we, as other ranks, showed ourselves ready to pitch in conversationally on such occasions.

That he had spoken of the arm-chairs there was no doubt.

> He looked so crushed and nervous afterwards I hadn't the heartlessness to ask him how it had all gone. Later he told Ron there was going to be 'a big enquiry' about the furniture.

> 13 November: Trotter intended going ashore today. Therefore we had a gale of classic proportions. It was calm at midnight and blowing a storm by dawn – which fortunately I did not see. The storm continued throughout the day and in the squalls blew more strongly than I think I have ever known before. In the afternoon I struggled to B Head and back, getting very wet.

It was an appropriate send-off from the Breakwater. Four days later I went ashore for what proved to be the last time.

16

A series of 'improvements':
Skokholm Island

> *4 December*: Two letters in the morning, one from Cowes, one from Holyhead.
> The former told me to write to the latter and to arrange to take my bedding
> with me. The one from Holyhead told me to be there on Tuesday morning. So I
> give up a week's leave to spend my seventh successive Christmas on a Rock
> station. Sent a strongly worded letter of protest which will probably do no
> good at all. [It didn't.]

Thus far I had known only reliefs done by local boatmen or contractors. Now, on
my eleventh posting, I was at last to encounter a 'Trinity relief'; that is, one carried
out by depot tender. The conclusion I was to come to on the basis of experience was
that I did not like it, and I do not think it would have improved on further acquaintance. It seemed to take up a great deal of time. It certainly meant a great deal of
travelling.

The hour of 0115 on 8 December found me on Crewe station at a low ebb. Crewe,
even at a less inhospitable time, is surely the armpit of the railway system to all but
the railway enthusiast. Holyhead, at five minutes to six on a pre-dawn winter's morning, was only marginally better. With time to waste I retired to the waiting-room the
better to enjoy the hard-boiled egg I had been keeping for just this moment. This egg,
in these abysmal circumstances, was going to hoist my spirits to the level of something with at least a distant view of contentment.

I took a bite – and the liquid yolk ran down my trousers.

I went out on to the platform and asked the only other occupant of the station, an
employee of the company, whether in the near future he was expecting any train that
I might throw myself under. He was unable to oblige. Forty years of marriage has not
seen a greater test of propinquity than that soft hard-boiled egg.

> I walked to the Depot, arriving at 0830. Presently several other keepers and
> lightshipmen turned up, but with no boat to take us anywhere we presently
> dispersed. The THV *Alert* is still gale-locked in Swansea at the other end of
> Wales. I saw the Chief Clerk, who was affable, and the Superintendent, who
> was unimpressive. I was told I would be going to the Skerries after a turn or

two at Skokholm. I could forgive much for the fact that I was reimbursed on the spot for my journey up from Portland via Birmingham – £5 and more. I spent the rest of the morning shopping after booking in at a comfortable commercial hotel.

Thus was day one.

9 December: Reported to the depot at 1000. The North relief had gone off at 0600 and we were to return at 1800 to embark.

The North relief would have been the Morecombe Bay light vessel and Skerries. I savoured further the delights of Holyhead in winter.

So at 1800 to the depot once again. There ensued a good deal of hanging around, taking gear down to the pier and so on, before we transferred to the Alert at about 2000. The ship started moving at 2045. Played cards before turning in at 2330. A gale was forecast but it didn't seem to be materialising. The accommodation is much better than I expected: amidships, curtained bunks to port, dayroom to starboard. But provision for feeding us seems to be non-existent.

The significance of the Morecambe Bay lightship and the Skerries being done separately is that the relieved men from both would otherwise have had to remain aboard until the *Alert* had travelled the length of Wales and back. Day two.

The Morecambe Bay Light Vessel being relieved by THV
Alert *in 1960.*

10 December: We steamed throughout the night and arrived off the South Bishop at about 0800. That relief done we went on to the Smalls. The South Bishop is a pile set upon a big rock – or a small island; the Smalls is a true tower with red and white horizontal bands. The landing there was very difficult and the men returned wet. But the relief was done. While the boat was there I went to the bridge to see the Captain and remonstrate about the non-existent feeding arrangements. I was told to go away and return when he was less preoccupied. I went back on being summoned. The discussion was inconclusive.

The problem arose simply because, administratively, we were not part of the ship's company. At the same time we had no access to food of our own or any facilities for providing for ourselves.

In fact the first offering since coming aboard last night was lunch at 1230. By the time this was produced it was blowing stiffly and I felt unwell. However, I swallowed a little soup [I remember seeing the globules of fat congeal in the wind as I ate it out on deck] threw the rest away, and immediately brought up the little I had eaten. Some time later we came up to Skokholm. The wind had by now increased to something like a six. The crew helped Samson (the Supernumerary) and myself to get our stuff on deck, we climbed into the launch, were lowered into the sea and went in. I spent most of my time looking into the bottom of a bucket but was able to observe a good deal of white water, with breakers romping up rocks which seemed uncomfortably close. We dropped the usual stern anchor, and then had difficulty getting it up again when the coxwain decided he didn't like the situation and pulled out.

It was a decision I had come to some time earlier.

And so it was back to the Alert, wetter and colder and with an even emptier stomach, and out with the gear again and presently round to anchor in Milford Haven. There I wrote a note to the captain, who must have thought he had already heard quite enough from me – 'Our compliments to the Captain … – asking if it would be possible for us to go ashore for a few hours. I might not be able to keep down any food but I still thought it could be important to take a little on board from time to time An officer took my message and presently the captain came out, quite amiable, and said we would presently be transferred to the Argus. My impression by now was that our gear had been moved at least as far by hand as by boat. Now it was once more put into the Alert's launch which took us across to the Argus, newly arrived from a refit. There was a different attitude in this, the district tender. Within half an hour we were given a substantial, though scratch, meal and a mug of tea. Television of a sort was on in the nominal saloon. I read, waited up long enough to have another mug of tea, and presently turned in. [Day three.]

11 December: At about 0700 the anchor came up. Once more we took the gear to the upper deck and loaded it into the launch. The sea had moderated

and the landing this time was quite good. The Principal Keeper and a Supernu-merary came off. The former had only last night been told that he was to take all his stuff ashore, an indication of the turmoil of comings and goings that seems to prevail on this district. He hadn't even been told which new station he had been appointed to.

At Skokholm the landing is three parts down the island from the lighthouse at the end and a Thwaites diesel dumper is used for transport. It took the two of us perhaps an hour to load the stuff and drive across the island in a Welsh drizzle.

The dumper had replaced a horse for which the Corporation had provided excellent stabling near the landing, but which it had never been persuaded to use. The horse was still on the island, buried where it had eventually fallen.

The island is a chunk of Wales in its character and colouring. There is colour-ing in the rocks as well as in the vegetation. Wherever one walks rabbits scatter. Mice apparently abound in the dwellings themselves.

I recall that they used to come out from behind the R/T table and play fearlessly on the floor.

The lighthouse is a barn of a place, built in 1915 with big, individual bed-rooms, tower, living-rooms, fog-engine room and scullery all under one roof. As far as living conditions go the station is a bit of a mess; the drinking water arrangements seeming particularly poor.

After lunch Mortiboys, the Keeper-in-Charge, went over the fog-engine starting sequence with me. The Supernumerary, Samson, is a negligible pin-head – his head does in fact go up to a point. Mortiboys is more interesting. A shambling fellow of about thirty he has been in the service some ten years and plans to 'work his ticket' presently on medical grounds. He has a child of twenty months, and another on the way, and thinks perhaps it is time he made the mother an honest woman. The putative Mrs Mortiboys' situation is at present precarious. She is in temporary possession of the Hire Purchase goods of a couple with whom she was sharing accommodation and who have recently done a 'moonlight flit'. When the Hire Purchase companies discover what has happened they will no doubt call and take the goods away.

I decided Mortiboys was possibly the most interesting colleague I had encountered since Genghis.

12 December: After lunch I went for a walk round the island. It took about an hour and three quarters, keeping as near as I could get to the cliff-top all the way.

15 December: I met a man and girl who had come across with a shooting party from Dale Fort unobserved. With them they had brought some lens

A series of 'improvements'

rollers which the *Argus* was even then on her way to Dale Fort to collect. So I presently went down to the landing with the dumper to bring them back and while I returned Mortiboys waited there for them to shoot a sheep for us.

Skokholm was privately owned. It had a population of black-faced sheep which every so often had to be culled. It was also a bird observatory with hides and rudimentary accommodation, unoccupied at this time of year. Our sheep shot,

> we went down to the observatory to collect it. I spent the rest of the day wishing heartily that I hadn't seen the cropped blonde I had met on the path. Incidentally the man with her was one of the Wooden Horsemen of the wartime prisoner-of-war camp episode. At 1300 we heard on the radio that *Argus* was coming down to land my gear, forwarded from Portland and arrived at last…
>
> 16 December: At breakfast I had gulls' eggs but to my regret find that I cannot accept them entirely. Likewise at lunch we had a stew in which the meat was the poore beastie we had shot yesterday, and I decided I preferred not to see my meat on the hoof before it appeared on the table.

It was indeed an extraordinarily tough beast and the most prolonged stewing did not seem to make it otherwise. On the other hand, in another sense, had it not been tough it would not have survived on Skokholm. The objection to the eggs was a different one. There was a notional line across the island that separated our half of the egg farm from that of the bird watchers. The 'hens' were great black-backed gulls and they laid their eggs in the open. You simply walked round and picked them up. Preservation was by laying them in barrels covered by successive layers of hydrated lime. They were duck's-egg in size, and free and plentiful, and it was a matter of regret to me that I presently began to find them nauseous. There was something repellent about the way the white frothed up into a cellular texture when they were fried; and the flavour was strong. Gulls were quite capable of catching a rabbit in the open and then dining first on the eyes. If I add that many of the rabbits on Skokholm at that time were infected with myxomatosis my decision to use gulls' eggs only in cakes may be seen as not wholly prejudiced or extreme.

> 17 December: Yesterday afternoon came news via the radio of several postings including mine to Skerries. No dates, however, so I might still do two months here. I hope so.

I suspect the hope expressed a disinclination to up sticks again rather than any formed opinion about Skokholm, though I think I was beginning to like the exposure and emptiness of the island. The weather continued the liveliness that had accompanied my departure from Portland Breakwater.

> Up to midnight it blew like the devil…Yet another gale last night had blown itself out this morning to the extent that the strength was a mere five…A day of fierce squalls superimposed on a steady gale. After lunch out into the

> weather for a brief walk. Tearing wind and flying spume. Monster seas dashing at the cliffs.
>
> *21 December:* In the morning with Mortiboys to the spring near the bird observatory where we filled six barrels with muddy water to replenish the supply of our eel in the drinking water tank.

The supply for our eel was also the supply for us.

Fortunately there was an intermission in the weather sufficient for our mechanic to get home for Christmas. He had been working on the lens.

> The *Alert* came on the radio at 1600 and said she expected to arrive after 1800. Some time before then we saw her lights and made our way across the island in the dark by torchlight – prematurely as it proved, for we must have waited at the landing for an hour before she came up from St Gowan light vessel. She made great play with her searchlight before sending in the boat to a difficult landing. Conditions had been good but by now the tide was making and in fact due to my carelessness the bow-rope was washed away and couldn't be recovered at the eyebolt. [I happen to remember that we had been distracted by an astronomical discussion.] Luckily they didn't have to make use of the impromptu one I strung together. The boat approached two or three times bows-on and each time we flung aboard cases and bags, and finally Rees. Three unimportant cases were left behind. And so back by 2030. To keep myself awake until midnight I listened to *The Importance of Being Earnest.* And by midnight, as predicted, the weather had begun to change for the worse.

Years later a stage appearance as Ernest in an amateur production was to provide me with my third standard nightmare, that of being about to go 'on' and not knowing my lines. One of the two others was of being in bed with my light 'stopped'.

I now began my usual series of improvements, it being my aim to leave every station a more effective, if not happier, place than I found it. One Principal Keeper had just left, another had yet to be appointed. The twain were unlikely to meet. I fixed a light to indicate lens rotation, re-sited the Fortin barometer and outside thermometer for more convenient reading, re-hung a door with the hinges on the other side, and contrived a formal play area with swings and a Ferris Wheel for our mice. (One thing we did not have was a still, though it was said that one had once existed on Skokholm. The isolation of lighthouses and their 24-hour watch would seem to suit them admirably to the manufacture of illicit liquor.) My activities met with no opposition from Mortiboys. He was, after all, going to 'work his ticket' and meantime had the preoccupations that went with it, 'scrounging around getting together bits and pieces for his home – brooms, saucepans etc.'

> *Christmas Day 1960:* My seventh lighthouse Christmas and, for better or worse, my last. For lunch soup, rice pudding, fruit and cream. For tea (only two of us – Mortiboys was abed, exhausted with the effort of foraging) ham, fruit and jelly, cake.

The weather was appropriate and I recall repeated excursions with a broom to sweep out rain being driven in under the outside door.

On almost the last day of the year Samson learned over the radio that his brother had been injured in a car crash. This was an unwelcome distraction because I was working on an idea which would make the flashing light in the kitchen show continuously when the driving weight neared the bottom of the tube. Fortunately he quickly learned that his brother had not been injured, then that he might not have been in an accident at all. I sensed a problem here and began to question Samson. How confident was he that this brother of his actually existed? Surprising though it might seem, mistakes were sometimes made. Had he ever seen a birth certificate? And so on and so forth.

Meanwhile Mortiboys was pursuing another tack. It was not in his nature to let any opportunity slip and he sniffed one here. All lighthouses and lightships had on their inventory a sealed bottle of brandy, kept locked in the medicine cabinet against the day when it might be required in an emergency. The following day Mortiboys broached ours, justifying it with the argument that Samson might not yet be completely out of the wood. In particular his continued insistence that he had a brother was becoming worryingly strident, even unbalanced. The situation needed watching, though it was not yet desperate.

'You can see he knows we're talking about him. That's a good sign.'

Justification for opening the bottle was needed because the seal was inspected for tampering on most visits by the Superintendent. Mortiboys now poured out a generous measure for himself and one for Samson, then decided to drink both on the grounds that we couldn't know which way Samson might go if exposed to alcohol. I had a small glass to settle my own nerves though I had no great liking for the stuff.

By this time the level was well down in the bottle and I suggested it was going to need some explaining. We put together a Three Page report which included the key phrase: 'Before agreeing to drink, SAK Samson insisted that Assistant Keepers Mortiboys and Lane join him, and in his then state of nervous agitation it was thought unwise to refuse.' I wasn't entirely confident this would 'go' but as Mortiboys seemed to be going anyway (and taking half the station with him) it seemed worth a try. In fact nothing more was heard of the matter. Samson's was the only dissenting voice. He seemed to regard the whole thing as a reflection on his character, which in a way, I suppose, it was.

> *4 January*: In the evening wrote thank-you letters to Christmas correspondents.

There were fewer here than there had been at the Eddystone, and so fewer replies to be written; but the writing in one particular case was more difficult. A lady in Malvern had sent us two left mittens and a rusty tin of fish. My customary warmth of expression may have been missing.

> *6 January*: Relief day. The boat came at noon, bringing the Superintendent.
> While he walked to the lighthouse and back with Mortiboys the launch landed
> a ton of coal and a ton of coke, a drum of diesel oil, some petrol and so forth.
> The Superintendent was pleased with the place – as he ought to have been
> considering the trouble Mortiboys took, personally, to hide away everything
> that might displease him, and which we have been trying to rediscover since.

Certain things we never did rediscover because Mortiboys took them with him. I
didn't hear of him thereafter and am left wondering whether he did, in fact, work his
ticket and legitimise his children. He had been good company. Evidently I had fulfilled the commission to write something for the Christmas *Flash* as the Superintendent mentioned it to George, but I never saw the issue. The possibility of two months'
leave before I took up my turn at Skerries was also bruited but – 'this isn't a promise,
mind'. It was to materialise as six weeks. As I noted at the time:

> The way this district operates there will be many influencing changes before
> then. We were back at the lighthouse with one load of gear at 1350, had a
> cup of tea, and I then went down to collect the rest with an Irish Supernumer-
> ary called James Bovaird. Bovaird is a pleasant intelligent fellow with a brogue
> it is difficult sometimes to understand. Robert Jones is Welsh-speaking [though
> I assume he also spoke English].

Routine resumed its course.

> In the morning brought back on the dumper with Bovaird 10 cwt of coke and
> 8 cwt of coal. And we cleared out the spring in readiness for drawing from it
> next week. In the afternoon I progressed with the book.

Leaving me in charge with two Supernumeraries (as I believe they were) was a
curious act of irresponsibility on the part of Trinity House, particularly in an inter-
regnum between two Principal Keepers, one of whom had left and another who had
yet to arrive. It was practically an invitation to anarchy.

> During the day took down the kitchen clock, cleaned it, oiled it, stripped the
> dial of its chipped enamel and painted it white. Its final décor will be modernis-
> tic, dots and dashes around the perimeter instead of the previous Roman
> numerals...took off the pantry door preparatory to hanging it more conven-
> iently on the opposite side.

A major entertainment was to fit an adapted acetylene headlamp to the dumper, run
off an old battery, to ease our occasional night journeys across the island. Unfortunately its effectiveness was limited by the 2 W bulb; we had nothing bigger.

My diary, curiously, makes no direct mention of one adverse feature of this month,
probably because it was so dire; but the consequences are hinted at.

> *13 January*: Felt famished at teatime so, unusually, had chips and a slice of
> processed meat, courtesy of James.

> *21 January*: Woke early with cold and hunger.

26 January: To bed to read in the afternoon and again lay down after tea. This idleness is partly unsettlement, partly poor diet. Up to midnight I made myself some chips.

31 January: Had some chips for an early breakfast while on middle watch.

Chips, this month, were the major element in my diet for a disastrous mistake had been made – by the store-keeper in Holyhead as I later discovered.

The explanation illustrates the frangible nature of our communications. Towards the end of my first month I had read over on the radio my order for my second month's food to the Smalls. Smalls read it back and some time later passed it on, again by radio, to the *Argus* which in due course conveyed it as a document to the shopkeeper in Holyhead. It was all pretty laborious and to simplify the transaction I had named only those few items on my first month's list that I did *not* want repeated, making it clear, as I hoped, that otherwise the list was to stand. When I opened my curiously light provisions box I found I had been sent *only* those few items named for deletion. My consolation during the month that followed was to anticipate my encounter with the shopkeeper on my return to Holyhead, when I was going to seize him by the neck of his shirt, haul him across the counter head-first and pile-drive him into the floor. It was a meeting which was frustrated only by the accident of returning to Holyhead, and leaving by train, long before his miserable emporium had opened for the day. Even if that had not been the case the advantage lay with him. It is difficult to maintain an emotional head of steam for as long as a month, even if it is fuelled by hunger. At the end of four weeks what had seemed a disaster had come to be viewed in terms of black comedy.

Yet, semi-starvation apart, it seems to have been a relaxed and enjoyable month. One of the light vessels conducted the evening radio test.

10 January: The three of us – 'Cheerio... Cheerio ... Cheerio (a major triad). This is Skokholm, your friendly station, saying Cheerio the Group. Remember! For relief from Skokholm, Smalls, South Bishop and other distempers take *Argus*, the wonder vessel. (Gong: spoon on shovel.)

We were still, unfortunately, within range of Radio Luxembourg.

And there was at least one lot of visitors.

16 January: In the morning of a somewhat disorganised day I repacked the two micrometer valves, then scribbled a note to M. The urgency was because a party of shooters had landed and it wasn't till they came up the island that we learned they would be staying till 1400. Directly after lunch I went down to the spring with the dumper and while there learned that they wanted to take a couple of dozen sheep carcasses with them. So we worked down from the lighthouse and took them down to the landing. Felt very annoyed with myself for not having a proper letter to M. ready.

We do not seem to have pressed to be allowed to have one of the carcasses; or if it was offered we declined.

> 14 *January*: *Argus* passed us going south in the night, and passed north at noon on her way to the South Bishop. We thought she might double back here but in fact she is off to Dublin for bunkering.

And luckily she stayed away from us throughout the month. We were also fortunate with fog.

> 20 *January*: On from 2000 and at 2345 decided to start sounding for the first time this month. Fortunately we only had ninety minutes. Just as I was turning in Robert came in and said it had cleared. So took him through the routine of pumping up and to bed again soon after 0200.

The intermittent blasts of the horn used air at high volume and low pressure but at the end of a run one charged the air tank to something 125 lb per sq.in. for the next engine start. The engines were horizontal Hornsbys of a nominal 5BHP but still the length of a small car with exposed conrods and eccentric valve-gear – a mechanical delight.

> 22 *January*: Ran the engine in the morning, booking it as fog. Poorish visibility was the excuse, but really I wanted to get the recorder chart working properly.

Air tapped from the coding machine was fed to bellows in a modified barograph and caused the pen to make an appropriate trace.

> In the afternoon I was writing when Robert reminded me that he was going to cut my hair. He did, too, more drastically than I liked.

Relief day was now approaching.

> 1 *February*: On from 0400 when I occupied myself with the end-of-month returns. It was a fine day and we completed the relief clean-up. In the afternoon for a walk over the island with James. Did some scrambling among the rocks in search of flotsam. Found none – the sea seems to make short work of anything it washes up.

> 2 *February*: Gale warnings were issued at midnight and they came true. *Argus* went out to Morecambe Bay Light vessel this morning but was unable to do Skerries. She will attempt to do it tomorrow and sail for these southern stations at something before noon. So it might be a night relief here – if the conditions are good enough. At the moment they are frankly bad.

> 3 *February*: Still blowing like the devil and there was nothing doing at Skerries.

> 4 *February*: *Argus* did Skerries in the morning and as we later discovered came down after doing Bardsey and spent the night in Fishguard. Conditions meantime are moderating.

We were kept informed of all this, of course, by the jungle telegraph of the radio-telephone.

5 *February*: Quite an eventful relief day. *Argus* went to the Smalls at about 0730 whereupon two things happened. The Principal Keeper, Walmsley, who was coming off, lost his personal cases overboard; and Hazelden, due to go on, had his leg crushed by the swinging launch as he was boarding it from the *Argus*. He had to be taken into hospital at Milford Haven from where *Argus* came round to us to do the relief at about 1245, by which time James Bovaird, who had been looking forward to a spell of leave, was already seeing the writing on the wall.

Presently the radio confirmed his worst fears: he was to take Hazelden's place at the Smalls. (To the disappointment of deferred leave was added the incidental hazard of having to take over Hazelden's choice of provisions which might not all be to his taste.)

For Skokholm it was a complete change of personnel, which was unusual. The three of us were replaced by the new Principal Keeper, Humphreys, Samson (back again) and Pearce. 'There was a heavy swell but I survived seasickness by good luck' – and, perhaps, it now occurs to me, as a consequence of a month's frugal living.

We did the South Bishop relief and then the Smalls, the latter being completed by about 1600 or so. From thence to Holyhead with hardly a movement of the ship (we were running with the swell) to arrive at two the following morning. I stayed aboard dozing till 0645 when ashore and presently by taxi from the depot to the station to catch the 0730 to Crewe, and thence home by late afternoon.

I had left Humphreys 'a long rigmarole' to introduce him to the various unorthodoxies he was going to encounter on his new station. I do not know whether he was a traditionalist. If he was I wish I could have been a fly on the wall. My 'improvements' will have caused him to froth a little.

17

The final posting:
Skerries

In fact, when I returned to Holyhead about the first face I saw there was that of PK Humphreys, on his way back, no doubt, to Skokholm. Being of a naturally retiring disposition I did not venture to speak to him, but I thought his expression, as he looked at me, was grave almost to moroseness. He did not have the appearance of a man who would have taken in his stride either Mortiboy's depredations or my various 'improvements'. At the depot, refreshed by three hours' sleep in the waiting-room at Holyhead station, I handed in my notice to Lewis, the Chief Clerk. He seemed slightly resentful: 'I hope you know what you're doing.' I might have told him I never had done in the past and that I was not hopeful of there being any change in the future. I suppose my departure meant for him a further shuffling of appointments in an already turbulent district.

> To my surprise he returned to me not only the 26 shillings expended on plimsoles and shirt but also the plimsoles and shirt for which I was claiming.

What this could have been about I now have not the foggiest idea, but money was money in those days and we all took it seriously. When I was at the Breakwater I had actually received a remittance for one shilling and sixpence (7½p) in the post from East Cowes.

I was going out to the Skerries with the Principal Keeper, Dai Higgins, who was returning there after five months away with a broken ankle. It seems to have been another complete change of crew, for with us was a third man, Dennis Jones. We boarded the *Alert* in the evening where I 'dossed down on the rather revolting mattress and stayed there until about 1530 the following afternoon, as the position proved best for combating sea-sickness'. We had sailed at 0700, heading north-east for the Morecambe Bay Light Vessel where we arrived at noon. Hence the late afternoon arrival at Skerries.

> The launch trip took a devil of a time and my stomach lost patience. The boat, slow ahead, was rolling to the gunwales and plenty of spray was flying. I suppose we were ashore by about 1615.

The Skerries lighthouse from half-way up the island.

The Skerries is a reef of several acres in area with the pile of the lighthouse at one end of it. The explanation of the extraordinary extensiveness of the buildings is that at one time they had provided accommodation for families as well as keepers. Then, it was rumoured, a child had died for lack of medical attention, after which it became a station for keepers only. It has the characteristics of buildings that have been added to over many years: construction on several levels, an initially confusing maze of corridors and stairways and, in part, arched doorways in a monastic style. Skerries had been one of the early conversions to electric illumination.

> There are single-cylinder, vertical two-stroke Gardner engines for the navigation light, twin-cylinders for the light and radio-beacon battery charging combined, and four-cylinders for the fog diaphones – an excellent example of standardisation: when Gardner want more power they add an extra cylinder.

Incidentally it was 29 March and there was waiting for me a letter dated 19 January, addressed elsewhere, which had been doing the rounds ever since.

Presently I went out on to the island, which was nothing like the size of Skokholm. At the far end was a well-constructed cairn built by 'Mad' Hicks. Hicks had been a name on the southern rocks when I was there, though even then he had been dead some years. It was PK Rictus who told me Hicks had predicted he would not live 'to make old bones', and that it had come true. He left the lighthouse service to qualify as a pilot at Penzance, then died of natural causes in his forties, leaving a wife and child. I carried out a little maintenance on his cairn as a tribute to someone who sounded as though he would have been fun to be with.

The Skerries lighthouse from the far end of the island with 'Mad' Hicks's cairn in foreground.

At just one place on Skerries there was marked out a small level area. I have recently been told this had been a vegetable garden, but it had been marked with an 'H' and was now a helicopter landing area. Beside it was a post carrying a mail box.

> 3 April: From after lunch we sounded for fog. A most colossal noise. And at 1400 the Coast Guards told us by radio that the helicopter would be coming. It did, at about 1600, and the four or five crew came up to the lighthouse for a cup of tea, bringing letters.

This was an *ad hoc* arrangement with the RAF station at Valley, on Anglesey. They combined their occasional training sorties in our direction with the role of postmen.

Among the letters they brought on this occasion was one from M. in which she mentioned in passing the annoying and continuing unreliability of our local phone box. It was something which no ordinary channels of complaint had been effective in remedying. Getting something done from the relative isolation of the Skerries presented a challenge to which I decided to rise. I gave the matter some thought – there is time for thought on lighthouses – then wrote four letters which went off with the next helicopter. The first was to the licensee of our local inn, a Mr Arthur Crump.

> Dear Mr Crump,
>
> Would you please note that I will be blowing up the telephone kiosk opposite your property at 10a.m. on the third of May. Only small charges will be used and I do not anticipate that there will be any structural damage to your premises. However, I would appreciate it if you would leave the windows open to lessen the effects of the blast.
>
> > Yours sincerely
> > Arthur Lane
>
> P.S. I trust Mrs Crump is keeping well.

The second letter was to Constable Smith, our local policeman.

> Dear Mr Smith,
>
> I am writing to tell you that I will be blowing up our village telephone kiosk at 10a.m. on the third of May. I do not anticipate any particular problems but I would appreciate it if you could be on hand to control the crowds.
>
> Yours etc.

The third was to the Rural District Council (as it then was). It was marked for the attention of the public refuse department.

> Dear Sir
>
> Would you please note that I will be blowing up a telephone kiosk…etc. etc. and I would appreciate it if you would have a refuse vehicle on hand to take away the rubble.

And the final letter was addressed to the Area Telephone Manager.

> Sir
>
> In the light of the continuing unserviceability of the public telephone in our village I assume you have ceased to have any interest in this facility and I will therefore be demolishing it with explosives on etc. etc. No charge will be made for this service but I hope you will feel able to meet any small policing and refuse disposal expenses that may be incurred.
>
> Yours faithfully
>
> A. J. Lane.

I sat back to await results.

4 April saw a repetition of what I had last experienced at Casquets.

> We sounded for fog until about 2230, and throughout the night birds, mainly starlings, drifted in the beams like snow. And not only in the beams. When I was undressing to return to bed at 0430, four came down the chimney, attracted by the room light, and I had to turn it out and encourage them to leave by the window. This morning dead and maimed were strewn everywhere.

We had been caught out, as sometimes happened. The migratory swarms did not always come with fog, but when we thought they would we had flood-lamps, supplied by the RSPB, with which we illuminated the tower to provide the birds – we hoped – with something to relate to.

And then it was the relief clean-up and my final relief day in the service of Trinity House.

> 26 April 1960: On from 0400 and Dai stayed up, expecting the boat early. In fact she didn't come till perhaps 1030 and then stayed while someone looked at the R/T batteries. There ensued a long slow trip to Morecambe Bay Light Vessel at which we arrived at 1715 and I am writing this as we return to

> Holyhead, probably to arrive at about 2300. The Master of the Morecambe Bay has just come off for the last time after being on the same light vessel for 38 years.

If this was not a mis-hearing it seems a phenomenal length of service at one station.

> We got back to Holyhead on a flat calm night with the shore lights lying along the water, drifting in to our anchorage. Ashore about 2315 I was given my documents by the District Clerk.

He also gave me my arrears of pay, managing to include two or three Irish florins in the loose change – an easy mistake to make in the half-light, rather harder during banking hours. Thence by taxi to the station to get the 0125 train through to Birmingham – and to digest the mail I had received on the relief boat. This included an invitation from an Inspector Foxall of our local constabulary to call on him at his convenience. He wanted to discuss my planned demolition of the telephone kiosk. I hadn't previously had commerce with a police officer of senior rank and I looked forward to the experience.

The meeting took place a couple of days later. He seemed nervous and I felt under an obligation to put him at his ease. 'Foxall', I said, shaking him warmly by the hand. 'An admirable name for a police officer – though an even more suitable one, if I may say so, for a villain. Your father or grandfather perhaps sailed on the windy side of the law and you have decided to redress the balance. Good. I expect you are familiar with the *Bouncer's Tale* from Chaucer: *"A bouncer he, full fleet-ee of foot-ee".'* No, it seemed Inspector Foxall did not know the *Bouncer's Tale* and he invited me to sit down and tell him about it. His courtesy set the pattern of the interview. I thought it was a pity PK Trotter could not have been there to witness such a civilised exchange of views.

However, nothing in this world is as it seems. The Inspector turned out to be not quite the man I took him for. It was after some fifty minutes of agreeable chat, in which I confess I did most of the talking, that he suddenly surprised me by calling in the help of a psychiatrist.

However, I am glad to say he eventually made a full recovery.

Our public telephone's recovery was more immediate. It had been attended to almost overnight and has never seriously looked back since.

Thus ended my 6 years and 277 days as a lighthouse keeper.

Thereafter I did something else, but when I look back, as one does in retirement, it is those years in the lighthouse service that I remember with a curious warmth. Lighthouse life suited me – which is not to say that I necesssarily suited it. I know I was a pain to many of my colleagues, and even those few who regarded me with curiosity not unmixed with astonishment ('He was a —ing nut!' was the reported comment, uttered with a guffaw, of one keeper I don't believe I ever served with) would probably have preferred to do so at a distance. To all these I apologise profoundly for not having been better company at the time.

There were signs at Skerries, even as I left, that it was all coming to an end. There were too many engines, too much noise, too much technology providing points of contact with the outside world. I like machinery; it is much easier to understand than people; but the silence of the night watches was no longer broken only by the hiss of the Hood burner, the gentle groaning of the lens clock, and the summer slop or winter roar of the sea. There was the intrusive Radio-Telephone and the twelve-minute cycle of the radio beacon. Most threatening of all, at Skerries there was television and the first-heard commercial jingle about someone's ice-cream, a memory trace to be expunged only by death.

Presently would come helicopter reliefs and one-month turns of duty, and instant accessibility to unwanted visitors in the poorest of weather. 'Last scene of all that ends this strange eventful history' of lighthouse keeping, was automation.

In the preceding pages I have used pseudonyms where it seemed kinder to do so. PKs Matey Rictus and Trotter are long dead, the latter surviving to a considerable age and dying, surprisingly, of natural causes. Genghis, I have been glad to discover recently, is still alive. For years I had been watching the press in vain for some such news item as 'An Englishman, identified only as G.Khan, was arrested by Swiss Guards at the Vatican today after committing what was described as a sacriligeous assault on the Holy Father. No details were given.' Perhaps, like me in my little dietary difficulty at Skokholm, Genghis found he couldn't maintain the necessary head of steam.